Global solidarities against water grabbing

Manchester University Press

**PROGRESS IN
POLITICAL ECONOMY**

Series editors: Andreas Bieler (School of Politics and International Relations, University of Nottingham), Gareth Bryant (Department of Political Economy at the University of Sydney), Mònica Clua-Losada (Department of Political Science, University of Texas Rio Grande Valley), Adam David Morton (Department of Political Economy, University of Sydney), and Angela Wigger (Department of Political Science, Radboud University, The Netherlands).

Since its launch in 2014, the blog *Progress in Political Economy (PPE)* – www.ppesydney.net/ – has become a central forum for the dissemination and debate of political economy research published in book and journal article forms with crossover appeal to academic, activist, and public policy related audiences.

Now, the *Progress in Political Economy* book series with Manchester University Press (MUP) provides a new space for innovative and radical thinking in political economy, covering interdisciplinary scholarship from the perspectives of critical political economy, historical materialism, feminism, political ecology, critical geography, heterodox economics, decolonialism, and racial capitalism.

The PPE book series combines the reputations and reach of the PPE blog and MUP as a publisher to launch critical political economy research and debates. We welcome manuscripts that realize the very best new research from established scholars and early-career scholars alike.

To buy or to find out more about the books currently available in this series, please go to: https://manchesteruniversitypress.co.uk/series/progress-in-political-economy/

Global solidarities against water grabbing

Without water, we have nothing

Caitlin Schroering

MANCHESTER UNIVERSITY PRESS

Published by Manchester University Press
Oxford Road, Manchester, M13 9PL

www.manchesteruniversitypress.co.uk

British Library Cataloguing-in-Publication Data
A catalogue record for this book is available from the British
Library

ISBN 978 1 5261 7244 0 hardback
ISBN 978 1 5261 7786 5 paperback

First published 2024

Typeset by Newgen Publishing UK

*I dedicate this book to everyone around the world
fighting against water grabbing*

Contents

Figures

All images belong to the author

Preface and acknowledgements

I finished fieldwork and wrote much of this manuscript during the Covid-19 pandemic, and I remember all of the lives lost, especially in the two countries where most of my work was grounded: Brazil and the United States. I edited this manuscript as the genocide in Gaza continued to unfold, funded with taxpayers' dollars from my own country. The atrocities of this world are manifold and, I believe, deeply interconnected. May this be one small act amongst the struggle that spans generations to create a world where people do not die because of greed, and where systems of oppression are dismantled. Our liberation is tied to each other. I offer my deepest gratitude to all of the organizers, activists, and militants in the United States, Brazil, Nigeria, and around the world who fight for the right to water each and every day. This book is dedicated to all of you, and to the fight for water justice. I am appreciative of the many coalitions, campaigns, and movements in which I have been involved over the years, and who have inspired and educated me. For every person who I name here, there are a dozen more who I cannot, to whom I am forever grateful. I trust you know who you are.

I first learned about the problem of corporations (including Coca-Cola, Nestlé, and their subsidiaries) bottling water and then selling it for a profit back in 2008 when I went to Brazil as part of my undergraduate studies. I visited the Tucuruí hydroelectric dam in the state of Pará and had various other experiences where I saw firsthand some of the environmental and social devastation caused by mining and dams. When I came back to the United States, I organized on my campus against water privatization and bottled water. My personal experiences with serious health problems – both my own and of loved ones – has also grounded my understanding of how the current structures that we take as givens are not working for the vast majority of us, and that people should come before profit.

My first memories of this are as a young child accompanying my mother and uncle to his doctor's appointments, where I witnessed the ignorance, homophobia, and cruelty directed toward people living with AIDS. On one occasion, upon arriving at the doctor's office, a nurse put an 'Out of Order' sign on the bathroom door and removed a bowl of candy from the waiting room. On another occasion, as we walked through the grocery store, with his IV pole in tow, I heard people yell homophobic slurs and that he deserved to die and would go to hell. After his death, my mother became involved in HIV/AIDS activism, working with people who were unhoused and living with HIV, and she always brought me with her. These experiences fueled me to become engaged in activism as a teenager. And, in college, I was active in various organizations and coalitions working to advance more equitable and just HIV/AIDS policies globally and domestically, and for there to be social, environmental, and racial justice on my own university campus. These experiences showed me how global financial institutions, such as the International Monetary Fund (IMF) and World Bank, created systemic barriers to healthcare and education, and perpetrated ongoing forms of colonialism. My experiences in Brazil in 2008 opened my eyes even more to how all these various forms of oppression and exploitation are interrelated; as well as to the possibility of resistance and change.

After college, I worked as a community organizer in Jacksonville, Florida, for four years on social justice issues that were not directly connected to water. During my time there, I organized hundreds of public meetings where many more hundreds of residents came together to discuss community problems and demand solutions. Organizing affirmed my belief in the power of people organizing for change and the capacity to create a different world.

I moved to Pittsburgh, Pennsylvania in 2015. The following year, in 2016, the Pittsburgh lead crisis broke. I felt personally connected to it (my house tested at 100 ppb lead level), so I was convinced that I had a responsibility to fight for clean, safe, public water in Pittsburgh. This reality, along with my previous understanding of the critical importance of the right to water and fighting against its privatization, is the somewhat abbreviated version of how I came to this topic.

This book marks the culmination of a dozen years of formal undergraduate and graduate study, which began at Ohio's Denison University. I thank all my undergraduate professors for fostering my love of research, writing, and language during my time at Denison, where my interest in human rights, as well as environmental and social justice were developed, encouraged, challenged, and supported. I especially express gratitude to the late Dr. Kent Maynard and to Dr. John Cort and Dr. Monica Ayala-Martinez for their continued mentorship, friendship, and support.

I would like to thank all the people I learned from in 2008 during a study abroad program based in Belém, Brazil, through the School of International Training (SIT). During this experience, my awareness of environmental social movements in Brazil and my anger at the extractivism and exploitation being done by US-based corporations grew. In particular, I thank the people of ACORJUVE in Juruti Velho, Brazil.

To Dr. Susan Paulson, the late Dr. Richmond Brown, and all the people in the Masters in Latin American Studies program at the University of Florida: thank you for all of your support of my academic pursuits during an incredibly trying time of my life. I would not have finished the program without you, and the work I did there provided me with an incredible foundation upon which to build my future research.

To Dr. Suzanne Staggenborg: thank you for the opportunity to work with you as your research assistant, to write a paper together, and for your always-prompt responses to questions and emails throughout the years. To Dr. Jackie Smith: thank you for your enthusiasm and support of my research topic, and for bringing Rob Robinson to campus to give a talk - this project would not have been possible without meeting him. To Dr. John Markoff: thank you for encouraging me back in 2015 to stick with my idea to do research in Brazil, and for pushing me to make a theoretical, not just empirical, intervention. To Dr. Gianpaolo Baiocchi: thank you for serving as my external committee member, and for your book *We, the Sovereign,* which has served as inspiration to my research and writing. To Dr. Marcela González Rivas: thank you for the opportunity to work together, and for the continued collaborations that we have had the chance to work together on. I have learned a lot and it has been wonderful to think through ideas with you, and then turn them into action!

To Luis G. Van Fossen Bravo: thank you for all your help in 2018 navigating the Institutional Review Board (IRB) process! The work in Brazil was supported by a Tinker Grant through the Center for Latin American Studies at the University of Pittsburgh, a Nationality Room Grant through the University of Pittsburgh Nationality Rooms Scholarship program, and an Andrew Mellon Predoctoral Fellowship through the College of Arts and Sciences at the University of Pittsburgh. I also received support through the Social Science Doctoral Dissertation Fellowship administered through the Department of Sociology at the University of Pittsburgh, and a Dean's Tuition Scholarship through the Arts and Sciences Office of Graduate Studies.

I would like to express much gratitude to Andreas Bieler for all your support through the book contract and writing process. Much thanks to Manchester University Press, especially Rob Byron, the editors of the Progress in Political Economy series, anonymous reviewers, and editorial team.

To my colleagues at the University of North Carolina at Charlotte (UNCC): thank you for all the incredible support and encouragement. I finished writing this book during my first year at UNCC and could not have asked for a better department to be a part of! Special thanks to: Dale Smith, Vicky Harris, John Cox, Joyce Dalsheim, Emek Ergun, Charles Houck, Garth Green, and Amal Khoury. Thank you also to Galen Miller and Alicia Ramirez, who helped me with appendices, the glossary, and references. Much gratitude to Rowan Grayson for fantastic and insightful copy edits, and indexing. Thank you to all my former, current, and future students, for grounding me in why I do this work, reminding me that education can be liberatory.

To Rob Robinson: thank you for all the work you do for justice around the world, and for introducing me to MAB. This book would not exist without you. Agradeço a Alexania Rossato e Yara Naí de Freitas por sua hospitalidade, carinho, e pelo convite em 2018 para aprender e lutar com o MAB. Sou grata por conhecê-las. Para a galera do Curso de Energia: foi uma experiência muito importante e uma grande honra participar do Curso com todes vocês. Para os e as camaradas do MAB, professoras e professores do curso, especialmente Flávia Braga Vieira e Luiz Felipe Osório, e toda a militância dos movimentos sociais e sindicais que lutam por um mundo mais justo: obrigada, obrigada! Sou grata por conhecer vocês. E vou traduzir este livro para o português!

To all the graduate students and organizers I had the chance to fight with for a union at the University of Pittsburgh: I am grateful to know you and to have organized with you, even though we did not "win." I trust that, soon, the graduate students at Pitt will be unionized.

For various forms of friendship, love, care, support, encouragement, learning, fighting together for justice, and – even in various cases – reading and providing feedback on drafts of book chapters, much gratitude to: Amanda Conley, Kristin Powell, Lisa Schilansky, Kit Jones, Chie Togami, Hillary Lazar, Patrick Beckhorn, Benjamin Case, Macarena Moraga, Tarun Banerjee, Michael Murphy, Patrick Korte, Marion Romero, Camilla Brito, Gessica Steffens, Luana Farias, Luiz Paulo Macedo Alves, Gabriel Gonçalves, Anderson Guahy, Raine, Edson Aparecido da Silva, Julio Sanchez, Deisy Paulina Avendaño Avendaño, Brandon Lazar, George Weddington, Hatem Hassan, Candice Robinson, Karen Rohrer, Andy Greenhow, Aly Shaw, Madeline Weiss, Neil Gupta, Kim Moulos, Talor Musil, Tom Hoffman, Emek Ergun, Ritika Prasad, Ella Fratantuono, and Kefaya Diab.

To my godchild, Kairo: may my words not be too abstract or boring and may the world you grow into be one with more justice than the one we currently have. And may we learn that together we can organize and make it so!

I am lucky to have so many aunts, uncles, and cousins, and I thank you all for the forms of love and support you have given me through the years. I love you. To my late grandmothers, Patricia Lee Gaines and Martha

Schroering: I miss and love you and know that you are always with me. To my late uncle, Charles Paul Gaines: your life and death has guided and supported me in my journey in understanding how all injustices are inter-related, and to be a part of fighting for a more just world. To my parents, Mark and Bobbie Schroering: I thank you for showing me from a young age the importance of caring for and loving our world, and the need to speak out against injustice. I am the person I am because of you. To Vincent Kolb: thank you for your support and belief in my work, for your own com-mitment to fighting for justice, and for solo taking care of our furry ones, Magic, Dora, and Frida (and later Frida and Mylan), when I was out of the country, and for reading many early drafts of chapters.

All royalties from this book will go to the social movements with whom I have worked.

Abbreviations

AEDAS	Associação Estadual de Defesa Ambiental e Social (State Association of Environmental and Social Defense)
ANA	Agência Nacional de Águas
ASCE	American Society of Civil Engineers
AUPCTRE	Amalgamated Union of Public Corporations, Civil Service Technical and Recreational Services Employees
BLM	Black Lives Matter
BRP	Blue-Ribbon Panel
CAP	Customer Assistance Program
CAPPA	Corporate Accountability and Public Participation in Africa
CDDH	Centro dos Direitos Humanos
COP	United Nations Conference of the Parties
CRC	Clean Rivers Campaign
DEP	Pennsylvania Department of Environmental Protection
EJ	Environmental Justice
ENFF	Florestan Fernandes National School
EPA	US Environmental Protection Agency
FAMA	Fórum Alternativo Mundial da Água (World Alternative Forum on Water)
FMA	Fórum Mundial da Água (World Forum on Water)
GCF	UN Green Climate Fund
GMO	Genetically modified organism
GWI	Global Water Intelligence
IMG	International Management Group
IPCC	United Nations Intergovernmental Panel on Climate Change
ITPI	In The Public Interest
LVC	La Vía Campesina (The Peasant's Way)
MAB	Movimento dos Atingidos por Barragens (Movement of People Affected by Dams)

MPA	Movimento dos Pequenos Agricultores (Small Farmer's Movement)
MST	Movimento dos Trabalhadores Rurais Sem Terra (Landless Worker's Movement)
NAWC	National Association of Water Companies
NRC	United States Nuclear Regulatory Commission
OPIP	Organization of Indigenous Peoples of Pastaza
OWC	Our Water Campaign
OWOR	Our Water, Our Right
PNAB	National Policy of Rights for those Affected by Dams
PND	National Privatization Program
PPP	Public–Private Partnership
PPS	Peer Performance Solutions
PSI	Public Services International
PT	Worker's Party
PWSA	Pittsburgh Water and Sewer Authority
SDGs	United Nations Sustainable Development Goals
SEC	US Securities and Exchange Commission
TCC	Transnational Capitalist Class
TNI	Transnational Institute
TSF	Tailings Storage Facility
UFRJ	Federal University of Rio de Janeiro
UN	United Nations
UNGA	United Nations General Assembly
WSF	World Social Forum

Glossary of key concepts

Academic imperialism The idea that academia can, intentionally or unintentionally, support or advance systems of imperialism, colonialism, or other forms of hegemony.

Austerity Economic and social policies which involve greatly reducing or cutting spending on healthcare, education, welfare benefits, or other government services.

Counter-hegemonic globalization/alter-globalization A form of globalization which resists the hegemonies associated with globalization as it exists now, usually taking on anti-capitalist, feminist, and decolonial views. It symbolizes the grassroots movements that fight against oppressive structures.

Cultural hegemony A concept advanced by Antonio Gramsci, which sees that the ruling class controls/manipulates (generally without force) the values of a society, so that those values become the world view.

Environmental justice The struggle for social justice which is explicitly connected to environmental degradation or harms linked to environmental degradation.

Epistemology The theory of knowledge, especially focused on where knowledge comes from – the methods, validity, and scope. Different people will have different conceptions of understanding something, which can be called their "epistemological stance."

Financialization When goods or resources are made into products which are integrated into the for-profit financial system.

Globalization The increasing flow of capital, cultural practices, and ideas between communities around the world. Some scholars argue there are two main categories of globalization: 1) problems related to it; 2) the concept or process of it.

Hegemony   Dominance of one state over others. In globalization studies, it is often thought of in terms of world empire (military, force, driven by state politics). Empires use language or ideology (shared culture) to create hegemony (manufactured consent).

Intellectual activism   The idea that scholars, intellectuals, and academics can use their work to advance social and political causes, in contrast to the idea that such work must be "neutral."

Liberation theology   An ideology of liberation for oppressed communities that is grounded in religious ideals, specifically Catholicism in the Latin American tradition. It applies religious ideals to the struggle against oppression and the fight for social justice.

Modernization theory (or "theory of the stages")   A theory of development that assumes a unidirectional and irreversible process: agricultural development, industrial development, infrastructure development. The United States is a model for what every other nation should/will become. The International Monetary Fund, World Bank, and other global financial institutions have imposed this particular development paradigm on countries, which has also indebted them and forced austerity measures domestically, which in turn hinder development around health, education, etc.

Neoliberalism   An economic ideology which emerged in the mid-twentieth century and prioritizes an orthodox, hardline, free-market approach to economics with marginal government presence. Refers to economic policies launched in the 1980s under Ronald Reagan and Margaret Thatcher (often referred to as the "Washington Consensus") that liberalized trade and increased state deregulation and privatization.

Positionality   How our "lens" of the world – including race, gender, sex, ethnicity, class, geographic location, etc – informs our understanding of the world and can influence research methods.

Positivism   The idea that there is one objective, empirical, and knowable truth.

Public–Private Partnership (PPP)   Operational partnerships between private entities (for-profit firms or organizations) and public entities, such as a municipal, state, or federal government or agency. Typically places all of the risk on the public side and all of the profit on the private side.

Translocal Learning Network   People, communities, and social movements that are linked to similar movements around the world, with an emphasis on building connections between the local and the global.

Western-centric/Eurocentric   The paradigm that prioritizes the interests of western powers or communities in the "west" – generally the United States, Canada, Australia, and western and northern Europe.

1

The global fight for water

Water is so fundamental we often forget how much we rely on it. Humans can survive a few weeks without food, years without proper shelter, but only a few days without water.

Despite numerous studies showing privatization decreases access to safe water and increases cost, multinational companies continue to buy water systems worldwide, turning water from something shared and held in common into a commodity for monetary gain. This threatens the survival of all life. Around the world, people are organizing to resist privatization and to reclaim the public sphere, including the human right to water and other necessities for life. These struggles demonstrate how people are linking their disparate fights to win against private profit-driven interests. This is ultimately a power struggle over who has a right to water. At its core, the conflict pits people and social movements who believe that access to clean, safe water is a basic human need, against capitalists who argue that they have the "right" to profit from the privatization of water. Too often governments endorse or collude with private interests for capital in so-called public–private partnerships. Strikingly, despite marked global disparities and differences, including of political and economic systems, this struggle over water is happening around the globe, from Pittsburgh to Lagos.

The chapters that follow are about effectively fighting global water privatization and increasing access to safe water for all. Water is at the heart of this book, but it is as much about collective struggle and popular organization as it is about water. Of course, water conflicts carry broader lessons about austerity, market deregulation, extractivism, and resource privatization, and the effects of water privatization cannot be separated from the effects of another pressing crisis of our time: climate change. In 2015, the UN Intergovernmental Panel on Climate Change (IPCC) noted that the world has not woken up to the severity of problems we will face regarding climate change and water. These intersections mean that this book is ultimately about how people around the globe are organizing for their right to clean, safe water and how they strive to both understand and to link this struggle to large-scale resistance against global economic structures that endanger human rights – and, indeed, jeopardize all life on our planet.

The global movement around water is organizing and growing, bringing together unlikely alliances of environmental, labor, human rights, racial and gender justice activists, and other advocates demanding clean, safe, (and public) water systems. As they fight against the privatization of water and for the world's ability to address the human right to safe water, the movement also focuses on imagining alternatives of what could be – a future aiming to secure our collective right to survive on the planet.

Grounded in fieldwork that spans three continents, this book focuses primarily on the privatization of drinking water and large dam construction; it also relates to bottled water. Privatization of drinking water, bottled water, and the construction of hydro dams all constitute forms of "water grabbing." Simply put, water grabbing refers to the appropriation of water by capital, placing profit over life (Bieler and Moore, 2023). There are six main forms of water grabbing: 1) privatization (of drinking water and sanitation); 2) bottled water; 3) water for extractive industry;[1] 4) land grabbing for export agriculture; 5) large dam constructions; and, 6) financialization (Bieler, 2021: 5–6; Bieler and Moore, 2023: 5–6 and 13). All forms of water grabbing have resulted in moments of resistance (Bieler, 2021). The financialization of water – referred to as the "privatization of life" because it turns what is necessary for life into a commodity for speculation – will increasingly drive the five other forms of water privatization (Muehlebach, 2023; Ideas for Development, 2020). I will return to this discussion in the next chapter.

Through examining water-based social movements, *Global solidarities against water grabbing: without water we have nothing*[2] explores how individual movements are frequently a part of larger movement communities. Thus, they are examples of translocal movements, in which people (citizens, residents, activists, and movement actors) engage with each other, the state, and the market to fight for community-driven partnerships, communal ideas of property rights versus private property rights, and for participatory, democratic, and horizontal governance structures (Banerjee, 2018: 812). This book makes three key assertions: 1) it shows how global communications and organizing are occurring around the public's right to water; 2) it argues that movements in the Global North are engaging with and learning from the Global South[3] with Global South movements playing a more prominent and innovative role than previous scholarship demonstrates; and 3) it shows how the struggle for water as a right, a public good, and a commons, rather than a commodity, is connected to a broader anti-systemic fight for livelihood that spans well beyond water. The pages that follow offer a dialogue between global environmental justice, resource conflicts, political economy, feminist and anti-colonial research methods, and social movement studies. I connect on-the-ground organizing with broader theoretical debates and pull areas of study, which are typically studied as discrete parts, together into a whole. This book advances the idea that the fight against water privatization is not relegated to the Global South or Europe but is active and growing in the United States in response to the failures of decades of neoliberal reforms and private sector "solutions."

In this book, I examine the interlinked efforts to reclaim the commons of water and show how grassroots movements drive the struggle and demand the prioritization of democracy, transparency, and human rights over corporate profits in public policy. As feminist scholars have pointed out, the "standpoint" of marginalized actors offers important insights into the operation of systems of power and strategies of survival and resistance (Collins, 2002, 2012; Connell, 2006, 2007a, 2007b). Transnational social movement scholars from the Global North have too often reinforced the idea that knowledge flows from the Global North to the Global South, despite research that has critiqued this dynamic as incomplete and an example of methodological nationalism (see Appe, 2022; Bracey, 2016; Connell, 2007a; Desai, 2009; Escobar, 1988; Hughes et al., 2018; Mohanty, 2003a, 2003b; Schroering, 2019a; Smith, 2022; Smith and Wiest, 2005; Vieira, 2015).

While there is literature that explores the linkages between Global South-led movements and argues the importance of those movements as producers of knowledge (including Barbosa, 2016; Bringel and Vieira, 2015, 2016; Desai, 2016; Holt-Giménez, 2006; Rosset et al., 2021; Vieira, 2011), the stance that ideas in transnational organizing flow from the Global North to the Global South persists in much transnational social movement literature coming from the West (Bandy, 2004; della Porta and Rucht, 2002; Hughes et al., 2018: 5). The research presented in this book demonstrates how efforts by the state and corporations to privatize basic resources[4] is being met with counter-hegemonic resistance – and how the need for survival is a transformative one that impels people to organize for democratic and public control of resources (Almeida, 2019; Markoff, 1997; Tilly and Wood, 2015).

Scholars have called for social movement theory to be more attuned to economy and structure (Hetland and Goodwin, 2013; McAdam and Boudet, 2012), to pay attention to what social movements are demanding (Barbosa, 2016; Bringel and Vieira, 2015 and 2016; Choudry, 2015; Cox, 2014; Cox and Flesher Fominaya, 2009; Falcón, 2016; Holt-Giménez, 2006; Icaza and Vásquez, 2013; Rosset et al., 2021), to address continued legacies of epistemic erasure, racism, colonialism, and imperialism, and for white scholars and those from the Global North to think about whiteness, positionality, and decolonial frameworks (Bracey, 2016; Connell, 2006; Go, 2020; Silva, 2016, 2018). Yet social movement studies have tended to privilege agency to the detriment of understanding the role of capitalist forces and focused instead on descriptive analysis, addressing the questions of how social movements maintain and who participates, while ignoring why movements arise and how they push for emancipation. Liberal approaches to studying social movements view civil society as separate from political society (Bieler, 2021: 8–14; see also Englehardt and Moore, 2017 and 2022; Moore, 2023: 14).

This book contributes to social movement theory in various ways. Principally, it calls for the need not to decontextualize analyses of movements from larger cultural, social, political, and economic structures, and to challenge conventional research assumptions that generate studies of pieces of movements – organizations, events, leaders – without situating them in long-term, local, national, global, and material struggles. It flows outside of neat boundaries set around problems, processes, and actors (including my own as researcher versus movement participant). It also contributes more broadly to decolonizing[5] social movement studies, which makes my intervention both theoretical and methodological.

Just as water conflicts involve power (Sultana, 2018), power is present in social movement resistance. It is present in the discourses of activists and scholars (Krishna, 2001). As Paulo Freire (2018 [1968]) outlines in *Pedagogy of the Oppressed*, a neutral education process does not exist. Neither does neutral theory, neutral methods, or neutral sociology. Since scholarship remains structured by choices and positionality, it is important for scholars to make these explicit. I maintain that there is a useful place in academia and activism for scholars to openly take a position. The sheer injustice involved in the privatization of water angers me and is a driving force in my research. Anger is an important catalyst, as Rachel Watkins powerfully states: "there's a political knowing that comes out of anger" (2019: no page). Her point relates to both theory and methods. Emotions – including, and especially, anger – can fuel action for change. Watkins speaks of the need for "ethical epistemology" (2018: 43) in scholarship – of producing knowledge with and from the community. Sociologist Patricia Hill Collins (2015) argues that "intellectual activism" is needed in scholarship.

In the rest of this chapter, I offer an overview of key conceptual frameworks that I draw from, provide a description of my cases, and follow with a discussion of my theoretical and methodological approach. Finally, I outline the remaining chapters of the book, explaining how they tie together.

Conceptual framework

There is an extensive literature that addresses the similarities and differences between campaigns, coalitions, social movement communities, social movement coalitions, transnational social movements, and transnational advocacy networks. Here, I will briefly address it for definitional purposes. Coalitions, such as Our Water Campaign (OWC) are alliances between organizations and individuals; campaigns, which the OWC is, refers to the specific and ongoing actions that a coalition pursues (della Porta and Rucht, 2002; Schroering and Staggenborg, 2021).

Relatedly, there is an ample body of work focused on transnational social movements (TSMs) and transnational advocacy networks (TANs). A TSM is a mobilized group that exists in at least two countries, and engages in contentious and sustained interaction (Tarrow, 2001: 11) that includes two or more states, a global financial institution, or other international institution (Piper and Uhlin 2004: 6; Tarrow, 2001: 11). The movements discussed in this book match these criteria. Margaret Keck and Kathryn Sikkink (1998) have completed much work to advance and understand the idea of TANs, which has been simply defined by Piper and Uhlin as "networks of activists motivated by principled ideas and values" (2004: 6). TANs seek to "change the behavior of states and international organizations" (Keck and Sikkink, 1998: 2). The cases in this book fit this description – even if, in the case of the OWC, the daily work is more locally focused. While I do not propose the elimination of TSM or TAN from our lexicon (something I address in Chapter 7), I argue that "translocal" better captures the anti-systemic and globally focused – yet locally/nationally rooted – movements with whom I work. I draw heavily on Subhabrata Bobby Banerjee's work and agree with his contention that "The ultimate challenge of a theory of translocal resistance is to conceive the inconceivable: an extension of the democratic that transcends nation-state sovereignty, perhaps even transcends citizenship" (2011: 337). In subsequent chapters, I further define this term.

My study of the privatization of water and the social movements that are resisting it relies on a framework that draws upon the concepts of "globalization," "neoliberalism," and "imperialism." Given the wide array of ways in which these ideas have been articulated and are understood, I will share specifically how they relate to my understanding of the systemic appropriation – and politicization – of water as well as of the people seeking to reappropriate our human right to this shared, public good. "Neoliberal globalization" can refer to economic policies and processes that have centralized wealth and power in the hands of a few, while dispossessing the majority of their wealth, labor, and land (see Harvey, 2004). But, what is "new" about neoliberalism? Immanuel Wallerstein writes:

> There have always been historical systems in which some relatively small group exploited the others. The exploited always fought back as best they could. The modern world-system, which came into existence in the long sixteenth century in the form of a capitalist world-economy, has been extremely

effective in extracting surplus-value from the large majority of the populations within it. (2014: 1)

This quote illustrates an important point: an exploitative economy is not a new phenomenon. To fully understand the processes of economic glo-balization and neoliberalism today, we need to look back to the long ori-gins and history of capitalism. Further, exploitation and injustice certainly predate the advent of capitalism. What seems distinct at present is a logic of "expulsion" (Sassen, 2014) fueled by speculative finance at work in the global economic system – whether we want to term it "neoliberalism" or "advanced capitalism" – that is different (or at least scaled up) to previous eras (see Chapter 2). Later, in Chapter 4, I discuss how the movements I have worked with distinguish between specific forms of capitalism. Globalization is not just about state and corporate power, but also about how movements respond to and shape the process. For example, David Harvey's notion of the "right to the city" argues that an alternative to the form of neoliberal globalization that we presently have will come from people uniting into a movement that demands access to public spaces and goods (Harvey, 2012) – i.e., the revolutionary movement will be concerned with seizing the means of survival (land and water) instead of the means of production, per se.

Vandana Shiva describes the current economic model as "corporate globalization":

> corporate globalization is based on new enclosures of the commons; enclo-sures which imply exclusions and are based on violence … In fact, globaliza-tion's transformation of all beings and resources into commodities robs diverse species and people of their rightful share of ecological, cultural, economic, and political space. The "ownership" of the rich is based on the "dispossession" of the poor – it is the common, public resources of the poor which are privat-ized, and the poor who are disowned economically, politically, and culturally. (2005: 2–3)

Shiva points to the complicated and interconnected dynamics of state and corporate power, and how social movements are responding to efforts to privatize the commons of water. For Shiva, and others, colonization of the "Third World" marks the beginning of globalization (Moghadam, 2005: 23; Shiva, 2005). According to Valentine Moghadam, "Many on the left regard globalization, at least its economic dimension, to be an exten-sion of imperialism. Thus globalization would be considered the latest (if not the 'highest' – apologies to V.I. Lenin) stage of capitalism" (2005: 23). Capitalism must keep finding new "frontiers" from which to extract profits; state (and corporate) violence[6] is key to this extraction (Patel and Moore, 2017; Robinson, 2013a).

Yet "capitalism does not just happen" (Sklair, 1997: 514). It is produced and reproduced through coercion and ideology. This invokes Antonio Gramsci's notion of cultural hegemony: dominant ideas, assumptions, and stereotypes of how the world ought to be can hold great power over people, affecting their daily experiences and consciousness (Gramsci, 2000; Sklair, 1997). Hegemony works by controlling knowledge and the production of knowledge. Hegemonic maintenance of the assumption that the world has to be the way it is works against envisioning a different world. Colonization throughout history and present-day capitalism both work by controlling knowledge systems and socialization systems. Hegemony is powerful because it is quiet, insidious, not visibly violent; people uphold it without realizing they are reinforcing it (Wallerstein, 2004: 58). Understanding this creates an opening to imagine different futures and ways of structuring our world (Scurr and Bowden, 2021). I discuss in the following chapters (especially Chapter 4) how the struggle against the commodification of water is also a struggle against hegemonic ideas, and the importance of "consciousness raising" and popular education in this fight.

A starting point for this is understanding and learning from the multitude of people who are working to change these oppressive structures which are traditionally accepted as "givens." Manisha Desai, for example, provides a slightly different understanding of "economic globalization" and focuses on the cross-border trade led by women (rather than corporations) to rethink economic globalization. Desai's gendered lens serves to "correct the myopia of the mainstream literature on economic globalization" (2009: 29). In other words, the grassroots or "bottom up" side of globalization can challenge us to reconceptualize its different forms (economic, political, and cultural) and, in so doing, allow new forms of globalizations (notice the plural) to emerge (Desai, 2009: 89). Desai contends that the global justice movement can look to this as an example of how to organize and counter the "neoliberal governmentality" that prevails (Desai, 2009: 94).

This relates to how market forces often shape/control knowledge production (Subramaniam, 2004), or how forms of domination shape the forms of resistance (Guha, 1989: 98). Yet the resistance shapes and changes the forms of domination, even if this has too often been made invisible, in particular as it relates to gender, including the role of women in the struggle. As Mangala Subramaniam notes: "Women have been largely invisible in debates about states and markets, despite considerable feminist writings on women's work" (2004: 637). According to Moghadam, the exploitation caused by capitalism today has created global anti-systemic movements: "a key characteristic of the era of late capitalism, or globalization, is the proliferation of transnational social movements, including the transnational women's movement and its organizational expression, the transnational feminist network" (2005: 3–4).

Capitalism is in large part maintained via the hegemony of the idea of the "free market": everything is or could be a commodity, including resources such as land, water, rivers, and oceans. In today's capitalist, everything-is-a-commodity world, the last commodity frontier is water. More so than other resources, it is often ostensibly under public rather than private control. But this could change in an instant. Many scholars differentiate between capitalism before and after the 1990s, which saw a worldwide rise of a specific type of capitalism – neoliberalism – that further weakened the working class. While neoliberalism has in many ways created specific problems related to water (see Chapter 2), my analysis is that the root of the problem is capitalism as a socio-political-economic system that is driving water privatization.

For most, Marx provided the foundational critique of capitalism based on its exploitation of human labor, and for the idea that unbridled accumulation of wealth could not be sustained (Foster, 1997: 127). Capitalism is inherently unsustainable, as its operation requires the alienation of humanity from humanity – it separates and forms unequal (and human created) divisions (Foster, 1997: 123). These points relate to the "second contradiction of capitalism," coined by James O'Connor, who draws on Marxist theory to contend that all societies face environmental limits, and therefore an environmental crisis will develop out of capitalism (Lidskog, Mol and Oosterveer, 2015: 348). As Schnaiberg, Pellow, and Weinberg (2002) describe, the "treadmill of production" serves to benefit politicians, elites, and investors, while leaving behind everyone else and destroying the environment. The current economic system is not compatible with sustaining life; the planet has limits, and capitalism requires constant expansion and has no limits. Samir Amin explains this succinctly, pointing out that: "Establishing a harmonious relationship between society and nature demands a radical break with the dominant logics of capitalism predicated on the essential destruction of the material basis of society and the reproduction of life on the planet" (2022: 44). In the chapters that come, especially Chapters 4 and 5, I will show how social movements employ these ideas and articulate alternatives for how we might live in the world.

Given the global nature of this work, imperialism[7] is another term related to capitalist extraction that needs to be defined. I draw on the definition outlined by CounterPower in *Organizing for Autonomy: History, Theory, and Strategy for Collective Liberation*:

> We define *imperialism* as a totalizing system of command and control based on the historical-geographical enmeshing of heteropatriarchy, capitalism, colonialism, and the state, whereby bodies, social relations, and natures are constantly made and unmade by the domination of abstract social forces moving

within and through the web of life. This is not to suggest that imperialism is *the world*, but that imperialism, as a social system, *articulates and produces a world* within which our bodies, creative social activities, and a multiplicity of natures are subordinated to certain systemic logics and path dependencies.
(2020: 48, emphasis in original)

This suggests that we need to reimagine the state today. Indeed, especially as many movements fighting against imperialism and corporate power are also fighting for a world that does not have the borders and boundaries that exist today. Imperialism is a totalizing system (not merely relations between countries), and those on the "periphery" experience it more directly. Those on the periphery – landless workers, peasants, and Indigenous people – are most directly affected by the extractive squeeze of imperialism.

Imperialism is a mechanism of economic, political, and cultural organization maintained in part by cultural hegemony. In practical terms, the media (newspapers, books, films, TV, and various other forms of entertainment and culture consumption) is a key part of getting the masses to support and maintain imperialism. A crucial function of discourses under control of cultural hegemony is to make imperial violence invisible (Said, 1993). It is not just popular media that serves imperial interests; too often, social science has as well (Guhin and Wyrtzen, 2013; Said, 1993). As Syed Farid Alatas writes, "social scientists may get involved in research that directly serves the imperialistic or hegemonic interests of a power" (2003: 601).

Knowledge production – the process which determines whose ideas are heard and seen as valid – is a part of this hegemonic system (Icaza and Vásquez, 2013). Of course, discussions of the need to decolonize knowledge, of academic imperialism, and critical pedagogy are not new (Alatas, 2003 [2000]; Fanon, 2007 [1961]; Freire, 2018 [1968]). As Walter Mignolo writes: "The need for political and epistemic delinking here comes to the fore, as well as decolonializing and decolonial knowledges, necessary steps for imagining and building democratic, just, and non-imperial/colonial societies" (2009: 161). Various scholars have advanced the notion that social movements ought to be understood as producing knowledge (Amin, 2022; Barbosa, 2016; Bringel and Vieira, 2015 and 2016; Choudry, 2015; Cox, 2014; Cox and Flesher Fominaya, 2009; Holt-Giménez, 2006; Icaza and Vásquez, 2013; Rosset et al., 2021; Vieira, 2011).

In fighting for a more equitable world, social movements are challenging long held assumptions about why social structures are inequitable and the environment is degraded. In doing so, they reimagine history and human beings' relationship to each other and to the natural world. They are challenging the "givens" of capitalism, offering a new paradigm of the "commons," and insisting that voices long ignored be included in the discussion. Referred to by various terms, including "alter-globalizations," "globalization from below," and "counter-hegemonic globalization," this reimagination is work being done by social movements to fight oppressive – and interrelated structures – of capitalism, colonialism, and patriarchy (Appadurai, 2000; Bakker, 2007; Brand and Makal, 2022; Falk, 1993 and 1999; Piper and Ulin, 2004). This reimagination has implications for the social sciences going forward.

Gabriel Hetland and Jeff Goodwin (2013) contend that while many seminal social movement scholars did see capitalism as an important force to be considered (including Anderson-Sherman and McAdam, 1982; Piven and Cloward, 1977; and Skocpol, 1979), more recent works have failed to examine its importance (Bieler, 2021). McAdam and Boudet (2012) suggest that social movement studies are overcorrected to focus on movements/agency, while not accounting enough for economy/structure. In writing about the present reality of social movement research, Anne Englehardt and Madelaine Moore argue the following:

> this literature lacks a certain political orientation, remaining at the level of a mid-range theory or methodology. This can be linked to the positivist turn in especially US sociological studies that has unfortunately resulted in the study of social movements and emancipatory politics developing in somewhat parallel but isolated traditions. As such, SMS tend to lack a theory of capital and class (or theory of the social more generally); they are good at providing description and tackling the questions of how social movements maintain themselves and who participates, but less adept at moving beyond the movement and asking why, or pushing an emancipatory position – struggle is a finished product rather than process, and class has been lost along the way. Conversely, critical IPE [International Political Economy] has often avoided the subject of social movements focusing instead on questions of hegemony and domination approaches. SMS looks at struggle, and critical IPE looks at class, each neglecting the other. (2022: 98)

I see that the role of capitalism is critical to the movements I examine as witnessed in their fight for a new mode of production and social reproduction. Capitalism has undermined social reproduction, and these movements are a response to that. As Englehardt and Moore put it, "the study of social movements – moments of collective struggle – is inherently political and should, therefore, be grounded in a theory of capital and class struggle" (2022: 98). The threat of water privatization is a part of the larger neoliberal trends and anti-systemic fights against capitalism, and many movements see themselves as part of a global fight against the threat of neoliberalism (Wood, 2005: 113).[8]

Piven and Cloward (1977) contend that people rise up infrequently and that, when they do, it signifies a moment of transformation. Moments of crisis often signal moments of transformation – or at least the potential for it. Today, we are in such a moment, with various counter-hegemonic movements organizing and fighting around the globe, including against water grabbing (Bieler, 2021; Moore, 2023; Muehlebach, 2023). David Harvey (2004) discusses this in the context of the "right to the city," and explains how this is a *collective* right. It is the right to create something new that does not yet exist (Harvey, 2004: 137–8). It is about the creation of a counter-hegemonic alternative to the present form of globalization (Harvey, 2004: 114; see also Escobar and Paulson, 2005; Machado, 2016). It often seems that "it is easier to imagine an end to the world than an end to capitalism" (Fisher, 2009: 2),[9] but movements *are* articulating alternatives to capitalist relations, including in efforts to fight against the privatization of water, as the coming chapters will demonstrate.

Similarly, scholarship focused on political ecology has created a theoretical framework for imagining a more equitable social order, which understands how social, political, environmental, and economic cannot be separated – everything is connected (Berkes and Folke, 1998: 8). Paul Robbins succinctly summarizes arguments defining people and nature, population versus consumption, and the subject of political ecology. He asserts that for political ecology to exist, there must be an opposite, apolitical ecology (Robbins, 2012: 14). Political ecology sees that human culture – with its political and economic constructs, which produce and reproduce systems of knowledge, power, and values – must be included in the understanding and study of ecology. Being both the shaper and the shaped, humans – and the cultures we create and that create us – are a part of nature. There is a tendency to exclude people from the equation of "nature," thereby holding humans as something separate from the environment. He argues that this is a false dichotomy and asserts: "The continued advocacy of an apolitical natural-limits argument, therefore, is implicitly political, since it holds implications for the distribution and control of resources" (Robbins, 2012: 18). For example, water shortages are not "natural" events but result from political structures (Bieler, 2021; Loftus, 2009), which I discuss in more detail in Chapter 2.

Further, capitalism cannot be understood without examining the history of colonialism, and colonialism cannot be understood without understanding how it was a racial project. This is the "coloniality of power" that continues today (Quijano, 2000). This created the Eurocentrism that continues to pervade within academia and knowledge production, which serves as the "coloniality of knowledge" (Quijano, 2007). That same coloniality is at work in studies of social movements that privilege social activism in the Global North. As Denise Ferreira da Silva explains, racism, colonialism, and "the 'means of production' or the 'raw materials' it uses for accumulation (the internal energy of African slaves and Indigenous lands) – now exists as the *form* of global capital" (Silva, 2018: final paragraph; see also Murphy,

2020; Murphy and Schroering, 2020). This form of global capital contin-ues to perpetrate environmental injustices[10] on Black, Indigenous, and com-munities of color, and other oppressed peoples around the globe. As Silva puts it, the "colonial and the racial have always been and remain integral to the functioning of global capital" (2016: paragraph 12). I add that it is critical to consider the "coloniality of gender" and how colonialism created and imposed divisions based on gender, making it an inseparable piece of the colonial project (Lugones, 2007).[11] Moghadam also notes the gendered dimensions of understanding the global economic/political system noting that it is not only "class and regional differences across economic zones, but it is also a gendered process, predicated upon gender differences in the spheres of production and reproduction" (2005: 192).

Gender is not the only erasure. Scholarship in world-systems analysis and transnational social movements often ignores race, coloniality, and whiteness (Murphy and Schroering, 2020). Yet this world-system cannot be understood – in history or the present – without interrogating race and, specifically, the project of whiteness. While whiteness, as much as any other racial category, is a social construction, a biological myth, it holds power as it is a category created to oppress and dehumanize. The existence of race and any sort of racialist structure or pattern of social organization always has social and environmental implications. The problem with ignor-ing whiteness in the study of social movements is that "The white racial frame privileges the thoughts and actions of whites over those of people of color" (Bracey, 2016: 19).[12] As Bracey details, the current hegemony of the West with its disproportionate power is "precisely because of their histories of racist domination and colonialism (Goldberg, 2002; Jung, Vargas, and Bonilla-Silva, 2011)" (Bracey, 2016: 12).

Contending with racist and colonial pasts and presents is imperative for confronting climate change. Carbon capitalism is at the root of cli-mate change. And, if we are to understand how capitalism has come to be, we must reckon that, as Carmen G. Gonzalez asserts, "Colonization and slavery were therefore central rather than peripheral to the Industrial Revolution and the birth of carbon capitalism" (2021: 118). This relates to what Silva argues: "in addition to the enclosures in England, conquest (colonization/settlement) and slavery are also integral moments in the found-ing violence of Capital" (2016: paragraph 16). Examining how racial capi-talism is bound up in the struggle for the water commons – and how climate change will amplify struggles for resources such as water – is imperative. We must consider the intersecting forms of systemic oppression based on class, race, gender, sexuality, and histories of "imperial globality" (Escobar 2008). Escobar argues that the "geopolitics of knowledge" are a part of this global system, and it begs the question: "Whose knowledge counts? And what does this have to do with place, culture, and power?" (Escobar, 2008: 4). He directs us to examine examples from Black and Indigenous activists of "counterwork" and "alternative modernities" to the status quo narratives of development, modernization, coloniality, etc. (Escobar, 2008: 10). The importance of listening to, valuing, and acting on knowledge production from social movements is a recurring theme throughout this book.

The above points to the dual problems of the erasure of dissenting voices from the periphery and the destruction of knowledge (Dotson, 2011; Escobar, 2008; Spivak, 1998: 282–3). There is a plethora of environmental sociology literature that is attuned to political economy and structure, as well as the more deleterious assaults of a Western-centric view of the world to both culture and nature. As Raul Pertierra wrote:

> One of anthropology's [*sic*] major responsibilities is to ensure that the variety of humankind's cultural insights is not discarded, following the increasing domination of a scientific-technological life-mode. As Scholte has argued, "epistemicide"[13] is a milder form of genocide but ultimately as threatening to the continuation of alternative approaches to life. (1988: 85)

The erasure, exclusion, and attempted destruction of non-hegemonic modes of knowledge(s) is one aspect of a larger conversation around knowledge production. Another is the colonial and positivist histories of the social sciences, especially around the process of research methodologies. Carolina Bejarano Alonso and co-authors note how too often social science has worked to maintain "Western imperial power" (2019). On the other hand, social science that is anti-colonial

> decenters the scientist as the principal actor in designing and enacting research. It recognizes the historical 'subjects' of anthropological research – themselves often the subjects of (neo)colonial aggression and exploitation – as more than merely the objects of ethnographic investigation. Rather, it acknowledges them as capable producers of knowledge and theorists of their own experience. (Bejarano et al., 2019: 136)

The discipline of sociology (especially in the United States) is not exempt. From the beginning of the discipline, there have been epistemic exclusions, with sociology focused on Anglo-European men. As Julian Go puts it: "It was only their knowledge that was valued; only their knowledge was taken as true sociological knowledge" (Go, 2020: 80). This is, as Bejarano et al., point out, a part of maintaining Western imperial hegemony. Epistemic exclusions persist in various forms today, especially around race, gender, sexuality, class, and geographic location. Go (2020) discusses how when Anglo-European scholars study the elite, or revolutions, or state formation, that work is not similarly considered "me-search" or seen as biased or subjective. Indeed, Weber, "a Christian white middle-class male in Europe, argued that white middle-class Christian males in Europe were the key to capitalism, his work was not called 'me-search.' To the contrary, his work is canonized and endowed with universal provenance" (Go, 2020: 89). I include this discussion because Go's work emphasizes a critical point: all social science, all theories, are partial and incomplete. As Chandra Mohanty Talpade wrote two decades ago:

> The contrast between Western scientific systems and indigenous epistemologies and systems of medicine is not the only issue here. It is the colonialist and corporate power to define Western science, and the reliance on capitalist values of private property and profit, as the only normative system that results in the exercise of immense power. (2003a: 512)

Emotional and ideological involvement – both conscious and unconscious – is always at play, which I will return to in the second to last section of this chapter.

Description of cases and methodology

The arguments in this book are built on three case studies, carried out between 2016 and 2022. The first one was conducted with the Our Water Campaign (OWC) – a coalition based in Pittsburgh, PA, USA. The second is with Brazil's Movimento dos Atingidos por Barragens (MAB) – a national, autonomous popular social movement. Nigeria's Our Water, Our Right (OWOR) is a third example that bridges the two primary cases.

My fieldwork with OWC reveals that there are grassroots mobilizations that resist water privatization in the United States and fight for more equitable, environmentally sound, and transparent governance. Movements have worked to draw attention to the role of private industry and neoliberal reforms – and not simply failed public governance – in causing water quality problems. Water struggles quickly flow into struggles over austerity and the role of the state and corporate power, and multi-issue movements are arising to fight for livelihood since it is connected with justice and equality. In other words: resistance against water privatization and for remunicipalization of water in the United States is political (González Rivas and Schroering, 2021).

The second case draws on my fieldwork in Brazil with the Brazilian social movement, Movimento dos Atingidos por Barragens (Movement of People Affected by Dams or MAB). I argue that the standpoint offered by Global South actors offers important insights into the operation of systems of power and strategies of resistance. I examine knowledge production and, specifically, how the work of the Brazilian movement is grounded in theory and praxis and is led by many young people who are adding to, critiquing, and changing theory, and, in so doing, building a national and international movement for the right to water (Schroering, 2019a). I discuss how MAB provides insight into how underlying systemic realities that cause struggles around water must be acknowledged by all – the problem is not solely one of scarcity versus abundance. I also examine how social identities, understandings of interests, and translocal connections are a part of how MAB builds a transnational struggle for the right to water and how this relates to a broader effort to redefine globalization.

These two cases are bridged with a third, where I explore other transnational movement connections, including data I collected when I had the opportunity to participate with Pittsburgh activists in a Human Right to Water Summit in Nigeria, organized by OWOR. This work centers a recurring finding in my research: just as governments, corporations, and global financial institutions interact globally, so too do social movements. Activists understand that movements can learn from each other and form transnational connections coalitions in order to more effectively advance goals and achieve favorable outcomes (Schroering, 2021a). My results demonstrate that activists see solidarity between movements and across national borders – especially in this political moment where there is a resurgence of authoritarian governments – as essential. I argue that the Summit in Nigeria is an example of translocal organizing (Banerjee, 2011, 2018; Mignolo, 2007; Shah et al., 2019) for water. These case studies expand the empirical foundations that can help illuminate the complex and multifaceted ways by which information and knowledge flows through transnational movement networks, thereby contributing to learning that can disrupt prevailing power relations.

MAB is a national popular movement that works in local communities but is a country-wide movement with national (and even global) vision and goals. OWOR is now a continent-wide organization, with many global partners. This contrasts from how the OWC operates in the United States, which is based in the city of Pittsburgh (even while making some national and global alliances). I see my study, however, as about a global fight against water privatization, grounded in local and national struggles, but connected to each other. While the hegemonic socio-political and economic forces have shaped political outcomes and repressed democracy and social movements, counter-hegemonic ideas and movements persist, often using explicit anti-systemic language – but sometimes it is more implicit, since an unequivocal anti-capitalist frame is strategically difficult, especially in the "belly of the beast" that is the United States. Nonetheless, the book provides examples of communities of people resisting expulsions and articulating a vision for how things might look different. These groups are not just criticizing the current system but articulating alternatives to the present form of economic globalization and capitalist relations. MAB does this in a head-on fashion and points to capitalism as the problem and argues that the right to water is inextricably linked with the right to land, to energy, to food, to education, to be safe from violence, to self-determination, and to sovereignty. The OWC conveys an understanding that these issues are inter-connected, and that solidarity and people power are necessary for change.

My data is drawn from extensive, in-depth participant observation. It includes fieldwork with MAB conducted in five Brazilian states over the span of four visits (each lasting between three and seven weeks) in 2018, 2019, 2020, and 2022, and virtually between 2020 and 2022. This includes thirty-one semi-structured in-person interviews and hundreds of hours of "observant participation" of daily activities, meetings, trainings, actions, marches, and informal conversations. For OWC, the book draws on fieldwork from observant participation of meetings, planning retreats, actions, city council, and other public meetings mainly between January 2017 and August 2020, although I remained engaged in OWC through 2022. Through work with OWC, in January–February 2019 I attended the Human Right to Water Summit in Abuja, Nigeria, and also visited Calabar, Lagos, and Ibadan, Nigeria. I amassed a collection of printed material (books, training manuals, posters, pamphlets, and other materials) from campaigns and movements, which I drew on in this book, looking at how the movements frame their work through published materials. The book also includes public content from web and social media pages. Please see Appendix A for more specific details on the fieldwork process and data collection.

A Note on Naming

In the chapters that follow, I use a combination of conventions to refer to the movement participants. I use people's full names if I am referencing a public event where the person spoke or if the person has requested that I use their full name. Due to changing political situations from when I began my research to the writing of this book and the ongoing nature of all of the cases (which means I need to be cautious about writing something that could harm that work), I only use someone's first or full name (outside of the above condition) if I could confirm permission. In some cases, people requested that I use their first or full name; others asked that I not use any part of their name. In MAB, there is a sensibility of speaking for the movement and the broader ideas it represents, rather than crediting individuals. I was asked in some cases to reference MAB as a whole instead of citing an individual. In other cases, I was not able to confirm if someone wanted me to use their name or not, and in both of these situations, I use a pseudonym or simply refer to the person as an "activist," "organizer," "participant," "leader,"[14] "militant," or "integrante," etc.[15] Finally, all tables, figures, photos, and language translations are my own, unless otherwise noted.

Navigating positionality in fieldwork and research, and linking theory with praxis

I came to the academic study of social movements from a background in organizing, and I have nearly two decades of experience in student, community, political, environmental, and labor organizing. When living in Brazil in 2008, I visited the Palmares II settlement of the Landless Workers' Movement (MST) and began to learn more about the largest social movement in the Americas.[16] I learned about conflicts and threats around land and resources, including water, mining, and other extractive industries. I witnessed environmental injustices and how the capitalist mode of development perpetrates ongoing forms of colonial appropriation. When I returned to the United States, I began a campaign to "ban bottled water" on my college campus and worked to educate students and faculty on why water should not be a commodity. Before beginning my graduate studies of social movements, I worked as a community organizer in Jacksonville, Florida, for four years with an affiliate of a national organizing network. The executive director of this network said the following to me before I left: Why would I want to go? To sit in the Ivory Tower and talk about social movements? Scholars don't do anything except talk about things. Movements are doing the actual work, he told me. I did not entirely disagree with this assessment, but I felt a strong pull toward academia, not only because I love to research and learn, but also because I believe education can be liberatory.[17]

More than a decade later, this tension between academia and organizing, and the role that research might play in transformative change, continues to agitate me. Yet, as Amita Baviskar instructs: "While we should be sensitive to the contradictions inherent in the researcher/researched relationship, we cannot allow our ethical dilemmas to immobilize us" (2004: 11). I have remained engaged in organizing work around various issues at a local, national, and global level. A critical aspect of academic activism requires being aware of power dynamics and the generation of mechanisms for collaborative/co-research. How do I produce research that does not reinforce, and actually helps dismantle, power hierarchies?

Michael Murphy suggests that an anti-colonial environmental sociology would do three things. First, it would place "human social activity within the manifold of associations that constitute the broader biophysical world"; second, engage with the multitude of views of "subaltern people to understand socioecological dynamics from their often overlapping, but sometimes conflicting standpoints"; and third, unearth "the colonial and imperialist foundations and ongoing entanglements of contemporary socio-ecological situations" (2020: 126). I find these elements instructive. I find the use of the term "anti-colonial" to describe my own research approach as more appropriate than "decolonial," given my own positionality as a white scholar from a settler colonial country.

The work of radical research is a constant and changing process of reflex-ivity. There is not a clear path nor a specific end goal. Thus, for me, a critical component of this struggle is to strive to produce work that is accessible to the movements with whom I work; one component of this includes lan-guage – creating work in Portuguese or translating the English version into Portuguese. On the other hand, I am cognizant of how MAB is not well-known (even among activists on the Left) in the United States. As MAB leaders told me, there is, then, a need to share the work and knowledge of this movement in English. The opposite is also true, however, as I have learned in the past few years: Knowledge flows must go both ways, and that includes using my positionality to share information and news from the United States with movement actors in Brazil. I discuss this process in more detail in subsequent chapters. Finally, I note that I have communicated and shared the process of writing openly with leaders in the movements with whom I do work. This has included sharing drafts of my work, receiving input, and permissions (that goes beyond the formal ethics review com-mittees in both the United States and Brazil through which my project had approval) on which photos to share and how to credit and cite leaders.

I have structured this book as episodes of encounters where translocal resistance becomes more visible and legible: the organizing space and work of the OWC, the organizing and training spaces of MAB, and the 2019 Summit in Nigeria. In all the empirical chapters, my voice is present as both researcher and movement participant to varying degrees, at times veering toward autoethnography. I have made choices about what to include and what to exclude for now, and what I choose to write is filtered by my per-spective. My inductive approach has led me to feminist and anti-colonial research methodologies and a process that is constantly learning with and from the movements with whom I work. I acknowledge that this informs not simply my fieldwork and data collection but my data analysis and writing.

While I do include interview data where I think it helps to paint a clearer picture of the landscape for the reader, the more profound stories come from conversations and interactions with people after building relationships and trust or turning off the tape recorder. In terms of methodology, in future projects – time permitting – I would choose to conduct interviews at the end, rather than the beginning, of my research process, after my knowledge and understanding of the topic had grown, and people gained trust in me. My work with MAB has brought me together with militants worldwide, including Chile, Venezuela, Cuba, Basque Country, Turkey, Spain, France, Bosnia, Guatemala, Mexico, Uruguay, Colombia, and the United States. While I do draw on and discuss this briefly, this is an area that I hope to include more in future work. Many of these connections have turned into continued communication and solidarity, despite the geographic distance and uncertainty of when we might all gather in a shared space in person again. My work with the OWC has built connections with water activists from elsewhere in the United States, in Nigeria, and other locales in the world.

The information I have gathered is informed by my positionality and how others perceive me. Race, class, gender, sexuality, and geographic location all matter (Crenshaw, 1989, 1991; Moraga and Anzaldúa, 1981; Richter et al., 2020). Indeed, there is a substantial body of work that calls for considering positionality when studying movements and argues that knowledge production needs to come with and from the community (see Bejarano et al., 2019; Collins, 2015; Conway, 2017; Escobar, 2008; Falcón, 2016; Icaza and Vásquez, 2013; Mohanty, 2003a, 2003b; Robnett, 1996; Vieira, 2015; Watkins, 2018). I am a white, queer cis, woman researcher from the United States, which shapes what is highlighted to me differently than if I had a different positionality. A repeated theme across my interviews, informal conversations, and participant observation is the importance of international solidarity. I recognize this stands out to me because of who I am: an academic and movement participant from the United States who has been invited to come share space with MAB as a movement actor from another space and place – and so, what I am going to be let into is likely more of the international solidarity than if I was, for example, a Brazilian researcher. This does not mean that international solidarity is not of critical importance or a real focus for MAB. Indeed, it is a point discussed in all of MAB's work and a core area of focus listed on their website. Instead, it means that I might see more of that than other aspects of MAB's work; for someone else, whose positionality differs from mine, this might look different.

Similarly, I recognize that my positionality as both researcher and movement participant in OWC shaped what I learned, including being invited to Nigeria and being in a space with others from the United States discussing, sharing, and learning from struggles elsewhere in the world. While I contend the Summit was a critical moment for those from the OWC who attended, I recognize that my positionality informs this view. For example, if I were a researcher only interested in Pittsburgh-based politics and movements, I likely would not have gone to Nigeria or participated in subsequent events connected to it and, as such, those aspects of the campaign's work would not be included in my analysis. I highlight this to connect to the idea that a purely objective, neutral researcher does not exist. Our positionality as researchers always informs what we see and, in turn, our analysis and writing.

With this in consideration, I argue that I cannot be a post-colonial, post-imperial, post-white supremacy, post-cis-heteropatriarchy, post-capitalism scholar. I live in a world where those systems are very much alive and at work. My positionality not only gives me certain privileges, it also shapes how I see the world, no matter how reflexive and critical I am. What I can be, however, is a scholar and person who interrogates the world-historic structures that shape what I see and what I know. I can seek with intentionality to be anti-imperial, anti-colonial, anti-racist, anti-cis-heteropatriarchy, and anti-capitalist. This is not just a theoretical stance; it is one lived out in praxis, and that means that theory and praxis cannot be devoid of taking an ethical standpoint.

To be clear: what I am calling for here is not new. Marx saw the need for "revolutionary practice" and that theory and action go together as part of a process to change society (Marx, 1845). W. E. B. Du Bois rejected disciplinary fragmentation, served as an extraordinary public intellectual, and saw theory and praxis as intertwined (Du Bois, 1952; Rabaka, 2006; Stewart, 1984). The Italian practice of "co-research," as articulated by Romano Alquait (and others) in the 1950s and 1960s, saw that collaboration between workers and researchers (sociologists in particular) could produce a new form of knowledge (Mohandesi and Haider, 2018), build revolutionary theory, and ultimately break down the distinction between scientific researcher and political militant (Sacchetto, Armano, and Wright, 2013; Wright, 2002). Or, as Carolina Alonso Bejarano et al. wrote of their endeavors to decolonize the process of ethnography:

> this approach did not originate with us, the authors of this book. Our intervention stands on the shoulders of the many individuals, schools, and perspectives variously labeled feminist, native, Black, collaborative, World, applied, engaged, practicing, and activist, to name but a few. (2019: 137)

Janet Conway argues the need for a "paradigm shift" in how we *study* movements (Conway, 2017). Laurence Cox addresses how scholars of movements could learn from movements: "We could, perhaps, learn something from listening to what movements (and social movement studies) have learned about the actual complexities of effective action for change" (2014: 958). Knowledge *is* produced outside of the academy and too often it is dismissed. Yet, as Aziz Choudry succinctly contends: "Whose knowledge is valued and by what criteria? What are the political, economic, and social conditions in which knowledge is produced, given that the academic mode of knowledge production is only one among many?" (2015: 56).

Social theory production can be – must be – a part of transforming society. While practices are shifting, the idea still remains in much of academia, and certainly within US based social movement studies, that there is somehow a detached, neutral researcher who critiques their research subjects.

This points to the challenges of overcoming methodological nationalism, disciplinary boundaries, and broadening the sociological canon. Paulo Freire wrote in 1968 how this notion of co-research is still under-discussed within academia, excluded by the non-dialogic pedagogies that reign hegemonic (Freire, 2018 [1968]). Decades later, there is still truth in his observation, even as there is a growing body of literature showing how peasant led social movements, as well as social movements more broadly in Latin America, are important sites of knowledge production (Barbosa, 2016; Bringel and Vieira, 2016; Holt-Giménez, 2006; Rosset and Altieri, 2017; Rosset et al., 2021), a point I will return to in Chapter 4. In the United States, I have noted growing attention to the ideas of decolonial research methodologies and community-engaged research, including at the University of Pittsburgh, with a series of panels held on this topic throughout 2020–2021. I have observed, however, almost no discussion within these settings of the problem of the neoliberalization of the university, why the economic system needs to change, or how the academy too often upholds and benefits from exploitative structures (see Sondarjee and Andrews, 2023, for an excellent discussion of how "decolonial" has been watered down and that caution should be taken, especially by Western scholars, in its use).

This conversation relates to a significant systemic problem posed by the capitalist and colonial university, which through neoliberal policies and practices has become what Giggi Roggero (2014) refers to as the "edu-factory." The university is both a site for the extraction of surplus-value and disciplinary exclusion/integration based on class, race, gender, sexuality, geographic location, citizenship, and politics. The opposite of the "edu-factory" is the space of the "undercommons" (see Moten and Harney, 2004), encompassing "networks of rebellious solidarity that interlace within, against, and beyond dominant institutions and power structures" (The Undercommoning Collective, 2016). I see that co-research can be a part of this undercommons and upset the order of the edu-factory, serving as a prospective site for the co-production and circulation of contested socio-technical-ecological knowledge(s)/power(s). In the spirit of a "right to the city" as articulated by Henri Lefebvre (1996 [1968]) and David Harvey (2012), I am interested in the processes and potentialities of a collective right to create alternative ways of organizing our world(s). Economic systems define who gets access to what resources and, in turn, defines systems of social relations. For capitalism, this is ordered around hierarchies and exclusions. However, other economic and social orders do and have existed that establish different priorities to govern social relations from the accumulation of capital.

I choose not to separate my militancy and scholarship. Or perhaps, as Freire (2018 [1968]) might say, I cannot separate the two. The bifurcation of research and practice has depoliticized research and enlisted scholars to reproduce hegemony, which works to the advantage of the hegemonic powers, who also fund research and academic institutions. As Choudry writes: "As some activist researchers themselves suggest, boundaries between research and organizing are sometimes blurred to the point of nonexistence. Such understandings challenge binary thinking that separates, fragments, and compartmentalizes activities into categories of 'research' and 'organizing,' and actors into 'researchers' and 'organizers'" (2015: 128). Rebecca Tarlau notes, "being an activist-scholar will never stop being a contradiction. However, I do think that social movement researchers dedicated to critical engagement, collaboration, and sharing can help to build a more robust understanding of activism and political struggle" (2014: 84). There is a reality of power dynamics amidst the world-as-it-is: as scholars, we have access to resources often denied to counter-hegemonic movements. As we work to change this system, there is an aspect of deciding to use privilege to work with (not on or for) movements.

The words in this book are my own, and I am responsible for them as such. At the same time, and in the spirit of the argument I make about knowledge production and anti-colonial methodologies, I could not have written it without the knowledge of every single person I crossed paths with on this journey. Some are named; many others are not. A few will read it, even more will hear about it, and some might not even know it was written.[18] However, since it is impossible – and presumptuous – to represent the nuances of each person's knowledge, fears, and hopes, the words on the page are mine alone.[19] People have given me their trust and shared their knowledge with me. Across the disparate social and geographic locations, everyone in the movements and campaigns that I discuss in this book see that water is a human right and should be available to all, without conditions. This book attempts to further that belief, even as the exact articulation is through my eyes.

Structure of the book

This book is organized in seven chapters. Chapter 2 will discuss the broader landscape of water privatization and how social movements have struggled against it. My analysis of such resistance against the political economy of water privatization is grounded within a discussion that is both local and global in its scope. The chapter explores how corporate malfeasance that is all too typical of international water privatization initiatives manifested itself in dramatic fashion in the United States in the water crisis in Flint, Michigan, and elsewhere. The chapter concludes with an examination of how the battle to see water as a commodity for profit versus water as a public resource for the benefit of all, plays out in an overlooked aspect of water grabbing: dams.

Chapter 3, my first empirical chapter, focuses on the social movement for the right to water in the United States based upon my fieldwork with a Pittsburgh-based coalition and the "translocal" (Banerjee 2011, 2018) aspects of it. The Pittsburgh case illustrates how privatization posed real and direct threats to people's health and living costs. I show how the struggle against water privatization is driven by political, not just pragmatic, concerns, and that it is part of a larger translocal struggle. The solution that emerged was to keep the water a public good managed by (local) government and to fight against corporate predation. The chapter argues that just as transnational corporations work globally, movements resisting privatization do the same: their struggles are locally focused, and organizing occurs at the local level, but these struggles are linked to more extensive national and global processes. Translocal activism is about people engaging with the state and markets, and fighting for participatory, democratic, and more horizontal governance structures, as well as the ideas of more communal notions of property rights, rights to livelihood, and social justice (Banerjee 2018: 812).

In Chapter 4, I explore how MAB offers crucial insights into the operations of systems of power and strategies of resistance. Purely technocratic approaches to solving water problems are destined to fail if they do not account for both the lived and theoretical knowledge produced and articulated by the people most impacted. Further, underlying systemic realities that cause struggles around water must be acknowledged by all – the problem is not solely one of scarcity versus abundance. This points to the need for a reorganization of social relations. MAB centers its struggle around the idea of water (and energy and education) as a commons rather than a commodity. MAB's counter-hegemonic work is about knowledge and imagination – a different world from the one in which we currently live cannot be realized if we do not understand the processes that shape the current one, nor if we cannot even imagine a different one. This includes considering the role of class, race, gender, and sexuality in organizing anti-systemic struggles, and centering the voices of people historically excluded from leadership and decision-making processes. MAB argues that solidarity between movements and across national borders is increasingly important. A critical component of this, I contend, is to learn about, from, and with Global South-led movements, who are producing theory and living it out in praxis.

Chapter 5 explores the implications of learning from knowledge produced beyond the academy and by Global South movements, and specifically MAB. I show that the what and how of my study (i.e., the questions I ask and methodologies I choose) cannot be separated from the who and why. Taking a collaborative and solidarity-based approach to knowledge directly shapes the theories and methods of analysis. I show that this enables the production of insights in real time of how to organize for the right to water, especially in terms of the role of popular education and training, spearheaded by many young people who added to, critiqued, and changed theory. Decolonized modes of knowledge production in turn helped cultivate alliances and collaborations that transcended national borders.

Chapter 6 examines efforts to reclaim the commons of water, and how grassroots movements drive the struggle and demand the prioritization of democracy, transparency, and human rights over corporate profits in public policy. As feminist scholars have pointed out, the "standpoint" offered by marginalized actors offers important insights into the operation of systems of power and the strategies of resistance. Transnational social movement scholars have too often reinforced the idea that knowledge flows from the Global North to the Global South. This chapter builds on scholarship that has examined the importance of Global South to Global North social movement connections, by bringing together my three empirical case studies. I argue that these three cases actually reflect a single case of a translocal movement for the right to water, with the National Summit on the Human Right to Water, Nigeria's Water Emergency: From Resistance to Real Solutions Against Corporate Control held in Abuja, Nigeria, in 2019 (referred to from here forward as the Summit), as one specific convergence space of translocal organizing for the human right to water.

Finally, Chapter 7 summarizes the main arguments and contributions of the book, and outlines some of the critical ongoing struggles around water grabbing and privatization in the world. I connect my cases and arguments to the new wave of water privatization occurring in Brazil right now, as well as growing discussion of water affordability and the role of federal money for private water infrastructure improvements in the United States. I argue that this work shows a re-organizing of social relations and people's understanding of interests and how they are met (or not met) through existing power relations. Through translocal right to water organizing, people from the Global North have shared experiences with people in the Global South regarding corporate power that results in unsafe water. These interactions challenge nationalist identities and alignments and begin to center global economic structures and how they determine policies and practices all over the world. Translocality allows for the maintenance of local specificity while creating learning networks that allow for movements to come together with others to build solidarity. Just as corporations operate together, so too does the resistance.

Global solidarities against water grabbing explores how capitalist exploitation and appropriation are being contested, and how movements are proposing alternatives beyond capitalism, with multi-scalar (translocal) dimensions of social movements and campaigns fighting against water privatization as part of a larger project of contesting capitalism. This book contributes to ongoing methodological and theoretical discussions about knowledge production and anti-colonial research methodologies. Taking a collaborative and solidarity-based approach to knowledge production – and being driven by my ongoing history as an organizer and activist committed to advancing the idea of water as a right for all – directly shaped the theories and methods of analysis that I used. In this work, I am a participant in and with the movements I discuss, and how I engage and participate is always under the invitation and guidance of the movements. In this sense, I am a subject of my analysis.

Notes

1 The book also directly relates to this third form: hydroelectric dams are inseparable from water for extractive mining industries and land grabbing for export agriculture, which is discussed in Chapter 2.
2 This footnote is inspired by a statement made to me by an interviewee who said: "If you do not have water, you do not have anything" – see Chapter 4.
3 As Chandra Talpade Mohanty writes, language is imprecise, and whatever terminology is chosen will therefore not be perfect in describing the situation and/ or explain the world in binary terms, when the reality is more complicated. Mohanty uses the terms "one-third" and "two-thirds" world to break up the world based on privilege and affluence, regardless of geography. A wealthy person in Brazil may very well have the same economic affluence as someone living in the United States. Perhaps more affluent people live in the United States than in Brazil, but both countries have people who are a part of the "one-third" world that uses most of the world's resources. On the other hand, a majority of the population in Brazil is impoverished, so is part of the "two-thirds" world. Some people living in the United States or other countries traditionally branded as "developed," are also impoverished and living on very little; as such, they too are a part of the "two-thirds" world (Mohanty, 2003a). I prefer this distinction to the alternatives in various ways. However, in this book, I use "Global South" and "Global North," as these are the terms most commonly used and understood, and also move us away from Western colonial notions of "developed" versus "undeveloped."
4 The term "resource" presumes a Western/Eurocentric understanding of how humans relate to nature. Language speaks to the episteme and ontology out of

which it comes. As I will discuss later, the binaries of culture/nature or people/environment, or the idea that humans can "own" something like water are based in understandings of the world that do not exist across time and space. However, I use the term "resource" here (just as I use "rights" (and various others), which I also discuss in Chapter 2), because that is the term that is commonly used and understood.

5 The term decolonize has gained more popularity and is used to mean various things that stray from its original use. I do not use this term flippantly, as I will discuss later in this chapter.

6 I argue that the question of violence is one that social movement studies needs to grapple with more in general. The current systems that organize and dominate our world create horrific violence to many, in the form of lack of sufficient calories, clean water, housing, healthcare, etc. Systems that center profit over life ought to be called out as violent. I return to this point later in this chapter and especially in Chapter 6. Additionally, the binary of what constitutes violence versus nonviolence in activism or organizing, as well as the role of violence in struggles for liberation, also needs to be interrogated (see Case, 2022).

7 Imperialism and colonialism are related, but different. The following statement by Edward Said succinctly distinguishes between the two: " 'imperialism' means the practice and theory, and the attitudes of a dominating metropolitan centre ruling a distant territory; 'colonialism', which is almost always a consequence of imperialism, is the implanting of settlements on distant territory" (1993: 8).

8 Leslie Wood's work is focused on the Peoples' Global Action (PGA) founded in Geneva in 1998 where 300 delegates from nearly twenty countries created a manifesto for collaboration, creating a transnational organizing framework. Included in the participants was Brazil's Landless Worker's Movement (MST). They used this collaboration to protest WTO meetings, including the 1999 Seattle WTO protests.

9 This quote is attributed to both Fredric Jameson and Slavoj Žižek, as Fisher notes.

10 Histories of colonialism and settler colonialism must also be acknowledged in considering environmental justice in the United States. As Kyle Powys Whyte writes, settler colonialism is defined as the "complex social processes in which at least one society seeks to move permanently onto the terrestrial, aquatic, and aerial places lived in by one or more other societies who already derive economic vitality, cultural flourishing, and political self-determination from the relationships they have established with the plants, animals, physical entities, and ecosystems of those places. Settler colonialism is an 'environmental' injustice" (2017: 9).

11 Lugones (2007: 187) argues for the need to go behind the ahistorical idea of the "heterosexualist patriarchy." She sees that Quijano's account of gender is "too narrow and overly biologized as it presupposes sexual dimorphism, heterosexuality, patriarchal distribution of power" (2007: 193). Lugones argues we must look at how race, gender, and sexuality are intertwined, and go

beyond the patriarchy. Brooklyn Leo in turn critiques Lugones for not interrogating the colonial history of cisgender violence: "If Lugones challenges us to see within colonial difference as itself a crucial feminist intervention into decolonial theory, then we must begin with a complex historical acknowledgement of how cisgender privilege is intimately tied up within colonial structure" (2020: 465). In future work, I intend to engage more in this discussion in the context of water justice organizing and understanding interconnected systems of oppression.

12 Bracey is specifically intervening in a strand of social movement studies called Political Process Theory. For too long, whiteness has dominated, and this shapes not just *how* but *what* movements are studied. While Bracey is writing specifically to the study of Black movements in the United States, his argument is also applicable to the study of movements beyond the United States. As Bracey notes: "Founding PPT theorists' reliance on the white racial frame manifests not only in the structure of the model itself (i.e., state centeredness), but also in the range of cases analysts select for empirical studies. Political process scholars have been criticized for focusing almost exclusively on movements in Western states (Wiktorowicz, 2004)" (Bracey, 2016: 19).

13 Following my commitment to an anti-colonial praxis, I would be remiss not to note the following: as of the final editing of this book, the news broke of the scholar Boaventura de Sousa Santos' sexual and moral harassment of multiple women. At the same time, attention is currently being drawn to the flaws in his scholarship, including that many ideas – including "epistemicide" and "ecology of knowledges" – did not, in fact, originate with him, nor in some cases did he even cite the original authors. Ideas and concepts are almost always communal processes, and I acknowledge that I will also most inevitably have omissions in my own work. In this particular case and moment, however, I made the decision to no longer cite Santos' work, and to instead give the space to other scholars who have been erased or ignored. And also to stand with and believe the voices of the women who are bravely speaking their truth. See here: https://web.archive.org/web/20231011194005/https://apublica.org/2023/04/brazilian-state-deputy-says-she-was-sexually-assaulted-by-boaventura-de-sousa-santos/

14 This work also addresses questions of leadership. Leadership is important to this work, especially as it relates to questions related to dismantling systems of oppression within social movements while also organizing to change those systems in the larger world. In subsequent chapters, particularly Chapters 4, 5, and 7, this is discussed as it relates to larger questions of how movements produce knowledge and organize. There is extensive literature on leadership within social movement studies; due to space limitations, I do not delve into it here.

15 These terms do have distinct meaning, especially the Portuguese "militante" and "integrante," which don't fully translate. Militante means militant in English and is commonly used by popular and revolutionary movements around the globe, including MAB. Integrante best translates to "members" in English and

is also often used. MAB militantes do not use/identify with the term "activist" and so I do not use it to describe them.

16 The MST mission is centered on access to land, which is a fundamental dimension of human–environment relations, and a basis for managing other resources such as water, forest, animals, and fertility of the soil. It has also, as Miguel Carter writes, emphasized education and "raising popular consciousness" of its members, using both the pedagogy of Paulo Freire as well as its own materials (Carter, 2011: 201). The MST formed out of the struggles for land reform by rural workers in the 1970s. It was officially founded in 1984 with the stated goal to obtain land for the millions of landless people left behind in the "Brazilian Miracle" of rapid economic growth and development. However, the MST came to see that access to land was not sufficient. People also need access to healthcare, housing, education, and credit. A critique developed, therefore, of the application of neoliberal economic policies, some of which included expansion of agroindustry via new methods of mechanized agriculture, which disenfranchised and left behind many rural workers. The MST's fight for agrarian reform, therefore, becomes linked with imagining a new, alternate model and reality (Boff, 2014; MST, 2023). As of 2022, the MST is organized in 24 Brazilian states, comprised of 450,000 thousand families and an additional 90,000 families in encampments fighting for land. The MST also operates 1,900 community associations, 160 cooperatives, and is the largest producer of organic rice in Latin America (MST, 2023; Pagliarini, 2023).

17 These same statements have also been echoed to me in various forms over the years, from many different people, across countries and continents, and that other "scholar-activists" have also written about (including from the United States, such as Bevington and Dixon, 2005; Dawson et al., 2012; Piven, 2010; Tarlau, 2014). In my own organizing and academic journey, I have also come to learn of the multitude of voices who have struggled with, lived into, and written about this same question. Due to the persistent colonial cannon, I only discovered many of these voices much later.

18 I intend to publish this book in Portuguese and see that as a critical piece of my own praxis.

19 I see that an important dimension of my scholarship is in citations and who I cite. I have attempted to cite thinkers outside the traditional "canon" and to include a range of representative voices. I am also aware that due to my own positionality, biases, education, and existing disciplinary boundaries and hegemonic dominance of scholars from the United States, I have likely missed critical work in my citations.

2

Water grabbing, privatization, and resistance against commodification

In March 2017, a meeting of activists from eleven countries asserted that "Water, food, and energy are not commodities!" Organized by Brazil's Movimento dos Atingidos por Barragens[1] (MAB), participants represented thirty-two different organizations, including the Pittsburgh, Pennsylvania Our Water Campaign (OWC). The gathering focused on organizing and building unity across organizations involved in struggles against the commodification of life-sustaining resources. The group argued in a joint statement that: "A collective effort is necessary for the building of unity of the widest range of organizations willing to struggle against capitalism and patriarchy and to build a new society" (Letter from The II International Seminar: *Food, Water and Energy Are Not Commodities*, 2017).[2]

On 5 October 2020, Veolia – one of the world's largest water privatization corporations – acquired 29.9 per cent of the shares of Suez, another water multinational, with plans to obtain eventual full control (Macleod, 2020; Veolia, 2020). After a bitter court battle, in April 2021, the two companies agreed on a $15 billion merger, and said that a final agreement would be reached by 14 May 2021 (White and Kar-Gupta, 2021). In 2022, the merger became finalized; Veolia's profit for the year grew to $1.2 billion (Morland and Mackos, 2022). It is now the largest private water operator in the world (Global Water Intelligence, 2022: 9).

The above two examples illustrate the point made in Chapter 1: this book is about how on the one hand corporations are organizing to accumulate capital through water grabbing, and on the other hand, social movements are organizing against it. This chapter examines water privatization (including how capital and multinational corporations operate in this realm) and how movements resist it. Water grabbing is a form of capitalist crisis driven expansion, and it is "always contested" (Bieler, 2021: 50). While capital is always coming back with new attempts to privatize, we "should not underestimate the transformative potential of water struggles" (Bieler, 2021: 166). The concept of water grabbing is useful because it helps us to understand how seemingly disparate processes are in fact intimately connected. A part of the problem of understanding the interconnected crises caused by capitalist expansion is the tendency to study each part as discrete. For example, lack of access to clean water for all is viewed as separate from the crisis of climate change, which is seen as disconnected from inflation and rising cost of food. Yes, there are differences, but in essence, all of these problems are connected because the same forces are driving them, with catastrophic results for all life. We must understand these problems as interconnected and caused by our socio-economic system.

This chapter connects the local to the global, providing context and understanding of the fight for the right to water in the United States, and how that fight is, like in Brazil, a struggle between competing world views. The dominance of capitalism as "the" economic system is powerful in the United States, a nation-state built on the idea of the "free market." As noted in the previous chapter, everything is or could be a commodity – including "resources" such as land, water, rivers, and oceans. Water, like air, is necessary for life. More so than other resources, it is often ostensibly under public rather than private control. The drive to privatize, however, continues, making water a new "frontier" for capitalist expansion. Many scholars differentiate between capitalism before and after the 1990s, which saw a worldwide rise of a specific type of capitalism, neoliberalism, that further weakened the working class. Yet, from the analysis of the movements with whom I work, the root of the problem is capitalism as a socio-political-economic system, even as the particular forms – neoliberalism and the austerity measures that come with it, speculative finance that financializes water – compound and worsen its extractive capacity.

I use the term "right to water" to refer to the idea of a collective right that articulates the conception that water is not a commodity but an essential source for the production and reproduction of human and non-human life. I use the term following the example of movement participants who I have met, worked with, interviewed, and learned from, who articulate the "right to water" as a struggle against water accumulation for profit. I want to note that increasingly corporations such as the water privatization giants Veolia and Suez are using and appropriating the language of rights as well. So, while it is a powerful narrative, it can be manipulated and abused, and this highlights the need to always be attuned to positionality and who the speaker is (see also Nowak, 2016).

Rights language can be used as part of a liberal, individualist, Western-centric approach, appropriated by transnational corporations; but rights language can encompass a more collective and transformative idea that sees water as a social and cultural good – a commons even – and that the "right to water" in struggles is often used to capture this idea and stand in opposition to neoliberal, capitalist logic (Bieler, 2021). I want to make clear: there are distinctions between thinking of water as a public good, a commons, a right, or a commodity. In this chapter, in the previous chapter, and in the chapters to come, I at times clarify these distinctions, and how I see movements using these terms. What is unambiguous, however, is this: there is an argument that water should not be a commodity – that it is not something for financial gain – and that all people need water to survive and therefore ought to have access to it.

The discussion around "rights" language also concerns how we think about property and property rights, which effectively serve as the right to exclude others. This differs from other rights since they often, in fact, threaten the rights of those who lack property and are commonly defined in arbitrary ways. Ideas can be patented and land or buildings can be owned and considered property, while labor is not (Dine, 2006, 2009). Much of our social structure today is built around this notion. On the other hand, the "right to the city" resists the enclosure of the commons and is based on the idea of public spaces and public goods. This is a collective right (Harvey, 2012: 72–3, 137).[3] It relates as well to the "political ecology of resistance" that conceptualizes property rights as something communal, rather than individual, and is a key component of many translocal struggles (Banerjee, Maher, and Krämer, 2023: 283). It is this conceptualization of rights – as something collective and in opposition to notions of individualized gain and control – that I mean when using the term "right" in this book, and I will discuss it more in the context of water shortly.

The struggle against the privatization of water is linked to the move to "enclose" and commodify water, discussed in the previous chapter. It is connected to water grabbing, which in basic terms can be understood as entities (usually corporations, but also governments, and sometimes individuals) claiming the control and distribution of water in a way that creates a significantly unequal distribution of the water. To recap the discussion from the previous chapter, there are five principal forms of water grabbing: 1) privatization (of drinking water and sanitation); 2) bottled water; 3) water for extractive industry; 4) land grabbing for export agriculture; 5) large dam constructions (Bieler, 2021: 5–6). There is a sixth form, which relates to all of the others: financialization (Bieler and Moore, 2023: 5–6 and 13). All forms of this water grabbing have resulted in moments of resistance (Bieler, 2021; Bieler and Moore, 2023). The financialization of water completely turns it into a commodity for speculation, and will be increasingly related to driving the five other forms of water privatization (Ideas for Development, 2020).[4] This book focuses primarily on the privatization of drinking water and large dam constructions, which is linked to water for extractive industry; however, it also relates to bottled water, which is discussed in Chapter 6.

Political economy of water privatization

In 2010, the United Nations declared access to water and sanitation a human right;[5] this right to water remains far from realized, however, both globally and at home. The "right to water" is a message embraced by movements that oppose its privatization. These campaigns and movements are often linked to the fight against other forms of resource privatization, as well as to efforts against climate change (Almeida, 2014, 2019; Bakker, 2007; Barlow and Clarke, 2002; Bieler, 2021; Broad and Cavanagh, 2021; Olivera and Lewis, 2004; Robinson, 2013a; Shiva, 2016; Subramaniam, 2014). Most of these actions have so far taken place in the Global South. Still, they are becoming more common in the Global North, particularly in response to the intensification of neoliberal policies, aging urban infrastructure, and state austerity programs (Bakker, 2007; Bieler, 2021; Robinson, 2013a; Snitow and Kauffman, 2007; Subramaniam, 2018; Sultana, 2018).

The struggle that took place in Cochabamba, Bolivia, in the early 2000s is heralded in the anti-water privatization movement literature as a "success" story of the movements for the right to water (Bieler, 2021; Laurie, 2011). Amid an era of state crisis at the turn of the twenty-first century, the Cochabamba struggle brought together a broad coalition of residents who successfully stopped the privatization of their water (Fabricant, 2012; Hylton and Thomson, 2007; Nowak, 2016). As Vandana Shiva writes, the Bolivian example shows "that real democracy, living democracy, cannot be delegated – to professional politicians, or any one sector of society. It can only be achieved through rainbow coalitions based on trust, not domination and control" (Olivera and Lewis, 2004: x).

In Latin America, water privatization is linked to the larger trend of neoliberal reforms that swept across the region in the 1980s and 1990s (Almeida, 2019; Harvey, 2004; Olivera and Lewis, 2004; Sassen, 2014; Sawyer, 2004; Subramaniam, 2014; Zimmerer, 2015). Paul Almeida (2014) reports how after a series of "modernization" and neoliberal reforms in Panama during the late 1990s, while certain types of privatization (electricity, telecommunications) passed without much opposition, water privatization was met with considerable social movement resistance. Likewise, resistance to water privatization also occurred in Honduras in 2007–2009 (Almeida, 2014: 92–97 and 150) and is connected to neoliberal reforms. During the 1990s, Brazil underwent neoliberal reforms, including the Programa Nacional de Desestatização or PND[6] (Bezerra, 2023; MAB, 2011; BNDES n.d). Similar plans and processes took place throughout the rest of Latin America during that time, including in Ecuador with the privatization of oil (see Sawyer, 2004) and Bolivia with water privatization (see Olivera and Lewis, 2004; Zimmerer, 2015).

Mangala Subramaniam offers an analysis of water privatization and neo-liberal state reforms in India. Subramaniam discusses how the neoliberal policies that privatized water and "common goods" caused the expropria-tion of local resources, and residents in turn resisted (2014: 401). She pos-tulates that the state (in this case, India) and the policies it implements play a significant role in shaping neoliberal globalization at the local and state levels. The reverse is also true: communities resist and challenge the policies that shape the process of globalization. Increasingly, however, it has proved to be a challenge for governments to manage water to meet social needs adequately (Subramaniam, 2014: 407). Subramaniam notes that the com-modification and privatization of water have led to resident mobilizations demanding a voice in water management. Although Subramaniam's study focuses on India, she argues that this contributes to the "accumulation by expropriation" scholarship (based on the work of David Harvey) and that her analysis of the fight for water rights is relevant to politics in other coun-tries (Harvey, 2004; Subramaniam, 2014: 395).

Olivera and Lewis discuss how the attempt to privatize water in Bolivia was the beginning of the struggle and that it is not just water but other resources such as oil and gas. They note that there are two types of pri-vatization that we must tackle. The first is "private property of transna-tional corporations." The second is "private property of the State," which seeks to control social wealth, without the word of the people, and without the word of democracy (2004: 156). This relates to transnational agrarian movements, such as La Vía Campesina (LVC): The dispossession of peas-ants as a result of capitalist expansion has become the point of coalescence for peasant mobilization and mobilizations against water privatization in Cochabamba stemmed from previous campesino resistance (see Chapter 4).

Today, around the world, people are coalescing to fight against the forces that seek to commodify and control life-sustaining resources. These actors are fighting against, to use Sassen's term, "expulsions" (2014: 1). Sassen's choice of the word "expulsions" relates to this experience, because it points out – using the active voice – that these expulsions are human-made. Sassen writes: "We are confronting a formidable problem in our global political economy: the emergence of new logics of expulsion." Expulsion is inequal-ity without limits. It is complex inequality (2014: 13 and 20), which can make resistance – and knowing who the target is to resist – more compli-cated. Land and water grabbing are forms of expulsions. While Sassen hints at the idea of resistance to expulsions, she does not delve into it. But social movements are, in fact, resisting expulsion, including around water.[7]

Yet there remains a dearth of studies on social movement mobilization against water privatization in the United States. Studies that have exam-ined remunicipalization (returning to public control utilities that had been privatized) in the United States have not focused on social movement mobilization. Some studies have argued that pragmatic (such as cost savings and service quality), rather than political, reasons have driven remunicipalization in the United States; elsewhere in the world, it has been more political and connected to social movements (McDonald, 2018; Warner and Aldag, 2019). I argue, however, that there are examples of resident mobilization serving as a critical impetus in fighting and preventing privatization in the United States and fighting for more equitable, environmentally sound, and transparent governance. Movements have worked to draw attention to the role of private industry – and not simply failed public governance – in causing water quality problems, including in Flint, Michigan. Water struggles quickly flow into struggles over austerity and the role of the state and corporate power, and counter-hegemonic, multi-issue movement formations are growing and emerging to fight for livelihood and connect issues of injustice and inequality. In other words: resistance against water privatization and for remunicipalization of water in the United States is political.

Decades of austerity reforms and disinvestment in public water infrastructure are driving efforts for remunicipalization and demands for infrastructure improvements. The country's drinking water systems are in dire need of infrastructure improvements:

> In 2017, the American Society of Civil Engineers (ASCE) gave the country's drinking water systems a grade of "D." Many of the millions of pipes that deliver water to households, factories, and commercial buildings were laid in the early 20 century with a lifespan of 75 to 100 years, meaning that many are at the end of their useful life. There are an estimated 240,000 water main breaks in the United States each year, wasting more than two trillion gallons of treated drinking water annually. Moreover, some pipes in older cities and homes contain lead, which can leach into water, causing serious health problems. The American Water Works Association estimates that $1 trillion over the next 25 years is needed to maintain and expand service to meet the country's water needs. (ITPI, 2019: 2)

While national attention to the problem of safe and affordable access to water in the United States might not have reached the national spotlight until the 2014 Flint water crisis, it has been a problem since long before then. As one example, in 2003, approximately 900 families a day had their water turned off in Detroit for failure to pay their water bills. As Laura Gottesdiener (2015: 20) discusses, people become delinquent on their water bills when the cost of water is too high to afford. Gottesdiener notes how some local officials argued that you do not get water service if you cannot afford to pay for your water. But this raises the issue of what water *is* – a fundamental right for survival and social good, or a commodity? The United Nations called the Detroit case a violation of international human rights. In turn, Detroit implemented a ratepayer assistance program.[8]

In the United States, there was a move in the 1800s and 1900s to create public water systems. This helped ensure and expand access to safe water, which significantly lowered disease and death rates. Public water is – and has always been – linked to public health, a point highlighted even more amidst the Covid-19 pandemic (McDonald, Sprunk, and Chavez, 2021). Nine out of ten people in the United States receive their water from a public utility, and the trend is toward remunicipalization, returning services that were privatized to the public sphere (Food and Water Watch, 2016). Globally, the remunicipalization of utilities, including water, that had been privatized is growing, suggesting a reversal of the trend of privatization that took place in the 1980s and 1990s (McDonald, 2018). Five hundred of the largest water systems in the United States showed that private utilities charged an average of 59 per cent more than publicly controlled systems (approximately $315 a year for 60,000 gallons versus $500 for a private company). In Pennsylvania, privatized water utilities charged 84% more than public; in New Jersey, people under private systems paid 79% more (Food and Water Watch, 2016). Studies and experiences show that privatization of water means higher rates and lower quality water. Consequently, places that have privatized water are turning to reclaim it as public. In a 2021 document entitled "Public Futures Database Report," the authors write:

> Much of what we know about global remunicipalisation has been the result of excellent investigative research over a number of years by the Transnational Institute (TNI)[9], and in particular a landmark report documenting, globally, 835 cases of cities, towns and regions on all continents that had taken privatised services back into local public ownership since 2000 (Kishimoto and Petitjean 2017; Kishimoto et al. 2020). The new Public Futures database includes a total of 1451 verified cases as of February 2021, of which 974 were de-privatisations (at the municipal, regional or national level) and 477 were cases of new public enterprises being established, so called 'municipalisations.'[10] (Pearson et al., 2021: 3)

There are various reasons for the global trend of remunicipalization besides increased cost and reduced quality under privatization (Bel, 2020; McDonald and Swyngedouw, 2019; Wait and Petri, 2017). Public water is shown to offer more accountability and transparency, and more room for resident participation in the governance structure (Lobina and Hall, 2008; Planas and Martinez, 2020). Public utilities are not automatically accountable and transparent to the public, but in comparison to privately run utilities, there is more space for residents to demand transparency and accountability (Holmsy and Warner, 2020; Kishimoto, Pettijean, and Steinfort, 2017;

Subramaniam, 2018). As Satoko Kishimoto, Lavinia Steinfort, and Olivier Pettijean put it:

> The promise of (re)municipalisation lies beyond the traditional concept of 'public' to embrace stronger, and in some cases novel, forms of democratic governance and control. We found clear evidence of the introduction or improvement of democratic mechanisms in at least 149 cases, ranging from increased accountability, transparency and information disclosure to establishing participatory governance in public corporations. (2020: 25)

In sum, cost is a significant reason for the remunicipalization turn; but another important reason is that public utilities are, by design, more accountable and transparent to the public. And when they are not, because they are publicly controlled, there is room to hold them responsible. In the discussion of the Pittsburgh case in Chapter 3, I delve into this point more.

While global struggles against water privatization and for remunicipalization have garnered considerable scholarship globally, and to a lesser extent nationally, the scholarship that examines the social movement resistance of these struggles in North America remains limited. Joanna Robinson's 2013 book, *Contested Waters: The Struggle Against Water Privatization in the United States and Canada,* examines resistance against privatization in two North American cities: Stockton, California, United States and Vancouver, British Colombia, Canada. Robinson (2013b) approaches these cases as two examples of local struggles that are part of a broader resistance movement against neoliberal globalization. Her focus is on the emergence, growth, and outcomes of the social movement resistance, making her study unique in the literature on water privatization in the United States.

While attention to water justice has been growing in the past few years, the scholarly study of water in the United States remains understudied by sociologists and social movement scholars. More interest in water has grown out of the Flint water crisis, and I am aware of various sociological studies (most currently ongoing) focusing on Flint (see the work of Jennifer Carrera in particular). Some studies have examined water scarcity and shortage problems, especially in the Western and Southwestern regions, and access to potable water and sanitation (for example, see the work of Stephen Gasteyer). Rising water unaffordability is documented in Baltimore, Cleveland, Chicago, Oakland, Pittsburgh, and elsewhere, and there are no permanent federal programs to help offset the cost of water for low-income people (González Rivas, 2020; Montag, 2019; Vanderwarker, 2012: 62–3). There is an explicit connection between race and water affordability, with Black communities and other communities of color disproportionately impacted by rising costs in the United States (Montag, 2019: 8). Since 2010, water bills in the US have increased by 80 per cent and two out of five US households have trouble paying their water bills. The Covid-19 pandemic has further worsened this crisis and highlighted how critical access to clean water is (González Rivas, 2020; Lakhani, 2020) (see also Chapter 3).

Scholarship has demonstrated that resident mobilization and opposition to privatization grow as people are faced with rate increases and other adverse effects of privatization (Bakker, 2007; Snitow and Kauffman, 2007; Subramaniam, 2018). The role of social movement pressure in pushing for public water and accountability, transparency, regulation, monitoring, and equity is critical. The water justice literature has shown that this social movement mobilization has been crucial in preventing privatization, reversing it, and shaping public water governance to be more democratic (Brown, Neves-Silva, and Heller, 2016; Holmsy and Warner, 2020; Robinson, 2013b; Subramaniam, 2014; Sultana and Loftus, 2012). This literature has touched on how these local movements fighting against privatization are linked to larger global economic structures and that communication between movement struggles is growing (Almeida, 2014, 2019; Olivera and Lewis, 2004; Robinson, 2013b; Subramaniam, 2018; Sultana, 2018; Sultana and Loftus, 2012).

Corporate malfeasance and contaminated water

In April 2014, residents of Flint, Michigan, turned on their faucets to see foul smelling, tasting, and discolored water flowing out of them; the water, poisoned with lead and other contaminants well in exceedance of EPA limits, was not fit for consumption. Since 2014, Flint has become a topic of national conversation and the site of various studies, articles, and books. Flint is a city of 100,000 people that is majority-Black, and what happened there has prompted more discussions of the problems of environmental racism in the United States. The Flint crisis, for example, has drawn more attention to the rampant problems of structural inequality and institutionalized racism (Menendian, n.d.) in the United States, as well as decades of disinvestment in public infrastructure and negligence on the part of elected officials, to serve their constituents (Clark, 2018; Pulido, 2016). What has received less attention, however, is the resistance to the contaminated water in Flint. Further, the critical organizing work done by resident groups led by Black leaders in Flint has been largely ignored by the media (Jackson, 2018).[11]

Further, the role of corporate actors (specifically Veolia and Nestlé) in causing the crisis has been largely ignored. There is blame to go around in Flint, for sure. However, as a Flint water activist noted at the Human Right to Water Summit in Abuja, Nigeria, in 2019 (discussed in Chapter 6):

> Veolia also implicated ... said it was fine to make the switch. Which was a lie. Then after the crisis, Nestlé stepped in and applied to drill in Great

Lakes (34 percent of nation's freshwater), and the governor, whose wife sits on the Nestlé board, allowed it. For 200 dollars a year, Nestlé pumps this ... (Fieldnotes, 29 January 2019; see also Glenza, 2017)

The activist talked about how their household uses four to five cases of bottled water a day and has to use it for everything, including pets. This puts people at the mercy of bottled water distributors. Out of this experience, community members decided to fight and created Flint Rising. Regarding Veolia, she added: "my heart goes out to you all ... when I heard about the possible contract with Veolia I thought, "They're still getting away with this?" Everyone in the world heard about Flint ... they killed people/helped to kill people and are still getting away with it" (Fieldnotes, 29 January 2019).

Veolia, its subsidiaries, and executives have been under investigation in multiple countries over the years (Fonger, 2019; Hosea and Lerner, 2018). In the United States, Veolia was involved in both the Pittsburgh water crisis and Flint, Michigan. The state of Michigan filed a complaint against the company, claiming that it ignored the contaminants in the pipes and worsened the situation. Veolia is one of the companies attempting to control the water supply in Lagos, Nigeria (the most populous city on the African continent), provoking criticism. As another Flint activist stated, "They have a history of poisoning black communities in the US and should not be poisoning the continent's largest African city" (Mark, 2018). This resonates with Rob Nixon's (2011) idea of "slow violence," a term used to describe the suffering, disease, violence, environmental destruction caused from toxins, climate change, war, etc., that capitalism causes. I return to this concept in Chapter 6, and connect it to thinking about racial capitalism.

As reported on by *The Guardian,* on 9 February 2015, the vice-president of development for Veolia sent an email to other company executives that asserted, "Do not pass this on ... The city however needs to be aware of this problem with lead and operate the system to minimize this as much as possible and consider the impact in future plans. We had already identified that as something to be reviewed." In another email to a company engineer, he added: "Yep. Lead seems to be a problem." These emails came to light after the Michigan attorney general filed a suit against Veolia, saying the company had given the city terrible advice and not advocating for more precautions against corrosion when it knew of the lead problem. While the case was thrown out for procedural reasons, over a dozen lawsuits have been filed by Flint residents. As *The Guardian* reported, "The internal Veolia emails show Veolia executives were quick to recognize that Flint's water system was fraught with problems that stemmed from lack of investment, outdated equipment, and unqualified workers." One Veolia executive sent an email (in February 2015) that the work in Flint could lead to a $15 to $30 million contract; Veolia contends that its recommendations were not at all influenced by business prospects (Holden, Fonger, and Glenza, 2019). Even before this news broke, in February 2018 Veolia decided to end "peer performance solutions" (a type of PPP here in the US), with industry analysts citing the public relations disaster of Pittsburgh as the reason (Global Water Intelligence, 2018: 12 and 2019).

People are fighting against privatization all across the world, and as a report by In The Public Interest (ITPI) argues: "The same failed, neoliberal policies of lowering corporate taxes and cutting public programs that have crippled Chile are hitting places like St. Clairsville – and Flint, and Baltimore … hard (Mohler, 2019)." ITPI defines "public–private partnerships" (PPPs) as the following: " 'Public–private partnership' or 'P3' is an imprecise term used to refer to different types of contractual arrangements between a governmental entity and a private entity. In the water sector, P3 typically refers to one of the following deal structures listed below. Note that both types of contracts can last decades, typically anywhere from 30 to 50 years." The risks of P3s include loss of public control over policy/planning decisions; profits driving decisions about what gets built (harming rural and low-income areas); limiting access and affordability; cost-cutting leading to cutting corners; workers experiencing lower wages; and loss of transparency and public input (ITPI, 2019: 3–4).

As Donald Cohen argues, Veolia's role in the Flint disaster is overlooked:

> Flint's water system needs to be fixed today regardless of costs. But one thing should be completely off the table: privatization. Often, the promises made by private water corporations – like Veolia – come at the expense of skyrocketing water rates and risks to public health. And customers in communities who sell or lease their water systems *pay more* than residents who live in communities with publicly owned utilities. Privatization is a page out of the "smaller government" playbook, the same playbook that Michigan Gov. Rick Snyder used when he *pushed through* a law allowing "emergency managers" to take over the state's cash-strapped municipalities and school boards. It was one of Snyder's emergency managers – who had unchecked authority over Flint's local elected officials – that decided to switch the city's pipes to contaminated water. In their report, Veolia praised Flint's government for being "transparent and responsive," but they were praising a government ruled over by one of Snyder's emergency managers. The same manager that overruled the Flint city council – democratically elected by residents – when **they voted to return** to the old, clean water after receiving Veolia's report. The manager *called* switching back "incomprehensible" because it would cost money. *So when people say Flint's tragedy is a failure of government they really mean it's a failure of running government like a business.* (Cohen, n.d., emphasis in original)

Corporate Accountability, one of the entities that brought to light the Veolia cover-up and emails, works to stop "transnational corporations from devastating democracy, trampling human rights, and destroying our planet." They have worked with Flint Rising, a group that arose out of the Flint crisis, "that has been leading the calls for accountability. Their demands include replacing lead service lines, 100 per cent bill reimbursements, and free health and education services for the community" (Corporate Accountability, 2021a).

As a result of the connection with Veolia, Corporate Accountability is a partner of the Our Water Campaign in Pittsburgh, bringing national and transnational aspects to an otherwise local campaign. Many (if not most) examples of anti-water privatization movements qualify as place bound because they are focused on local struggles for water control. In Brazil, MAB clearly articulates its struggle as one for national sovereignty. Yet, in all the examples I discuss, these place-based movements are about sovereignty and defending the commons (of water specifically) against corporations and politicians who seek to profit from the commons that all should share. This directly contradicts the extractive logic of capitalist globalization, which privileges the global scale at the expense of the local. In this sense, the issue identification of these movements is not bound only to place, since these groups articulate an interest in connecting their local effort to a broader, global, anti-capitalist struggle for water as a human right (Banerjee, 2011, 2018; Desai, 2016; Escobar, 2008; Schroering, 2021a; Smith, 2017a).

Some of these local struggles have worked to ban water privatization. Baltimore became the first United States city to ban water privatization. In November 2018, 77 per cent of voters turned out to approve the charter amendment prohibiting the privatization of water and sewage systems. Rianna Eckel (2018) reported:

> Baltimore is the first US city to amend its charter – the city's constitution – to prohibit water privatization. And it is part of a global water justice movement to realize the human right to water. In 2004, Uruguay voters amended their constitution to become the first country to ban water privatization. Around the globe, cities have committed to keep water services in public control, most recently Berlin and three other German cities.

While Baltimore is the first city to ensure by law that its water and sewer system cannot be privatized, other cities are moving in that direction. Bieler and Moore write of the importance of the concept of water as a commons and how it is interlinked with a broader counter-hegemonic effort:

> In struggles against water privatisation in Europe (Bieler, 2021: 158–73), one of the key contributions of the Italian water movement was the conception of water as a commons, which is jointly governed, jointly enjoyed and jointly

preserved for future generations. It is thus a way of organising water manage-ment, which goes beyond the dichotomy of private versus public. It includes a direct link to forms of participatory democracy resulting in the movement's motto: "It is written water, it is read democracy"' (Fantini 2014: 42). It is this combination of a new understanding of democracy and a new way of how to run the economy and, importantly, of how these two dimensions are closely and internally related, which brings with it a transformative dimension beyond capitalism. (2023: 15–16)

These successes do not mean that the threat of water privatization is over. The recent decision to begin trading water on Wall Street (Chipman, 2020) is part of a move by corporations to argue that commodifying water and encouraging private control will help lower costs and improve environmen-tal sustainability.

Water privatization and dams

In some parts of the world, and especially Brazil, the struggle around hydro dams is directly connected to the fight against water privatization, with the argument that water – rivers, lakes, dams, and all its forms – ought not to be privatized and should be treated as a commons, not a commodity. Struggles against water privatization, including in the United States, share this lens regarding fighting for drinking water that is publicly controlled (Robinson, 2013b; Schroering, 2021a). Thus, the "right to water" is linked to move-ments of people affected by dams via the larger struggle against the com-modification of water. It is also linked to the various yet connected forms of water grabbing, noted earlier in the chapter. In particular, it is directly related to the third form, water for extractive industry.

Since the 1980s, discussions about the social, agrarian, and environmen-tal impacts of large dam projects have been ongoing. There have been large-scale resistance movements for environmental justice led by those impacted (Guha and Martinez-Alier, 1997; Johnston, 2018; Martinez-Alier et al., 2016). Many of these movements have networked with each other (Boelens, Shah, and Bruins, 2019; Shah et al., 2019). I first learned about dams when I decided to write a paper about salmon for my Environmental Studies 101 class as an 18-year-old undergraduate student. I spent my teenage years in Oregon, and salmon – and diminishing populations of salmon – in 2005 was a topic of conversation. The declining salmon population was directly linked to hydro dams. Yet even though I work on water justice issues, I have not spent much time thinking about dams in the United States. On the sur-face, it would appear that dam conflicts are not an issue in the United States today. But this is far from the reality. As studies worldwide have shown, dams and dam failures have catastrophic socioenvironmental consequences, and the United States is not exempt from this.

From the Americas to Asia to Africa, the communities most impacted by dams are excluded from the political process and decision-making. In the twentieth century alone, large dam projects displaced 40 to 80 million people globally, primarily indigenous populations. Only 37 per cent of the world's rivers remain free-flowing. Hydro dams have destroyed freshwater systems, threatened food security for millions of people, and contributed to the decimation of various freshwater nonhuman life (Bakker and Hendriks, 2019; Baviskar, 1995/2004; Boelens, Shah, and Bruins, 2019; Del Bene, Scheidel, and Temper, 2018; Fox and Sneddon, 2019; Moore, Simon, and Knudsen, 2021; Shah et al., 2019). As Amita Baviskar (2004: 32) writes, governments justified most of these hydro dams under the guise of development and advancing national interests, yet the projects have tended to "diminish poor people's ability to control and gainfully use natural resources." She discusses how this is not specific to India – her nation of focus – but that it is "embedded in contemporary global structures such as the arrangement of the world into nation-states, and the expanding system of international capitalism" (Baviskar, 2004: 35).

On 25 January 2019, one of the worst human-caused environmental crimes in Brazil's history resulted in the loss of 272 lives (Costa, 2021; Stropasolas, 2020). Today, thousands more continue to be adversely affected by the socio-environmental damage caused. A dam, owned by transnational mining company Vale (the globe's largest iron ore producer), collapsed in Córrego do Feijão in Brumadinho, Minas Gerais, Brazil. What made it a crime is that Vale knew something like this could happen. Brazil is a resource-wealthy nation: it holds 12 per cent of the world's fresh water, and it is home to large quantities of iron, bauxite, and other minerals. What happened in Brumadinho is not just for the Brazilian people to bear. The extraction of resources – and the actions of Vale – are part of a global economic system in which we all participate. Too often, this extraction of resources is for the 'benefit' of those of us in the Global North, while devastating to communities like Brumadinho.

As discussed in detail in the previous chapter, while colonialism is no longer an economic policy (Smith, 2008), its legacy remains through corporate control and international financial structures. Indeed, as Stephen Gasteyer et al. (2012) argue, water grabbing is a new form of colonialism, dispossessing indigenous and peasant populations from their land in the name of investor profit. The mining industry in Brazil has been pivotal in "post-colonial" capitalist development, with all too often catastrophic human rights and environmental abuses. Vale has been in operation since 1942. The Brazilian government privatized it in 1997 during a wave of neoliberal economic reforms that swept across the world, seeking to privatize resources previously managed by the state or communally. With this move, the only incentive for Vale was profit-making, with little of that wealth remaining in the country to benefit the common good (Schroering, 2019c, 2020a).

This point speaks to the heart of an article published in the Brazilian news source *Brasil de Fato*, which called out the dam collapse as a crime and not an accident, asserting: "The process of privatization and the denationalization of Vale is emblematic of the neoliberal project in Brazil. There was no record of tragedies such as Brumadinho while the company was state-owned" (Tricontinental: Institute for Social Research, 2019). In other words, "Vale is the symbol of what privatization means in Brazil" (Tricontinental: Institute for Social Research, 2019).

The Brumadinho collapse was due to a tailings storage facilities (TSF) failure. TSFs "are one of the main liabilities associated with mining activities, and approximately 600 of these structures are found in Brazil" (Salvador et al., 2020: 137). In Brazil, between 1986 and 2019, ten TSFs have failed – six within the past six years. As Salvador et al. wrote, "The country sets among the record holders of this kind of disaster, behind the USA (29) and China (12) (Abdelouas, 2019)" (Salvador et al., 2020: 138). They point to the role of privatization in these failures:

> What we observe is a process of privatization of regulatory powers in this sector (Santos and Milanez, 2017), where the whole process of licensing, monitoring, and assessment of environmental recovery following disasters is led by the companies themselves, clearly raising several conflicts of interest. This is also true for the Brazilian national dam safety plan, which aims to assist the companies in managing the safety of their dams (Brasil, 2010). Again, companies are responsible to implement the plan and to provide the information about the stability of its own dams to the government, which in turn must supervise those structures. However, the lower number of surveillance officers to analyze more than 600 Brazilian TSFs put the supervision capacity in check. (Salvador et al., 2020: 139–140)

Most of Brazil's 24,092 dams are for agriculture and irrigation (41 per cent) (Guimarães, 2019). As of the end of 2017, Brazil had 219 hydroelectric plants in operation, representing a growth of 60 plants from a decade earlier (Leturcq, 2019: xiii).[12] While 75 per cent of Brazil's energy does come from hydropower (Fearnside, 2017), it is important to note how much of the power generated from them in Brazil will not fuel people's homes; it is to serve multinational industry and mining. Only 29 per cent of Brazil's energy is for domestic use (Fearnside, 2021). A report by the Agência Nacional de Águas (ANA) in 2017 showed that 780 of the dams were mining tailings dams (like the one that collapsed in Brumadinho). Brazil (like the US) has no central regulatory entity for dam inspections. There are 43 different inspection entities; four are federal and 39 state-run (Guimarães, 2019). According to the ANA's 2019 report on dam security, there was an increase of 129 per cent between 2018 and 2019 in the number of dams that raised security concerns by inspection agencies, with 156 in critical condition. In 2018, the number was only 68. Of the 156 dams, 63 per cent were privately owned. Eighty-one of the 156 critical dams are located in Minas Gerais – the same state where the Brumadinho tragedy occurred – and 21 of them are dams owned by Vale or its subsidiaries (ANA, 2020).

More than 45 per cent of Vale's shareholders are international, including some of the world's largest investment management companies based in the United States. BlackRock and Capital Group hold about 5 per cent of shares each in Vale. BlackRock claims to put sustainability and climate change at the center of its work. Vanguard Group also owns shares in Vale and says that it works for environmentally responsible operations. These companies manage trillions of dollars each. Vale itself accrues more profit each year, even as this accumulation comes at the expense of life – of people and the environment (BlackRock, 2023; Schroering, 2019c; Trocate, 2019; Vale n.d.; Vale, 2019; Vanguard, n.d.).

While Brumadinho is considered one of the worst socio-environmental crimes in the history of Brazil, it is not the only example of a dam breach. In 2015, a dam collapsed in Mariana, also in Minas Gerais,[13] killing 19 people when two dams ruptured at an open-pit mine (Septoff, 2020). That mine is operated by Samarco, a project between Vale and the Australian company PHP Billiton (Lazare, 2015). The impacted communities still suffer the effects and are without integral reparations[14] (Brito, 2022). On 4 January 2021, the second anniversary of the Brumadinho collapse, a dam collapsed in Santa Catarina (MAB, 2021a). On 25 March 2021, a dam in Maranhão state, owned by a subsidiary of Equinox Gold (a Canadian-owned company), collapsed, polluting the water reservoir of the city of Godofredo Viana, leaving four thousand people without potable water (MAB, 2021b; MAB, 2021c).

When you fly over Minas Gerais, you can see large gaping holes in the ground that are iron mines. In 2018, iron ore was the mining industry's best-selling product with exports of $23.4 billion (it accounted for 20 per cent of all exports from Brazil to the US) (Presidency of the Republic of Brazil, 2019). Brazil is the world's second-largest producer of mineral ores (Salvador et al., 2020). Vale (or its subsidiaries) owns 175 dams in Brazil; 129 are iron ore dams, of which 102 are in Minas Gerais.

In the region impacted by the Brumadinho collapse, people can no longer grow food; they cannot drink the water. The Paraopeba river is contaminated, filled with iron, aluminum, and mercury; people are displaced, and illnesses – including mental health illness and suicide – are rising in the after-math (Aun, 2020). In theory, many affected communities are considered a "traditional" population that receives protection; in practice, receiving legal recognition is rarely secured. Dam projects particularly threaten these com-munities. This speaks to a more extensive, historical process of colonialism, exploitation, and erasure of ribeirinho[15] and Quilombola[16] communities (Fearnside, 2020). And Brazil has even more hydro dams planned. As Philip Fearnside (2017) writes of the planned dam construction:

> Should Brazil's unfettered dam construction continue at the current pace, the country will essentially take all of the major free-flowing Amazon tributaries east of the Madeira River – in effect, half of the Amazon basin – and turn them into continuous chains of reservoirs. This would mean expelling all of the traditional residents from two-thirds of Brazilian Amazonia. (paragraph 4)

Many people assume that dams are "clean" energy; in the face of cli-mate change, we must build dams, and hydropower is a better, cleaner energy source than fossil fuels. But this is a complete misconception. Research has shown that approximately 20 per cent of human-caused methane emissions come from reservoir surfaces. However, a 2016 study by Deemer et al. showed that dams contribute 25 per cent more than this to climate change contributing emissions. Reservoirs emit around 1 billion tons of carbon dioxide yearly, which is more than the entire country of Canada. On the other hand, free-flowing rivers trap carbon. Dams disturb ecosystems, creating a situation where it is harder to adapt to climate change – especially as we will continue to see more unpredict-able weather patterns and more flooding (Deemer, 2016; Hudson, 2017; Moore et al., 2021).

In the United States, there is little conversation today about dams and dam safety. When the Brumadinho dam collapse occurred, it barely made inter-national news, let alone garnered sufficient attention in Brazil. Yet a large transnational corporation was behind it, and it was their errors that caused this catastrophe – this crime. MAB asks: energy for whom? What happened there, and participating in the first anniversary of the collapse (discussed in Chapters 4 and 5), including conversations with people affected by dams from around the world, making me wonder: what is the state of dams in my own country, the United States, in 2020?

Are there safety concerns? Could a dam collapse like what happened in Brumadinho happen here? Who controls these dams – and who "benefits" from the energy? Posing these questions, in turn, unfolds various others – and to adequately address all of them would require its own book. Here, I attempt to outline the basic situation of dams in the United States today. I have seen with my own eyes the tremendous power trapped behind a dam and the devastation it can cause when it breaks. Yet these safety-related concerns of hydro dams are not in the consciousness of much of the right to water organizing that I have observed in the United States, which tends to be more focused on distribution, regulation, and affordability of drinking water systems. Yet, as discussed earlier, all forms of water grabbing are connected to each other; the struggle against privatizing drinking water is related to the other forms, which includes large hydro dam projects.

However, my work with MAB has shown me how hydro dams, water privatization, and bottled water are all linked and constitute various forms of water grabbing; and in turn, so too are struggles against the commodification and privatization of water. Further, these struggles exist on every continent except Antarctica. This is not a problem of "somewhere else;" the problems of "there" and "here" are related (especially in terms of corporate power and wealth concentration).

At 770 feet high, the Oroville Dam is the tallest in the United States. The state of California is considered as the leader in "dam safety management" in the United States. But in February 2017, it almost collapsed. This forced the evacuation of nearly 200,000 people and cost over $1 billion in repairs. As Jacques Leslie (2019) writes:

> It took its place as a seminal event in the history of US dam safety, ranking just below the failures in the 1970s of two dams – Teton Dam in Idaho and Kelly Barnes in Georgia – that killed 14 and 39 people, respectively, and ushered in the modern dam safety era. The incident at the half-century-old, 770-foot-high Oroville Dam, which involved partial disintegration of its two spillways during a heavy but not unprecedented rainstorm, signaled the inadequacy of methods customarily used throughout the country to assess dam safety and carry out repairs. It occurred as federal dam safety officials have made substantial progress in updating methods of dam assessment, in the process propelling dam safety practices into the 21st century. But federal and state dam safety officials have been unable to procure from disinterested state legislatures and Congress the tens of billions of dollars needed for repairs to the nation's aging dam infrastructure. (paragraph 3)

In 2017, the American Society of Civil Engineers (ASCE) gave a "D" grade to the country's 91,000 dams – this is the same (nearly falling) grade the nation's dams have received since 1998 when the ASCE began giving report cards. The ASCE further estimated that around $45 billion needs to be spent on repairs on dams "whose failure would threaten human life;" to fix all the dams that require repairs, it would cost over $64 billion (Leslie, 2019). Most residents are completely unaware of this reality, including those who live near dams. Leslie describes the situation in the United States, asserting: "scientists say the likelihood of dam failures – which not only threaten lives but release toxic sediments trapped in reservoirs behind many dams – will increase as extreme precipitation events become more frequent in a warming world" (2019: paragraph 6).

In the United States, approximately 1,500 dams are owned by federal agencies. Aside from these, however, safety regulations are a state (not federal) responsibility that varies drastically. Leslie asserts:

> Across the nation, each state dam inspector is responsible on average for about 200 dams, a daunting ratio, but in some states the number is much higher. Oklahoma, for example, employs just three full-time inspectors for its 4,621 dams; Iowa has three inspectors for its 3,911 dams. Largely because of its legislators' distrust of regulation, Alabama doesn't even have a safety program for its 2,273 dams. (2019: paragraph 7)

The statistics on dam failures, people who have died due to failures, and the significant lack of regulations around dams are troubling – especially as climate change will exacerbate these problems. While "high-hazard-potential" dams are supposed to be inspected every two and a half years, the duration between inspections is often much longer; some states do not even check dams deemed as "low-hazard-potential" (which constitutes ones that do not threaten property or lives). California is the state that spends the most money on dam safety ($21 million in 2017). Yet, as the Oroville example shows, there are still significant problems. A 2018 report illustrated that the Department of Water Resources (which oversees dams) was understaffed and lacked much-needed expertise (Leslie, 2019). Between 2005–2013, there were 173 dam failures and nearly 600 dam events that likely would have been failures if not for speedy action. In the US, human deaths as a result of dam failures are rare. A dam collapse in Hawaii in 2006 resulted in seven deaths. No more fatalities as a result of dam failures occurred until 2017, when a dam in Nebraska "gave way to epic floodwater, sweeping away a house with a man inside it in the floodplain below" (Leslie, 2019). One person died when this dam breached, and a lawsuit filed by the spouse of the deceased alleged that the dam collapse was the result of negligence. In 2023, the family lost its appeal with the Nebraska Supreme Court. This dam was ranked as a "significant" risk not "high risk," which suggests there are more "high risk" dams in the United States than are being recorded as such, especially with increasing "severe storms" as a result of climate change (Hammel, 2023; Lieb, Casey and Minkoff, 2019).

Around 20 per cent of United States dams deemed high risk lack hazard emergency plans. While dam safety lags seriously behind Western Europe, Australia, and Canada, it is more stringent than in most of the world. In recent years, fatal incidents have occurred across the globe, including in Nepal, Laos, Kenya, Brazil (Leslie, 2019), and most recently India, when a melting glacier caused a dam collapse, with an estimated death toll of

150 people (BBC News, 2021). Historically, there have been horrific dam breaches in the United States. Generally, these accidents are due to a lack of funding and proper regulations and repairs. In Johnstown, Pennsylvania, in 1889, 2,209 people were killed when a dam failed (Ho et al., 2017). Another significant problem with dams in the United States (but is an applicable point globally as well) is that of "hazard creep." As Leslie reports:

> dams are vulnerable to so-called "hazard creep": their danger increases as development occurs downstream. A dam that was rated "low-hazard-potential" when it was built because nobody lived in the floodplain below may become a "high-hazard-potential" dam once people move into the area. As a result, even though new dam construction in the US virtually stopped in the 1970s, the number of high-hazard-potential dams has grown from 9,314 in 1999 to 12,557 in 2017. High-hazard-potential dams must conform to a more rigorous safety standard than lesser-rated dams, but if funds aren't available, the necessary upgrades won't be made. And dam safety officials are often slow to reclassify dams. Neither Kaloko nor Spencer dams, for example, were rated high-hazard before their fatal collapses. (Leslie, 2019: paragraph 18)

As of 2020, the majority (70 per cent) of the nation's dams are over 50 years old (Griggs, Aisch, and Almukhtar, 2017). Most of the 90,000 dams in the United States are small dams – and some environmental groups argue that it would be less expensive and better for fisheries to decommission small dams. Between 1912 and 2016 (with most occurring in the past two decades), 1,384 dams have been taken down in the United States (Griggs, Aisch, and Almukhtar, 2017). Large dams, on the other hand, can be more costly to decommission than to repair. Further, "Efforts to dismantle large dams on major rivers, such as the Snake River in the Pacific Northwest, have faced strong resistance from business groups and utilities, which defend the dams for generating hydropower and creating reservoirs used to ship grain and other commodities" (Leslie, 2019). As Ho et al. (2017) argue, there must be more attention and examination of dams' role in our water future in the United States.

In the United States, "a majority of dams are privately owned, about half the states have shifted to owner-responsible inspection systems, in which dam owners are required to hire inspectors and pay for the inspections themselves instead of relying on state inspectors" (Leslie, 2019). While most infrastructure (roads, bridges, and sewer systems) is publicly owned, 97 per cent of dams are not federally owned (Ho, 2017).[17] Like in Brazil, most dams in the United States are not for energy generation but are used for irrigation (mostly privately owned and used for big agriculture and cattle ranches and flood control) (EIA, 2020). As noted above, the effects of megadam projects around the globe have had devastating socio-environmental effects. In 2004, after returning to the Sardar Sarovar Dam on the Narmada River in India, Baviskar (2004, 258) wrote:

> In the contentious politics of place-making in the Narmada valley, the terminal geography of dams seems to have triumphed. The rising level of water in the reservoir, that was once a river, is a physical manifestation of the state's success in swallowing adivasis [indigenous people] into the belly of the nation-space.

Too many people around the globe have been and continue to be swallowed by nation-states and corporations placing "progress" or "profit" ahead of life.

On 22 January 2021, MAB held a virtual international press conference to commemorate two years of the Brumadinho collapse.[18,19] MAB noted how this is a global fight and international solidarity matters because corporations know no borders and can extract, exploit, and take human life – and do so with impunity. A significant reason for this is that Vale was turned from a state-owned company into a privatized one. MAB asserts that this privatization has robbed people of their sovereignty and wealth, operating from a "logic of profit" rather than a logic of life. Neither the dam collapse nor the pandemic stopped production or profits, even as workers died.

As Joceli Andrioli, MAB militant, asserted in the press conference, "Two years of impunity for Vale … Vale values profit over life" (Fieldnotes, 22 January, 2021). People made the point at the press conference that Vale has created propaganda filled with untruths about the negotiations for reparations. All of these meetings between Vale and government officials have been without the participation of those affected. Meanwhile, people are without potable water, agriculture and fishing are disrupted or halted; and people live in chaos. This is a region where thousands of people depend upon the water affected by the collapsed dam to survive, but the water is contaminated.

At the press conference, Jôelisia Feitosa, an affected person from Juatuba (one of the affected communities from the dam collapse), noted how in 2019, nearly 300 lives were lost; now with the after-effects of the collapse, compounded by the pandemic, lives continue to be lost. Feitosa talked about how people are suffering from skin diseases that were not present before due to the contaminated water; how small farmers cannot continue with their livelihood; how people who relied on fishing can no longer do so; and how many people have had to leave. She said that at present, there are "not conditions for surviving here" anymore. The lack of potable water (in an area that, before Vale's crimes, did have potable water) has created an emergency. And, Feitosa argued, "Vale is manipulating the government, manipulating justice." She spoke about how there are more than 100,000 atingidos (people affected) in the region and that people do not know what will happen or when emergency aid will come. A final critical point to this is that Vale make the decisions as to who is or isn't an atingido for the purpose of reparations, which is another way they manipulate the process. Feitosa said that "people are still dying, and we need justice." People need emergency aid for survival and justice so that this type of crime doesn't happen again: "We want dignity and justice" (Fieldnotes, 22 January 2021).

Feitosa reflected on one success: through organizing with MAB and working with The Associação Estadual de Defesa Ambiental e Social (AEDAS or State Association of Environmental and Social Defense), they were able to secure technicians. AEDAS conducted an assessment and report in collaboration with more than seven thousand residents in the regions impacted by the dam collapse. This report shows that, depending on the town (the collapse effects vary from those buried in mud to those affected further downstream), 55 to 65 per cent of people lack employment due to the dam disaster. The report details emergency measures that need to be implemented immediately for the survival of fisher people and farmers, including proposals for how to address the immediate need for potable water (MAB, 2021d). This work with AEDAS is an example of the importance of resistance and organization and working in partnership with other entities and movements to demand that Vale and the state include those most impacted. As Joceli said during the press conference: the inclusion of those affected in the process is critical, as is the fight to ensure that 106,000 people do not lose aid and that there is a plan in place (for which MAB is fighting) to recognize the rights of the people who Vale left out of the original emergency aid.

On 4 February 2021, the government and Vale reached an accord. *The New York Times* reported that Vale awarded nearly $7 billion to the state of Minas Gerais (making it the largest settlement in Brazil's history), and that company officials were charged with murder (Andreoni and Casado, 2021). MAB, however, argues that this accord, made under false pretenses, is not legitimate; that it is a lie that Vale and the government included the affected population in the process. They further argue that the dollar amount awarded does not begin to cover the irreparable and continuing damages caused by Vale, or that the money will go to those who are most impacted and need it. As José Geraldo Martins (a member of the MAB state coordination in Minas Gerais) said to me in an email interview, Vale's "Crime destroyed ways of life, dreams, personal projects, and the possibility of a future as planned. This leads to people becoming ill, emotionally, mentally, and physically. It aggravates existing health problems and creates new ones." José added, regarding the accord:

> The first violated right is the right to participate in decisions that involve their lives, their future, and the full reparation of the damages caused. Those

affected were not even able to participate in the hearings, and the terms of the agreement were negotiated under secrecy. For this reason, the values do not meet the needs for independence from the collective moral damages suffered, most of the listed projects are not of interest to the affected region, and the "participation" provided for in the agreement does not resume choosing from a list of which projects will be prioritized. (Personal interview, 2 March 2021)

MAB said that they are committed to continued resistance and will bring the case to the Supreme Court (MAB, 2021e)[20].

In the larger, global struggle of those affected by dams, there is a recent victory and glimmer of hope for movements fighting against the devastating effects of dams. After decades of struggle, in November 2020, an agreement was reached between dam owners, First Nation's people, and farmers to bring down four dams along the Klamath River in Oregon and California in what is now called the United States. As Moore et al. (2021) wrote:

This is an important step in restoring historic salmon runs, which have drastically declined in recent years since the dams were constructed. It's also an incredible win for the Karuk and Yurok tribes, who for untold generations have relied on the salmon runs for both sustenance and spiritual well-being. (paragraph 2)

It represents the world's largest hydropower dam removal and a significant win for tribal communities (specifically the Yurok and Karuk), and the salmon runs so critical to their survival and culture (Moore et al., 2021). In November 2022, the Federal Energy Regulatory Commission gave final approval to allow moving forward with the removal and restoration; several dams on the Klamath are planned to be removed in 2024 (National Fisherman, 2023).

Ultimately, the struggle of those affected by dams continues, and just as corporate and government actors organize to control and profit from water, movements organize and fight against water grabbing in its various forms. However, the extent to which these struggles are isolated occurrences or part of an interconnected global movement remains under-examined in the academic literature of social movement studies in the United States. Water grabbing – whether in the context of a hydro dam, drinking water, or the other various forms – and the resistance against it is a conflict between two logics: the logic that capitalists must be able to control and profit from resources versus the logic that resources must be in control of the people and used to support and sustain life for all. These competing narratives are not exclusive to any one struggle or country. The various (yet interrelated) ways people are organizing against the commodification of water is the core of the content in the following chapters.

Notes

1 Movement of People Affected by Dams in English.
2 The "2nd International Seminar: Food, Water, and Energy Are Not Commodities" was held at Rutgers University, Newark, NJ, 12–14 March 2017, and sponsored by various programs, including the International Institute for Peace at Rutgers, at the university.
3 See Chapter 1.
4 See Chapter 6.
5 The United Nations General Assembly recognized the human right to water and sanitation on 28 June 2010 through Resolution 64/292.
6 National Privatization Plan in English.
7 It is useful to situate *Expulsions* (2014) in relation to an earlier article in which Sassen contends that global capitalism is entering a new phase, pointing to a deep systemic crisis (Sassen, 2013). This is "advanced capitalism," different from traditional capitalism, she argues, because it is "marked by predatory dynamics rather than evolution, development, or progress" (Sassen, 2013: 200). Whereas Keynesian capitalism valued "people as workers and consumers," advanced capitalism does not. Primitive accumulation is still at work, but it is dominated by speculative finance, which she argues has caused systemic transformation characterized by expulsions of increasing numbers of people who are no longer valued as consumers or workers. Advanced capitalism expels people – from both the Global North and Global South (Sassen, 2013: 200–01). I argue – as discussed in the previous chapter – that it is not the particular form of capitalism (neoliberalism or "advanced capitalism") that is the root of the problem but rather, capitalism as a system of socio-economic organization. I don't think that "expulsions" are a new phenomenon, but I am persuaded by components of Sassen's argument: advanced capitalism is scaled up in the speed and scope of its rapid rapaciousness to accumulate (Sassen, 2014: 150–1 and 200). This is a problem of accumulation by dispossession: in the quest to accumulate greater profit, capitalism seeks new ways to lower production costs and to increase sales revenue (Wallerstein, 2004). This causes dispossession of people and environmental degradation. In the era of speculative finance, the global economic system is complex, and with a more complex system often comes more brutality (Sassen, 2014: 2–4). It can also make organizing more complicated, as it is not one "bad actor" to target, but rather a whole system, which often makes the various actors within it invisible. We can see this at play with multinational investment firms.
8 The payment plan program was implemented poorly. Six months later, of the 24,000 residents who initially registered for it, it was found that fewer than 300 were actually current on their bills (Gottesdiener, 2015).
9 An NGO and think tank committed to "building a just, democratic and sustainable planet" (from TNI's website at: www.tni.org/en)
10 Twenty-two per cent of these cases are in the water sector.

11 Even Anna Clark's well-documented book *The Poisoned City: Flint's Water and the American Urban Tragedy* (2018) does not discuss the community group Flint Rising (Flint Rising, n.d.), and while she does delve deeply into problems of structural racism, she also largely ignores the role of Black activists.

12 With many more planned. There are 158 dams in operation or under construction in the Amazon Basin and over 351 proposed as of 2019 (Fearnside, 2020).

13 The affected region is throughout the Rio Doce River basin and includes the state of Espírito Santo.

14 According to Camilla Brito, integral reparations would include the following: mitigating damage; return of assets; fair compensation for damages, including emotional/moral and immaterial damages; collective and individual compensation for everything that is not possible to refund or calculate a compensation amount; rehabilitation with measures that enable the resumption of economic, social and cultural activities; guarantee of satisfaction of those affected and those affected by the results of the repair; and finally, that the same crime will never happen again (Brito, 2022: 35). Brito's study examines how the damages caused before and after the Mariana collapse have disproportionately harmed women and how the process of reparations has too often excluded affected women. The affected women are also majority Black, and so the study points to the intersecting problems of environmental racism and machismo (Brito, 2022). MAB continues to struggle for reparations for those affected, throughout the region.

15 Ribeirinho refers to people who live near rivers that the Brazilian state classifies as "traditional" (but not Indigenous) inhabitants of the land who rely on subsistence farming and fishing.

16 Quilombolas are communities founded by people of African descent who escaped enslavement and formed their own communities. Quilombola communities continue to exist and resist today and are also defined by the Brazilian government as traditional communities.

17 The largest dams, however, are mostly regulated and owned by the federal government (FEMA, 2019). The United States is fourth in generating capacity, behind China, Brazil, and Canada (Reve, 2020).

18 MAB has a skilled communication team that makes use of online media, including holding frequent talks and panels broadcast via Facebook Live.

19 I attended this press conference, and some of the content from it is published in a piece in *Roar Magazine* (See Schroering, 2021b). The MAB organized commemoration surrounding the first anniversary of the collapse is discussed in Chapter 5.

20 This struggle is ongoing and developing, and MAB continues to advocate for reparations; more recent information can be found on MAB's webpage, www.mab.org.br, with some articles translated into Spanish or English.

3

The Grinch stole our water: translocal resistance for the right to water

As the holidays approached in the United States city of Pittsburgh in December of 2017, the Our Water Campaign (OWC) held a public action outside the district attorney's office under the slogan, "The Grinch Stole Our Water," deploying a well-known Christmas story to drive home their point (see Figure 3.1). In this story, the Grinch was Veolia,[1] a company contracted for a public–private partnership (PPP) with the water authority to improve the quality of water and provide more cost-efficient service to residents. Instead, they made things worse. The private part of the partnership was an international corporation that was profiting while also causing similar problems in other cities around the world. The residents of Pittsburgh organized to take back their right to clean, safe drinking water. Their actions exemplify how a translocal network (discussed later in this chapter and also in Chapter 1) of activists can organize for the human right to water.

This chapter examines the social movement struggle for the right to (safe and accessible) water in the United States focusing on this Pittsburgh-based coalition. The Pittsburgh example demonstrates how organized social movement resistance can successfully organize against water privatization and for accessible and clean water for all. Privatization is always driven by profit. If water supplies are run by private corporations, profit will always take priority over service to residents. Either the price of water increases, or costly maintenance required for clean, safe water will diminish. In both cases, the public will lose. PPPs should be recognized as a form of privatization (see Chapter 2). Local organizers in Pittsburgh understood this and established a coalition for safe water. They declared that "Pittsburgh's water system is for us, the people of Pittsburgh, so we have clean and affordable water; it is not for generating billions of dollars for Wall Street billionaires!" (Fieldnotes from OWC Messaging, 2018)

The above quote relates to the Bolivia struggle (introduced in Chapter 2), and how there are two logics of privatization to be countered: the "private property of the transnationals," and the "private property of the state," both of which seek to control social wealth without the input of the people,

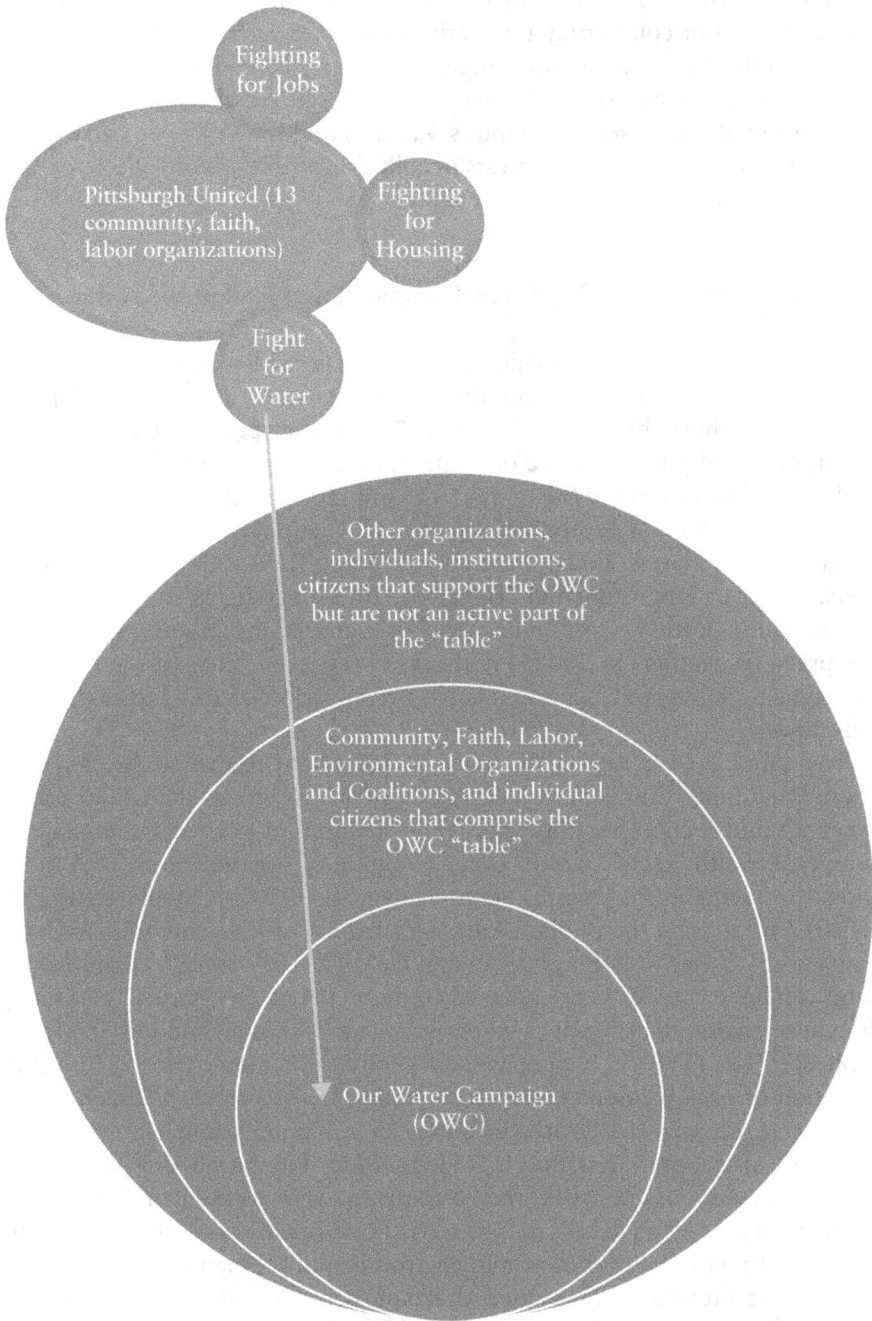

Figure 3.1 OWC organizational structure

without the voice of democracy (Olivera and Lewis, 2004: 156). In many ways, it is about countering a narrative of private versus public control of social goods – a narrative not unique to Bolivia.[2] Indeed, much of Olivera and Lewis' discussion of the Cochabamba struggle parallels that of MAB's fight in Brazil (discussed in Chapters 4 and 5) and the OWC in Pittsburgh. Increasingly we see private interests in collusion with the state, via so-called PPPs, as discussed in the previous chapter.

Background: the Our Water Campaign and lead in the water

In 2016, a lead crisis hit Pittsburgh, which is where I lived at the time. I felt personally connected to it – my own house tested at a level of 100 ppb, nearly seven times the safe level – and that I had a responsibility to fight for clean, safe, and public water. For context, Pennsylvania's Lead and Copper Rule establishes a limit of 0.015 mg/L (15 ppb) for lead in water. The United States Environmental Protection Agency (EPA) stipulates that action must be taken if lead levels in water are above 15 ppb (EPA, 2021; Pennsylvania Department of Environmental Protection, 2021). Having spent time organizing against bottled water (one aspect of water privatization, as noted in the previous chapter) in 2008, I understood the importance of the fight for the right to water and fighting against privatization of this life-sustaining substance.

I was involved in the OWC since its inception, participating in meetings, community outreach and actions, canvassing, town halls, and other meetings and events (see Appendix A). A coalition of environmental, labor, women's health, racial justice, other community organizations, and individual residents in Pittsburgh, Pennsylvania, the OWC formally coalesced in 2017 to address the public health catastrophe of lead contamination in Pittsburgh's water (Pittsburgh United, n.d.a). The individuals/organizations who comprise the OWC are referred to internally as the "table," and have fought to ensure that the city's water is "safe, affordable, and publicly controlled."[3] The OWC is a campaign of Pittsburgh United, which is itself a coalition of organizations (labor, community, faith, and environmental) in the Pittsburgh area that works to create "a community and economy that work for all people" (Pittsburgh United, n.d.b). Pittsburgh United is affiliated with a national network, the Partnership for Working Families, a coalition of nineteen regionally based advocacy organizations that work for solutions to national economic and environmental problems.

Previous literature has argued that anti-privatization or remunicipalization efforts in the United States have been driven by pragmatic reasons such as increased cost and reduced service quality, rather than political/

ideological opposition to privatization and the idea that water should be held in the public trust (McDonald, 2018; Warner and Aldag, 2019). In what follows, I recount the struggle for clean and public water that both serves as a counter example to this literature and provides an example of translocal organizing (González Rivas and Schroering, 2021a).[4] As discussed in the previous chapter, Pittsburgh is an example of how around the world, people are mobilizing to fight corporate control and greed, and for the idea that water should be a right and not a commodity.

Like many other cities in the United States, Pittsburgh has an aging infrastructure in need of significant repairs. The Pittsburgh Water and Sewer Authority (PWSA) – the city's public utility company – has been plagued by administrative problems and financial difficulties caused by the 2008 financial crisis, when the Authority lost around $100 million after investing in risky interest rate default swaps (Shaw, 2019). To "fix" these problems, PWSA sought help from a private company – like other cities in the country that sought short-term savings by entering into PPPs, which were defined in the previous chapter. PWSA hired Veolia in 2012 to manage operations, and the contract stipulated that Veolia would keep up to 50 cents for every dollar saved under its management (Lurie, 2016).[5,6]

The changes made under Veolia's management of PWSA included switching to a new billing system to modernize it. This resulted in significant billing errors and overcharging. In May 2015, some Pittsburgh residents sued Veolia North America Water for billing errors. By the end of 2015, PWSA had laid off 23 workers,[7] including safety and water quality managers. In addition, heads of finance as well as engineering and the lab staff, who were responsible for testing water samples, were cut in half. According to Veolia, at this point, they were in a consulting, not management role, and did not accept responsibility for the layoffs. In his later audit of the PWSA, City Controller Michael Lamb found that "cost savings from reduced staffing at the lab" were part of "improvement initiatives that Veolia negotiated and for which they were paid" (Office of City Controller, 2017: 13). In December 2015, in the face of the citizen class-action lawsuit, Pittsburgh terminated the contract with Veolia and returned all control back to publicly accountable officials (Lurie, 2016).

In 2014, while PWSA was under Veolia's management, a switch was made to the corrosion control, swapping out a more corrosive but cheaper chemical. This change caused more lead to leach into the system, and occurred without testing or authorization from the Department of Environmental Protection (DEP), the PWSA board, or the City of Pittsburgh (Addison, 2017). In October 2015, the PWSA maintenance superintendent appeared to take credit for replacing soda ash with the cheaper caustic soda in an email to staff, lauding the cost-saving benefits. However, others, including

PWSA spokespeople and Pittsburgh's mayor, continued blaming Veolia for the change, noting that it occurred under their management. DEP cited PWSA in April 2016 for not notifying them of the chemical switch; PWSA released statements placing the blame on Veolia.

During the summer of 2016, PWSA informed 81,000 homes that Pittsburgh had a significant level of lead in the water problem; approximately 20,000 homes had lead service lines. In October 2016, PWSA sued Veolia for causing the lead crisis; in 2017, Veolia countersued for defamation. The parties ultimately settled out of court (Addison, 2017; Fieldnotes, 2017; Lurie 2016).[8]

Water is an environmental justice and human rights issue

The United States Environmental Justice (EJ) Movement began with a focus on the disproportionate exposure to toxic waste dumping faced by communities of color (see Brulle and Pellow, 2006; Bullard, 1993; Cole and Foster, 2001; Taylor, 1993, 2016). The Latin American context has historically been more focused on conflicts over resource (see Altieri and Toledo, 2011; Carruthers, 2008; DiChiro, 1998; Lewis, 2016; Roberts and Thanos, 2003; Sawyer, 2004). Environmental justice scholar, Robert Bullard (1993: 19), contends that all environmental injustice issues are connected because the roots are always found in economic and racial exploitation, oppression, and an overall devaluation of life. As I have suggested, this is indicative of the role of the global economy in exploiting people and degrading the land. In the context of the fight for the right to water in Pittsburgh and the OWC – an environmental justice campaign of Pittsburgh United – the conflict centered around *who* controlled the water, as well as the struggle for drinking water and rivers that are not contaminated with lead and sewage.

The OWC viewed water as a human right that should be publicly controlled, safe, clean, and affordable. Members of OWC attended Pittsburgh Water and Sewer Authority (PWSA) board meetings throughout the campaign, with individuals registered to speak during public comment at most meetings. Attendance varied, but there were often ten or more people who would hold up a banner for "Our Water Campaign" while different residents, who represented the campaign, spoke. This experience showed a combination of a "carrot and stick" approach with PWSA: offering accolades for moving in the right direction and speaking to the importance of keeping the Authority public to respond to resident demands. For example, at one PWSA board meeting, an OWC volunteer said the board had shown courage with their efforts, especially around the fight for green infrastructure, to put a moratorium on shut-offs and stop partial lead line replacements. The

EJ organizer for the OWC told the board to keep having the courage to keep PWSA public and clearly expressed that the OWC was opposed to any form of privatization, including PPPs. Another person talked about the need for not just a moratorium, but a total ban on shut-offs and called for more strategies to mitigate the impacts of water rate hikes for low-income residents.

After approving a budget increase for the 2018 lead service line replacement program, a PWSA board member noted that PWSA had so far replaced 605 lead service lines, leaving a bit over 700 to complete in 2018. He said: "our speaker was right, it does take courage to approve a $44 million project, but it has to be done" (Fieldnotes, 15 December 2017). This idea that people have an inherent right to water guided the work of the OWC, including in its advocacy for a moratorium on shut-offs. The campaign by OWC was successful and, in October 2017, PWSA issued a winter moratorium on water shut-offs. The OWC joined the Clean Rivers Campaign (CRC)[9] (at the time, the two were separate campaigns)[10] to expand the Customer Assistance Program (CAP) to 250 per cent of the poverty level.

Transparency

As I wrote in my fieldnotes in June 2017, the water landscape in Pittsburgh was (is) complicated, and the lack of transparency prevented residents from knowing what was going on:

> [most residents] aren't aware of the efforts to privatize and what that means ... they aren't aware of how bad the lead problem is ... and the perception that (Mayor) Peduto doesn't want to privatize is not wholly accurate. Although he is on the public record of so doing, his statements behind closed doors tell a different story. (Fieldnotes, 15 June 2017)[11]

It became clear that in this struggle for the right to water the meaning of "privatization" was at stake, which did not include PPPs in the definition for many elected officials, including the mayor. The examples that follow illustrate this. The mayor of Pittsburgh put together a Blue-Ribbon Panel (BRP)[12] in March 2017 to look into the restructuring of PWSA. In the post-Veolia PPP landscape (which ended in 2015), this was the first time the threat of privatization appeared again. The lead contamination crisis – with some discourse amongst political leaders eager to place the blame exclusively on PWSA while completely ignoring the role that Veolia played – had created a challenging situation for PWSA. This was compounded by other problems, including water main breaks and continued billing errors, which was something that began under Veolia's management (Members of the Mayor's Blue Ribbon Panel, 2018).

In the fall of 2017, the consulting firm IMG (a pro-PPP firm chosen by the city) presented recommendations to the BRP, including various forms of privatization. The OWC and other civic and community groups participated in these public input meetings, asserting the need to keep PWSA Public. They cited Veolia as a reason why PPPs are not in the best interest of the city. The OWC did outreach to encourage residents to attend and for each coalition partner to commit to a certain number of people who would attend.[13] The representatives of the coalition, other partners, and individual residents emphasized the following:

- We already experienced Veolia coming in and cutting staff and implementing dangerous cost-cutting measures that led to the lead crisis in our City.
- Private companies will always prioritize profit over the needs of Pittsburgh residents.
- Our need for safe and healthy drinking water is too important to be left in the hands of corporations.
- We need to expand public, democratic control over vital resources to allow our communities to thrive.

Following these meetings, the BRP convened a public meeting to share their final recommendations. The OWC planned to participate in this meeting and prepared for it. At a meeting before the BRP meeting, the discussion focused on the need to emphasize that maintaining public governance and control is about democracy and creating structures that preserve public accountability (Fieldnotes, 24 January 2018). On 30 January 2018, the BRP held a meeting on PWSA restructuring and cited lead, decaying infrastructure, and boil water advisories as reasons why this was needed. In the course of the report, speaking to a room of approximately 60 people, the panel noted the previous advocacy of citizens and the OWC, and one member of the BRP said, "We want to hear from you ... [we] don't want it to be a monologue." The BRP's key finding was that while PWSA has made vital progress in the past few months, more was needed. The mayor's executive order from 22 January stipulated the need to make governance changes by 31 March 2018. Allotted just two minutes to do so, more than a dozen people voiced various concerns during the public comment period, including the need to ensure public accountability, democracy, representation, and transparency in any new governance structure.

One of the BRP members said, "water is not an inalienable right that should be free." An organizer connected to the OWC replied that the OWC believes water *is* a human right and should be accessible to all: the best way to ensure this is to keep it public. Further, any changes made to the structure of PWSA must increase democracy and transparency. This speaker was followed by two more members of the OWC, one of whom handed the BRP a printed copy of recommendations (crafted by the OWC) for restructuring the governance structure. I gave public comments at this meeting, speaking to the need to focus on equity. Ultimately, while early discussions and public meetings involving the BRP included the possibility of another PPP, in the end, the BRP recommendations were against privatization "at this time" (Blue Ribbon Panel, 2017; Lindstrom, 2017).

The above is an example of the critical role social movement resistance can play in reversing or preventing privatization. Social movement studies have been focused on outcomes, which are important, but they can be hard to assess without close attention to the complex and long-term processes of change making. Social movements can be key actors in preventing or reversing privatization and promoting local voice and equity and environmental policies (Almeida, 2019; Robinson, 2013b). Privatization – including and especially PPPs – are part of the hegemonic script of policy recommendations promoted globally and enthusiastically by the World Bank and other powerful institutions, including states. Government actors are often reluctant to challenge recommendations that they assume are tried and tested, or that challenge the prevailing hegemonic order and corporate power (Miraftab, 2004; Nowak, 2016; Sager, 2011).

In the case of the OWC, activism served as a critical driver of reversing privatization and in shaping the meaning of public water. This shift in policy can only be explained by the presence of the OWC's organizing. My work with the OWC shows that its mobilization, along with pressure from allied public officials and other community organizations and residents, halted the possibility of another PPP. A new PPP could have occurred at various points, and specifically during two points in time: first after the BRP recommendations, and next with "Peoples Water," discussed below. The OWC's efforts of coordinated public education, mobilization, and political pressure encouraged and mobilized residents who might have been opposed to privatization but would not have turned out to public meetings and other events (Krauss, 2019; Weinman, 2019a).

The campaign carried out political education with local officials to help them understand what constituents want and why it was important to take an anti-privatization stance. It is not about "credit" to one entity, but rather about furthering the goal of public water that is accessible to all, with transparent and democratic governance. In the case of the OWC, "people power" changed the trajectory of what could have occurred, and that included pushing public officials (who are also residents) to take heed and listen to their (organized) constituents' demands. Mobilizing residents (and public leaders) to oppose the hegemonic line of seeing PPPs as beneficial, required organization and education against the hegemony of the pro-business and anti-government logic that prevails in our society today.

The argument of the OWC that water *is* a human right versus that it is "not an inalienable right that should be free" (Fieldnotes, 30 January 2018) is important to highlight. It showcases the point first made in the first chapter of this book: struggles over water grabbing are about *who* has a right to water. Conflicts around water grabbing are fundamentally between, on the one side, people and social movements who believe that access to clean, safe water is a basic human right, and on the other side, capitalists argue that they have the "right" to profit from the privatization of water.

Disrupting hegemony: Global South to Global North

Following a Gramscian analysis (outlined in Chapter 1), I argue that one of the most important outcomes of movements is to challenge hegemony, which includes affecting how residents are thinking about an issue, such as PPPs. Broad and Cavanagh's book, *The Water Defenders* (2021), discusses a story of "unlikely allies" who fought against corporate mining extractivism and water privatization in El Salvador. The struggle brought together a broad and complex slate of local and global actors; together they formed a counter-hegemonic force that won the fight. The same held true in the Pittsburgh case. Disrupting hegemonic narratives is insufficient alone; but it must be a starting place. Due to colonialism and imperialism, the Global South has more experiences with the failures of neoliberal logic, including PPPs around water. But the failures of decades of neoliberal reforms and austerity in the Global North are now becoming more visible, with the Pittsburgh water case serving as one example. A key part of the OWC's work was to challenge the hegemonic narrative that privatization is the solution.

The OWC's focus on public water and against privatization came out of the previous failed experience of a PPP with Veolia and activists learning about the failed experiences with PPPs globally. As noted in the previous chapter, Veolia is or has been connected to investigations in numerous countries (Fonger, 2019; Hosea and Lerner, 2018; Global Witness, 2023). As Leana Hosea and Sharon Lerner (2018) report:

> The company's methods have also come under scrutiny outside the U.S., with controversies in Canada, France, and Gabon. In 2015, Romania's anti-corruption agency launched an investigation into Veolia's Romanian subsidiary, Apa Nova Bucuresti, and individual executives for allegedly running a multiyear, multimillion-euro bribery scheme in order to dramatically raise water rates. Veolia's subsidiary allegedly used sham contracts to funnel over 12 million euros to public officials or their affiliates in order to get approval for water rate hikes. The investigation has since expanded to France and the U.S. Securities and Exchange Commission. (paragraph 49)

Between 2006 and 2012 alone, more than 50 documented campaigns against Veolia existed (Brown, 2019).[14]

The OWC's push for public water emerged from understanding the role Veolia played in the Pittsburgh lead crisis, research on other locales which had experienced PPPs, and connection to others who had experienced poor water quality and rising rates due to PPPs. From its early days, the campaign has been focused on ensuring that the water stays public and that the public utility is held accountable for providing safe and affordable water. This conviction was evident at a community meeting organized by the coalition in November 2018 about green infrastructure. The invited speaker (from another city) said to the audience of approximately 50: "how do you privatize green infrastructure?" and in response, you could hear vocalizations of disagreement, head shaking, and even some people stating aloud "no" to the idea of privatization. He clarified that he was not talking about privatizing PWSA, but about private sector solutions for implementing green infrastructure. I share the point here because it showed the commitment against the idea of privatization as a solution to problems that the water justice community in Pittsburgh has developed (Fieldnotes, 19 November 2018). This opposition includes so-called "public–private partnerships" (also known as PPPs or P3s), discussed in Chapter 2. Chapter 6 delves into this in more detail, but public–private partnerships are the most common form of water privatization in the United States, which are worse than full privatization because all of the risks are turned over to the public side and all of the profit to the private side (Bel, Bel-Piñana, Jordi Rosell, 2017; Kishimoto et al., 2017).[15]

In many ways, the concept of a PPP is a reflection of the fight around ideas that I began this book noting: on one hand is the idea of using water to extract corporate profit (and the global economic and political systems that support it), and on the other hand is the idea that water should be a public good and a right.[16] One of the strategies of the elite/market forces has been to appropriate social movement ideas. This has manifested in the practice of PPPs and calling them a public and democratic alternative to privatization. In this sense, the term itself reflects a response to movement pressure (Smith, Plummer, and Hughes, 2017).[17] The use of the term PPP further complicates how movements fight against hegemonic forces and privatization, since the phrase "PPP" suggests collaboration and partnership and includes the word "public." To shed light on the problematic aspects of PPPs, the OWC put considerable energy into education about what the term means. The OWC focused and organized from its earliest days for public water and against privatization (including PPPs). When in 2018, a private utility began actively working to enter into a new PPP with PWSA, the OWC noted the need for more education around what does and does not constitute privatization.

This education took place in two main ways: first, with public and elected officials, and second, with residents and the public

Within a few years of the Veolia contract termination and post-BRP recommendations, rumblings of a new PPP with PWSA began. The OWC (along with other allied individual residents, public officials, and organizations) fought against new PPPs proposed and led by Peoples Gas (the private gas company in the city), Penn American Water Company (the private water company that provides water to a small segment of the city), and Aqua America Water Company (a major private water company in the United States),[18] and the Allegheny Conference (a Pittsburgh organization representing the business sector interests) (Shaw, 2019).

In May of 2018, Peoples Gas began meeting clandestinely with members of City Council; in June 2018, the OWC started to advocate against "Peoples Waters,"[19] a plan created by Peoples Gas to create a PPP with PWSA led by the President and CEO of Peoples Gas, as well as the former chief of staff to the mayor (hired by Peoples after working for the mayor on the Blue Ribbon project), who also claimed to be against privatization (Shoemaker, 2018a). This turn of events brought to light the blurry meaning of privatization: it was not just Peoples Gas arguing explicitly that what they were proposing was *not* privatization. It was elected leaders and others, even some who had espoused opposition to privatization, advocating for this PPP. It became clear that some people did not understand "PPPs" as privatization until the OWC helped illuminate how they do in fact constitute a form of privatization (Shoemaker, 2018b). The OWC spent time discussing how to address the need for more education about PPPs, and the need to push city officials to oppose private companies. While there were some concerns about taking on a big target[20] and fear that the coalition lacked the power to stand up to Peoples, ultimately the OWC decided that it must remain committed to its anti-privatization stance and take on the corporate actor involved in it (Fieldnotes, 29 March 2018). As one leader put it, "We've built enough power that they [Peoples] are asking[21] us to stay quiet – we need to use our power" (Fieldnotes, 24 May 2018). The OWC successfully intervened to challenge the hegemonic logic that private companies can do things better than governments.

Throughout the years, OWC met regularly with local elected officials; I attended over a dozen of these, especially when the elected official was one of my representatives. The OWC, upon hearing suggestions of the proposed Peoples PPP, scheduled meetings with elected officials to talk about why a PWSA/Peoples Gas partnership was not in the best interests of Pittsburgh residents. I share one such meeting here, which serves as an illustrative example, showing the dynamics around PPP education and fighting the potential Peoples PPP.

In May 2018, eight members of the OWC (myself included) met with a local elected leader to discuss the recent move by Peoples gas to try to enter into a new PPP with PWSA. Each person had the opportunity to share reasons for being against a new PPP in the meeting with this elected official. I made the point that water is a public good and human right, not a commodity, and that our need for safe drinking water should not be left in the hands of corporations: Pittsburgh needs a fully public authority that is accountable to the people. An OWC leader argued in the meeting that when private companies (like Veolia and Peoples Gas) claim they will bring "efficiency and cost savings" to water systems, this obscures the reality of what is happening: using their power to lobby politicians to remove barriers to water privatization so that they can make billions of dollars. Another person made the case that Pittsburgh residents deserve and will demand transparency. Backroom meetings behind closed doors between elected officials and private corporations are not transparent.[22] After hearing the arguments for why privatization would not be good, this elected leader said, "That's why I promised to keep our water public" [during the previous campaign].

This statement illustrated how this public official's definition of public included public–private partnerships. This interaction showed three main things: 1) that this corporation had successfully pitched the PPP to elected officials as an environmentally sustainable solution that could replace all lead lines without raising costs, all while keeping the conversation behind closed doors and out of public scrutiny; 2) pitches like this sound appealing to politicians beholden to the hegemonic logic of capitalism that argues government ought to be scaled back, and this is especially true when there is not organized resistance against hegemonic "solutions;" 3) the role of education about P3s and their negative impact on the public is critical. After the meeting, this leader soon became (and has remained) opposed to PPPs, demonstrating a change from their expressed view during the meeting that PPPs do not constitute privatization. That this pressure from constituents matters, and that those residents then make the issue public – when corporate and government players would liked to have kept it quiet for longer – matters.

While it is impossible to "prove" that social movement resistance stopped a new PPP, shedding light on what was happening mobilized resident resistance, and I contend that is what stopped the deal from moving forward. It suggests that (at least in some cases) when exposed to information and arguments that lie outside the hegemonic logic of the neoliberal order and question its basic assumptions, some public officials' views change – especially if they think their election or re-election might depend on it. This highlights the importance of people power: one individual constituent contacting their elected official or speaking out and sharing information is unlikely to have much impact; it is only when there is significant pressure (coming from many people) that public officials might "hear" the information and change their stance.

On 13 June 2018, the OWC held an action at Peoples Gas headquarters opposing the Peoples Water plan and announced a petition drive to keep PWSA public. The OWC created messaging to organize around why a new PPP with Peoples Gas would not serve the interest of the people. The points included the following:

> For the past year and a half, the Our Water Campaign has fought for safe, affordable, publicly controlled water. We're winning: PWSA has begun replacing lead lines, developed a Customer Assistance Program, fixed their billing system, taken steps to reduce lead in the water, and instituted a winter moratorium on water shutoffs. We now have safer water, and more equitable rates for everyone, from a public water authority that is more accountable to the public than ever. And we're not done yet; PWSA continues to work with us on behalf of the people of Pittsburgh to improve their services across the board. Despite all of this progress, Peoples Gas continues to try and privatize our public water system. They want to create a giant corporate monopoly that controls our water.
>
> Handing over control of our water to a private company is what got us here in the first place. Paris-based private water company Veolia took over management of PWSA in 2011, and we've been cleaning up their mess ever since.
>
> Water is a public good and human right; not a commodity. Our need for safe and healthy drinking water is too important to be left in the hands of a private equity firm on the other side of the country. Pittsburgh's water system is for us, the people of Pittsburgh, so we have clean and affordable water; it is not for generating billions of dollars for Wall Street billionaires. (Fieldnotes from OWC Messaging, 2018)

This turn of events brought to light the blurry line of privatization: it was not just Peoples Gas arguing that what they proposed was not privatization, elected leaders and others, even some who had publicly expressed opposition to privatization, agreed. In 2020, Aqua America acquired Peoples Gas (Krauss, 2020). The website created for Peoples Water (Shoemaker, 2018a) is currently a dead link,[23] but until 2020 it asserted that they were still interested in being a part of the "solution" to Pittsburgh's water troubles.[24]

In January 2021, one of the prominent newspapers published a letter to the editor from a pro-private water lobby, arguing that Pittsburgh should privatize its water. The OWC EJ organizer at the time, Madeline Weiss, and a city councilperson co-published an op-ed in response, arguing the following:

> Private water corporations often cut corners to reduce operating costs, negatively impacting water or service quality, or both. It's laughable to tell people

in Pittsburgh that the best way to fix their water system is to privatize it. Following Veolia's management, the private water corporation walked away with millions of dollars, while the city and residents were left to pick up the pieces. When everyone saw what Veolia did, there was a social movement to prevent water from being privatized again just a few years ago. From community members to the mayor, Pittsburghers agree that our water is not for sale. (Weiss and Strassburger, 2021)

As a leader in the OWC said in 2017, in the context of mentioning examples of water privatization failures the world over, "privatization never works anywhere" (Fieldnotes, Winter, 2017). Indeed, as noted in Chapter 2, communities with privatized water services always end up paying more, and the quality of the water declines (Cohen, n.d.). Privatized water means that the company's goal is to make a profit; they must extract profit. This means that rates will always rise and/or the company will stop investing in upkeep and maintaining the water system, leading to a decline in quality.

Strategies and tactics

The organization of the OWC combines a formalized structure with elements of grassroots organizing. The campaign has a paid environmental justice organizer, staff from other member organizations, as well as individual residents, with ties to diverse constituents and organizations in the progressive movement community. The OWC uses a variety of tactics that are well-known among activists: attending public utility and city council meetings, canvassing door to door in the community, and organizing town halls, direct actions, trainings, and meetings with public officials. Sometimes the OWC uses petitions and pledges. Especially during the initial years of the campaign, community canvassing and phone banking was carried out often, because educating and engaging the general public was vital to the struggle. The OWC held trainings on canvassing and phone banking, to help prepare participants with the skills needed to be successful. The OWC and partners did targeted canvassing to find people who had partial line replacements, and people who had elevated lead levels in their water. Through this work, early on, the campaign better understood which communities were receiving lead line replacements and which were not, how water filter distribution was being implemented, and other community concerns. During canvassing and phone banking, people were given information on how to sign up for lead testing kits and filters. Canvassing served as a way to connect with residents about problems and concerns, provide education on the topic, and direct people to available resources. Figure 3.2 is an example of an OWC handout.

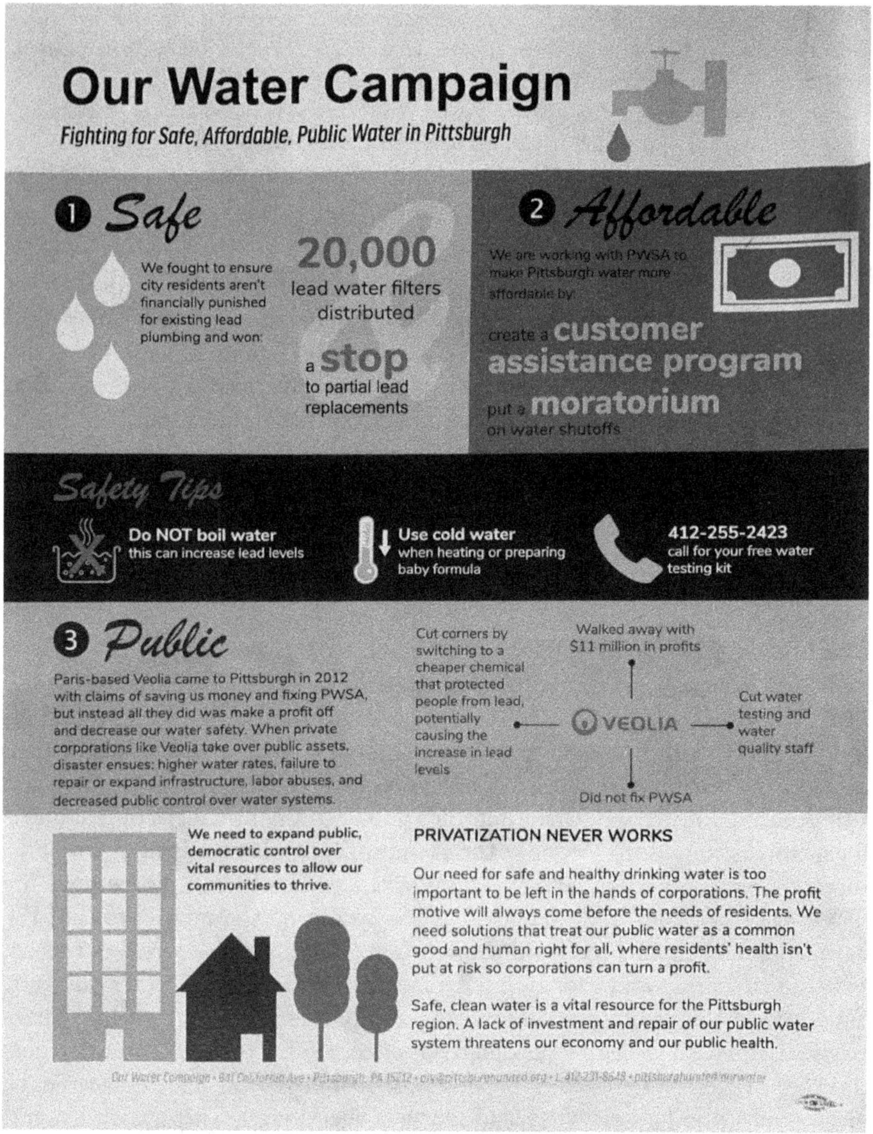

Our Water Campaign

Fighting for Safe, Affordable, Public Water in Pittsburgh

❶ Safe

We fought to ensure city residents aren't financially punished for existing lead plumbing and won:

20,000 lead water filters distributed

a **stop** to partial lead replacements

❷ Affordable

We are working with PWSA to make Pittsburgh water more affordable by:

create a **customer assistance program**

put a **moratorium** on water shutoffs

Safety Tips

Do NOT boil water this can increase lead levels

Use cold water when heating or preparing baby formula

412-255-2423 call for your free water testing kit

❸ Public

Paris-based Veolia came to Pittsburgh in 2012 with claims of saving us money and fixing PWSA, but instead all they did was make a profit off and decrease our water safety. When private corporations like Veolia take over public assets, disaster ensues: higher water rates, failure to repair or expand infrastructure, labor abuses, and decreased public control over water systems.

Cut corners by switching to a cheaper chemical that protected people from lead, potentially causing the increase in lead levels

Walked away with $11 million in profits

Cut water testing and water quality staff

◎ VEOLIA

Did not fix PWSA

We need to expand public, democratic control over vital resources to allow our communities to thrive.

PRIVATIZATION NEVER WORKS

Our need for safe and healthy drinking water is too important to be left in the hands of corporations. The profit motive will always come before the needs of residents. We need solutions that treat our public water as a common good and human right for all, where residents' health isn't put at risk so corporations can turn a profit.

Safe, clean water is a vital resource for the Pittsburgh region. A lack of investment and repair of our public water system threatens our economy and our public health.

Our Water Campaign • 841 California Ave • Pittsburgh, PA 15212 • owc@pittsburghunited.org • 412-231-8549 • pittsburghunited.org/water

Figure 3.2 OWC canvassing handout

Channeling anger

The OWC discussed how to build the coalition and how to do community outreach. At a base-building meeting in 2018, the organizer for the OWC at the time said: "In February, people are going to get 28 per cent rate hike [on their PWSA bill]. We need to use the anger [people are going to feel] and channel it into something productive" (Fieldnotes, 11 January 2018). The OWC understood the need for rate increases for infrastructure improvements to keep the utility public, while at the same time saw the imperative to advocate for assistance programs to prevent rate increases from disproportionately impacting the city's low-income and most vulnerable residents. It worked to educate residents on examples of water utility PPPs' failures (including high rates) and mobilize people to push for safe, clean, public water. OWC's messaging included this point: "PWSA must remain controlled by and accountable to the people of Pittsburgh. Public control of our assets, like water, is critical to a healthy democracy, and a healthy citizenry." The campaign argued against the potential Peoples plan stating: "Are we to believe that a private equity firm will keep rates affordable? The best way to ensure that no one is priced out of water is to keep the water authority accountable to the people."

Much of the OWC's work consisted of planning ever-changing strategies and tactics. One way this occurred is through annual planning retreats where goals, successes, and tactics were reviewed and planned for the coming year. But discussions of strategies and tactics often consumed a considerable portion of the table meetings. For example, earlier in the campaign, there was consensus: total lead line replacements needed to happen to address the issue of lead in the water. Scientific data showed that partial lead line replacements are dangerous (McCormick and Andrade, 2022; Women for a Healthy Environment, 2021: 17). The goal was clear, but the target (the person who has the authority to make the demanded change happen) less so. Was it the mayor, the health department, or the PWSA? Ultimately, it was a combination. Achieving lead line replacements required the work and commitment of many individuals, including many elected officials – but the OWC directed and pushed this and held public officials accountable to their commitments, as I will describe in the text that follows.

The OWC pushed elected leaders, the health department, and PWSA to provide clear messaging and action about the situation. The coalition worked with local officials and PWSA on this information gathering. Initially, PWSA's focus on lead line replacements was not in the Hill District or Homewood, both majority Black neighborhoods, and instead focused on where new gentrification projects were happening. PWSA was also doing partial lead line replacements (replacing the public street side but not the private side), which is shown to increase lead levels for up to six months (Fellet, 2016). These partial line replacements were mandated by the State Department of Environmental Protection (DEP). But, in the face of pressure organized by the OWC, some public officials, and other community members, PWSA halted these in May 2017. This required temporarily breaking the DEP lead line replacement mandate. Work had to be carried out on a local level to change regulations to legally conduct full lead line replacements (Fieldnotes, 18 May 2017 and 15 June, 2017; PWSA, 2017).[25]

PWSA now has one of the country's most comprehensive lead line replacement programs (Del Cielo, 2021). At a table conversation in summer 2017, someone noted that Lansing, Michigan, replaced all the lead service lines, but it took them ten years to do. Across the country, 10 million homes are served by an estimated 380,000 lead lines, and it is estimated that up to 20 per cent of most people's exposure to lead comes from this tap water. In 2016, the City Council in Cincinnati, Ohio, passed an ordinance to replace their 39,000 lead lines over the course of 15 years (Barna, 2019). In Green Bay, Wisconsin, the city replaced its 2,000 lead lines over the period of five years (Hart, 2020). While PWSA still has much room for improvement in various areas, its lead line replacement program is a success, assuming it stays on pace.[26] The commitment of the OWC to focusing on accountability, transparency, and democratic governance and pushing PWSA and elected leaders to follow through on commitments was critical to this effort.[27] As Lauren Del Cielo wrote:

> "The program now I think is one of the best in the country," said Aly Shaw, environmental justice organizer for Pittsburgh United. Shaw and Pittsburgh United helped secure a legal settlement mandating lead service line replacement. "We are replacing lines at no cost to the residents and they are doing it really quickly. Last year, they replaced over 2,000 lines and this year they will do even more than that. I think other cities can learn from our eventual response to the crisis. Community engagement has been crucial in PWSA's response," Shaw said. The authority has an advisory committee with people from the community to help shape the program in a more community-oriented way. PWSA also holds community meetings to raise awareness of the solutions available in the program. (2021: paragraphs 6–7)

The OWC focused on affordability, advocating for expanding PWSA's Customer Assistance Program and a moratorium on shutoffs. This served as a place where the OWC pressured PWSA on what they had done wrong previously and needed to get right, using messaging about how residents have had to deal with inaccurate bills, questionable water quality, and now rate increases. While PWSA showed leadership in creating an affordability subcommittee to look at a moratorium on water shutoffs until a Customer Assistance Program was in place, more action was needed for low-income ratepayers. The OWC also focused on why water shutoffs needed to be eliminated: They burden low-income families by making simple tasks – like cooking, cleaning, and bathing – more complicated, and create unsafe conditions, especially for children, older people, and the sick. Shutting the water off when there is a lead line can increase the lead content when water service is restored. The OWC and other advocates argued for stopping the practice of water shutoffs and for a CAP, that will help protect low-income ratepayers in the PWSA service area. (Fieldnotes, throughout 2017–2018).

World Water Day: claiming wins

In the section focused on disrupting hegemony, I detail the OWC's work with elected leaders around what actually constituted privatization and why PPPs are not in the best interest of Pittsburgh. Similarly, the OWC spent considerable focus on trainings and events to bring together residents to discuss these issues. On 22 March 2018, the Our Water Campaign organized an event for World Water Day to "celebrate the human right to safe, affordable drinking water by learning what water rights you have as a PWSA customer!" The event began with dinner and included a speaker from the Pennsylvania Utility Law Project – a legal aid firm that provides assistance and advice about utility bills to residents. The OWC did outreach through canvassing, sharing the event with the networks of organizations that are a part of the OWC, and creating a Facebook event page. The OWC launched a yard sign campaign on 31 October 2018 (see Figure 3.3) with signs that said: "protect our water, keep it public," and the OWC worked to distribute these to supporters across the city. This campaign made visible the fight for maintaining a public water system. During this time, other work for the campaign continued, including community canvassing and meetings to hear community concerns. The organizing efforts also branched out into surrounding municipalities.

In July 2019, the OWC[28] put together a flyer detailing the victories of the campaign. It read:

> The campaign includes twelve social, environmental, and racial justice groups. For nearly a decade, our campaign has stood with ratepayers from all around the region to fight for water equity and a sustainable future in the face of climate change. Together, we've won: The distribution of thousands of free water filters; Stopping of dangerous partial lead line replacement practices in Pittsburgh; Full lead service line replacements that come at no cost to the homeowner; New water affordability programs in Pittsburgh and the region; Keeping the Pittsburgh Water & Sewer Authority publicly owned and operated. (Fieldnotes, 16 July 2019)

All too often, the work of organizing is slow, with seemingly intangible benefits, with wins constantly feeling like an impossible or distant reality. People become discouraged and resigned to the situation, and it is hard to keep up momentum. Claiming wins and victories and sharing that with supporters and residents is essential. It helps inspire hope and keep the focus on

Figure 3.3 OWC yard sign

why everyone is involved in this work: because everyone deserves access to clean water and because that right is attenable.

On 23 March 2019, the OWC held another World Water Day event, this time focused on activist training for a lobby day with elected officials where they would be asked to pledge their support of a ban on all privatization (see Figure 3.4). Leading up to the event, the OWC organized outreach to residents, including phone banking. Like other events (phone banking and canvassing), the table had a "script" for people to use when calling:

Hi is ____ there? Hi my name is ____ I'm a volunteer with the Our Water Campaign [or Clean Rivers Campaign], we're fighting for safe, affordable, public water in Pittsburgh. I'm calling to ask you to join us in celebrating World Water Day by holding our elected officials accountable. We're hosting a water activist training where you can learn more about local water issues, how to talk about them to politicians, and then join us in meetings with your representatives. Are you available to come to the training on March 23rd from noon to 2 pm?

Depending on the answer, people were given further instructions, directions, or asked to do something else (such as share the information with a friend or on social media). The training itself began with lunch and then a welcome, and community agreements. This was followed by campaign updates and discussion of the pledge before moving into training breakout groups and role play. There were different groups to prepare for visits with City Council and county, state, and federal reps. Attendees also signed up for lobby day visits.

The campaign update section focused on the following points:

- when rates go up, low/moderate income people need to be protected;
- everyone in the City – including big businesses and large "nonprofits" – ought to pay their fair share;
- update on PWSA's new CAP and winter moratorium shutoff;
- why corporations should not make a profit off of water;
- decision makers should be publicly accountable to people, not to shareholders;
- decisions are transparent and open to the public;
- public water is 59% cheaper than private water; and
- public utilities pay workers 8% more, give workers more benefits.

A graph of what constitutes a P3 was shared, citing Veolia as an example (see Figure 3.5). The need for green infrastructure in public investment and ensuring that good union jobs with benefits are a part of the workforce to make that happen was also discussed. Various interests, however, wanted to see water privatized in the form of a new P3, including some of the same entities noted earlier. Because of this, the OWC created the "Our Water, Our Rivers Pledge" (an image of which is shared in Chapter 6). The main goal of these lobby visits was to get elected officials to sign onto the pledge. While no one thought that a pledge alone would result in action being taken, it was a visible, public means to hold officials accountable and continue to push

SAT. MARCH 23 | 12PM-2PM | 1 SMITHFIELD ST, 15222

WATER ACTIVIST TRAINING AND LOBBY DAY

Hosted by the Our Water Campaign and Clean Rivers Campaign

March 22nd is World Water Day - a day when water activists from all over the world come together to work towards water justice. To celebrate, we're holding a training where you'll learn more about local water issues, meet other activists, and practice holding your representatives accountable before you meet with them.

Our local elected officials have critical decisions to make about Pittsburgh's water future:

Should a corporation have control over Pittsburgh's drinking water? (NO.)

Should we invest in sustainable solutions to stop dangerous flooding? (YES.)

Should our region make sure no child has to drink lead-tainted water? (YES.)

Figure 3.4 OWC World Water Day activist training

them on. The training discussed how to react to various responses, including explaining that a public–private partnership is a form of privatization, just as bad or worse than full privatization, because PPPs allow private companies to make decisions about the water system and when things go wrong,

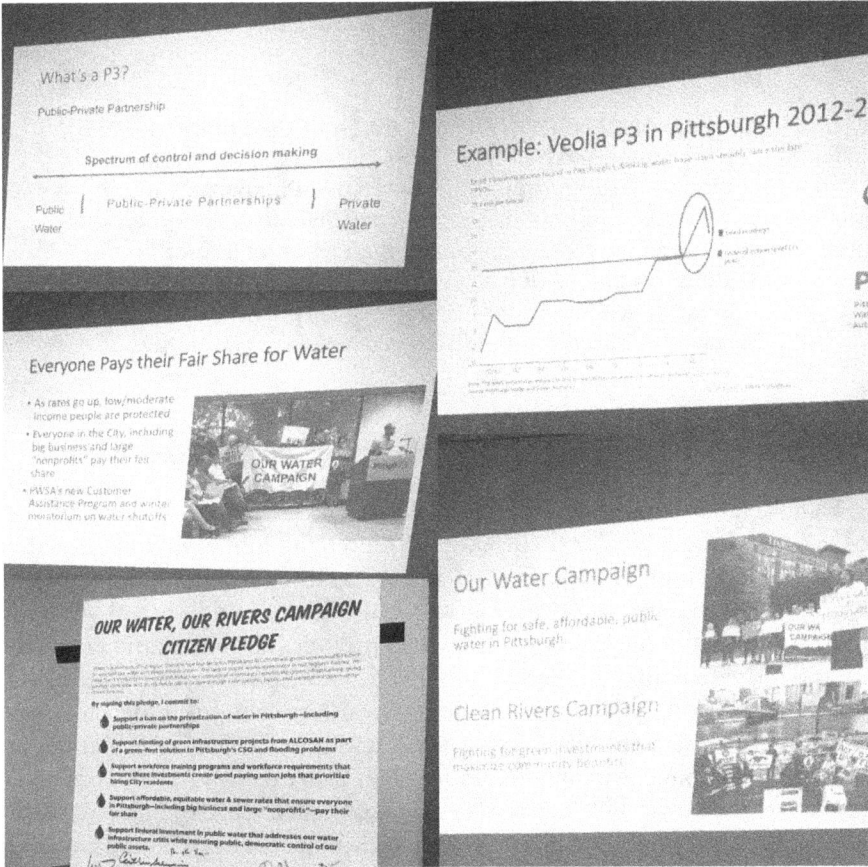

Figure 3.5 OWC 2019 World Water Day training

the public side is left liable and cleaning up the mess (like with the Veolia PPP) (Fieldnotes 23 March 2019).

After this training, participants received a certificate of completion for attending. Throughout the next couple of weeks, over 80 constituents participated in lobby visits with 22 elected leaders (City Council and County Council members, the Mayor of Pittsburgh, and State Representatives and Senators). Ultimately, 11 officials signed the pledge. I participated in several of these visits and, in two (where I was meeting with my representatives), the elected officials signed the pledge (Fieldnotes, 3 April 2019). In June 2019, members of the OWC attended a PWSA meeting. The authority passed the pledge, asserting its support of public ownership of Pittsburgh's water and sewer infrastructure and commitment to investing in green infrastructure

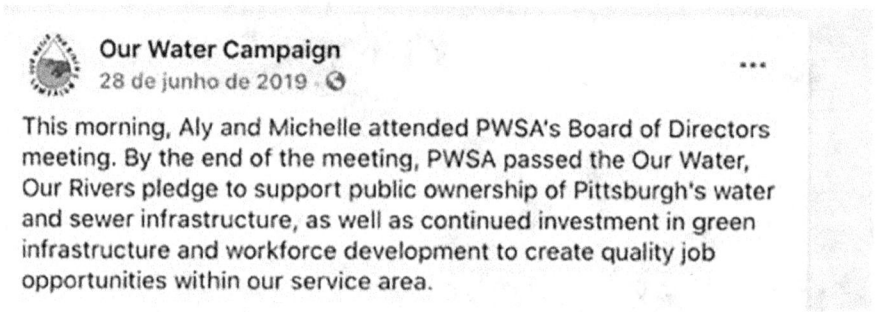

Figure 3.6 Facebook post, PWSA commits to OWC pledge

(Krauss, 2019; see Figure 3.6). More outcomes of these lobby day visits are
noted in Chapter 6.

Pennsylvania congressperson Mike Doyle became a co-sponsor of the
2018 federal WATER Act[29] (Byrd, 2018) after the lobby visit. The Water
Affordability, Transparency, Equity, and Reliability (WATER) Act of 2021,
which was introduced by Bernie Sanders in the Senate and Brenda Lawrence
and Ro Khanna in the House, was backed by over 70 Democratic lawmak-
ers and more than 500 advocacy, labor, and faith-based organizations from
almost every state, who urged United States President Joe Biden to back
this critical legislation. Pittsburgh United and other organizations that sit
at the OWC table were included in this list. It is the same as the previous
year's version of the bill (Corporate Accountability, 2021b). The WATER
Act would: provide $35 billion a year to drinking water and wastewater
improvements; create up to 1 million jobs across the economy and protect American workers; prioritize disadvantaged communities with grants
and additional support; expand technical assistance to small, rural, and
indigenous communities; dedicate and increase grants for indigenous communities; fund projects to address water contamination from per- and poly-
fluoroalkyl substances (PFAS); help homeowners replace lead service lines;
provide more than $1 billion a year to update water infrastructure in pub-
lic schools; upgrade household wells and septic systems; and promote safe,
affordable, publicly controlled water for all (Food and Water Watch, 2022;
Lakhani, 2021). As of the writing of this book, it has not passed, but was
again introduced in March 2023 and, in June 2023, had 72 co-sponsors
across the Senate and House versions, with over 500 non-governmental
organizations endorsing it (Bonnie Watson Coleman, 2023).

As an article published in *The Guardian* as part of a series on water
affordability on 24 February 2021 notes, federal funding for water systems

in the United States has decreased by 77 per cent since 1977. Climate change adds to this crisis, with most water and wastewater systems unequipped to handle increasing climate chaos. In this article, Senator Sanders is quoted as saying: " 'It is beyond belief that in 2021 American kids are being poisoned by tap water … Not only do we allow corporations to pollute our waterways, but the government has failed to keep up with critically needed improvements to our drinking water and wastewater infrastructure,' said Sanders, who warns that further privatization would drive up prices and reduce access" (Lakhani, 2021). Water is a human right; but in the United States, it is treated as a for profit industry (Sanders and Lawrence, 2020). The continued disinvestment in water systems has not been felt equally: Black, Indigenous, and communities of color have been impacted disproportionately.

As Monica Lewis Patrick of We the People of Detroit (a supporter of the WATER Act) asserted, "Water is a human right, but our current water systems are a breeding ground for environmental racism and trauma" (Lakhani, 2021). Pittsburgh, named as one of the country's most livable cities, has positioned itself as a city with a strong commitment to sustainable development, and city officials have pledged to make Pittsburgh a leader in municipal efforts to implement the United Nations Sustainable Development Goals (SDGs), which includes equitable access to clean water and sanitation. At the same time, the city has come under fire as being the worst locale in the country for Black women (Howell et al., 2019), where inequalities in race, class, and gender persist. One of the city's challenges relates to water infrastructure, quality, and affordability (González Rivas, 2020). The United Nations General Assembly recognized the human right to water and sanitation on 28 June 2010, through Resolution 64/292.[30] SDGs establish concrete targets and timeframes for achieving this right, yet these global standards and expectations remain far from realized, including here in Pittsburgh. As Marcela González Rivas (2020: 295 and 302) writes regarding the landscape in Pittsburgh:

> According to the U.S. Census, 21% of residents live in poverty – well above the state (12.2%) and national (11.8%) averages – while 40% of the population are eligible for assistance programs (U.S. Census 2018). It is important to note that there are significant dynamics of inequality across race and gender along various dimensions, including health, income, employment and education. For example, a recent report comparing Pittsburgh's race and gender inequality to similar cities in the U.S. shows that the poverty rate among African-American[s] is higher in Pittsburgh than in 85% of similar cities, and more Black children in Pittsburgh grow up in poverty than in 95% of similar cities. (Howell et al., 2019: 29)

Further,

> In Pittsburgh, low-income communities include communities of colour, refugees and immigrants. In surveys of organizations providing services to refugees and immigrants in the summers of 2019 and 2020, water affordability was identified as the number one challenge, and there is lack of information about assistance programs (González Rivas 2019, 2020). Language is sometimes a barrier leading to a lack of knowledge about the programs, even though PWSA has contracted out interpretation services for customers who do not speak English.

Like elsewhere in the world, Covid-19 compounded challenges, especially as moratoriums on water shutoffs (and evictions) expired.[31] PWSA does have more protections in place for low income residents than the private water authority in the area that serves slightly under 20 per cent of the city's residents. However, as González Rivas notes, they could do more work to expand these programs and make them more accessible (González Rivas, 2020).

OWC as a translocal learning network: South to North

"Translocal" activism, as defined by Banerjee, is:

> the ability of translocal engagements to 'both transcend territorial locality and change the local spaces from which they emerge' (Banerjee, 2011: 331). Communities inhabiting these spaces interact with particular configurations of market, state and civil society actors and form relationships with local activists, community groups, domestic and international NGOs, and political parties. (2018: 811)

While the literature has typically focused on translocality in the context of actors who reside in the Global South, this concept is valuable for understanding OWC and the right to water organizing in the United States. As water justice and human rights scholar Farhana Sultana argues, "water justice is never just local, but cross-scalar and global" (2018: 489). The OWC is an example of how communities organize to take control over local governance, shape new economic futures, and ensure that basic needs and rights are observed. It is an example of "translocal" activism, introduced in Chapter 1: activism rooted in a specific community, but that engages with local, national, and global movements, government, and markets, to place the human right to water above profit. I argue that the OWC is an example of a "translocal learning network" (Banerjee, 2011, 2018) where people are engaged in a counter-hegemonic struggle for the right to public, clean, affordable water and are connecting with and learning from each other "across locales and across national contexts as they confront some of the same corporate entities that threaten local livelihoods" (Manski and Smith, 2019: 8).

Scholarship on water has discussed the role of Global North/Global South partnerships and transnational organizations in the fight for the right to water (see Bakker, 2007; Bieler, 2021; Sultana and Loftus, 2012). Much of this literature has focused on how organizations and movements in the North partner to assist those in the South, as noted in earlier chapters. These translocal connections are learning from and with each other to subvert this order, and connections can flow from South to North. The OWC serves as one such example of a translocal learning network, where activists learn from others with similar experiences but adapt to the local contexts and form alliances to fight against corporate control and other alliances (Schroering, 2019b, 2021a).[32] In translocal activism, citizens and residents engage with each other, the state, and the market. They fight for community-driven partnerships, communal ideas of property rights versus private property rights, and for participatory, democratic, and horizontal governance structures (Banerjee, 2018: 812), demonstrating how the right to water movements are fighting against the idea that water is a commodity. This presents a competing ideology to that of corporate and state actors. As Sultana puts it: "The rising commodification of water means that water is given an economic value driven by a market logic (McDonald, 2016)" (2018: 485). Ultimately, translocal resistance seeks to "change the logic of the political economic system (Mignolo, 2007)" (Banerjee, 2011: 339). In the pages that follow, I explain how the Pittsburgh mobilization employs such translocal resistance.

Translocal resistance in the context of water has significant consequences since it is so fundamental to life itself. As Sultana writes:

> The remarkable thing about water is that [sic] seeps across all boundaries and all aspects of life, as it is simultaneously social, economic, political, institutional, cultural, spiritual and ecological. Water plays a central role in various aspects of our lives that we may take for granted or not be aware of: from urban planning, industrial production, agriculture and food production, international development, and economic policies to political strife and conflict, geopolitical instability, ecological sustainability, people's cultural practices and sense of self, and their spiritual and religious practices. Water needs to be a lens through which we understand and appreciate complex social and environmental issues (Boelens, Hoogesteger, Swyngedouw, Vos, & Wester, 2016; Budds & Sultana, 2013; Zeitoun et al., 2014). This underscores the importance of understanding hydrosocial cycles (water–society connections) rather than just paying attention to the hydrological cycle (Linton & Budds, 2014). (2018: 484)

Since the system causing water strife is global, many activists increasingly see the need to "globalize the struggle." Translocalism enables building global-scale analysis and action while retaining sensitivity to place, life, and community rooted in the local. I apply the term translocal learning network to the OWC because it fits Banerjee's definition (described above) of a community facing different state and market actors, and pushing to have a say in how governance is done and to be included in shaping the decision-making process (Banerjee, 2011 and 2018). It also represented an example of political, not simply pragmatic, factors driving the mobilization, as discussed earlier in the chapter.

In April 2017, during the first year the Our Water Campaign coalesced, they organized a town hall titled "Not Another Flint."[33] The OWC invited activists from a Flint based community organization called Flint Rising[62] to speak at the event and provided food and information on lead testing and filters (and some free filters). This event is important because it set the stage for citizen resistance and mobilization, without which Pittsburgh could have become another Flint. I will now provide a few additional illustrations of how the OWC exemplifies a translocal learning network, specifically in how it engaged and organized the community. Further, the OWC case represents a movement for public water that is rooted, from its inception, in a political position against privatization.

In December of 2017, OWC held the "The Grinch Stole Our Water" action introduced at the beginning of this chapter. The action epitomizes the idea of a translocal learning network: it included activists from outside of Pittsburgh who were familiar with similar organizing against water privatization and Veolia in different parts of the world. At this event, various speakers – mainly from Pittsburgh, but also someone from Corporate Accountability – spoke about the history of Veolia, locally and globally, and that people have a right to clean and safe drinking water, and the need for Veolia to be held to account for their role in the lead problem. As the OWC organizer asserted at the event:

> It's important to remember how we got here: a French-based water company, private water company, Veolia, took over management of our water authority ... the OWC is standing with the residents of Pittsburgh and echoing the call of local elected officials and announcing our filing of a formal complaint against Veolia North America on behalf of the citizens of Pittsburgh for their role in Pittsburgh's lead crisis. (Fieldnotes, 18 December 2017)

The couple dozen attendees sang "satirical Veolia Carols" (with the disclaimer that they are "intended to be satire and not literal accusations").

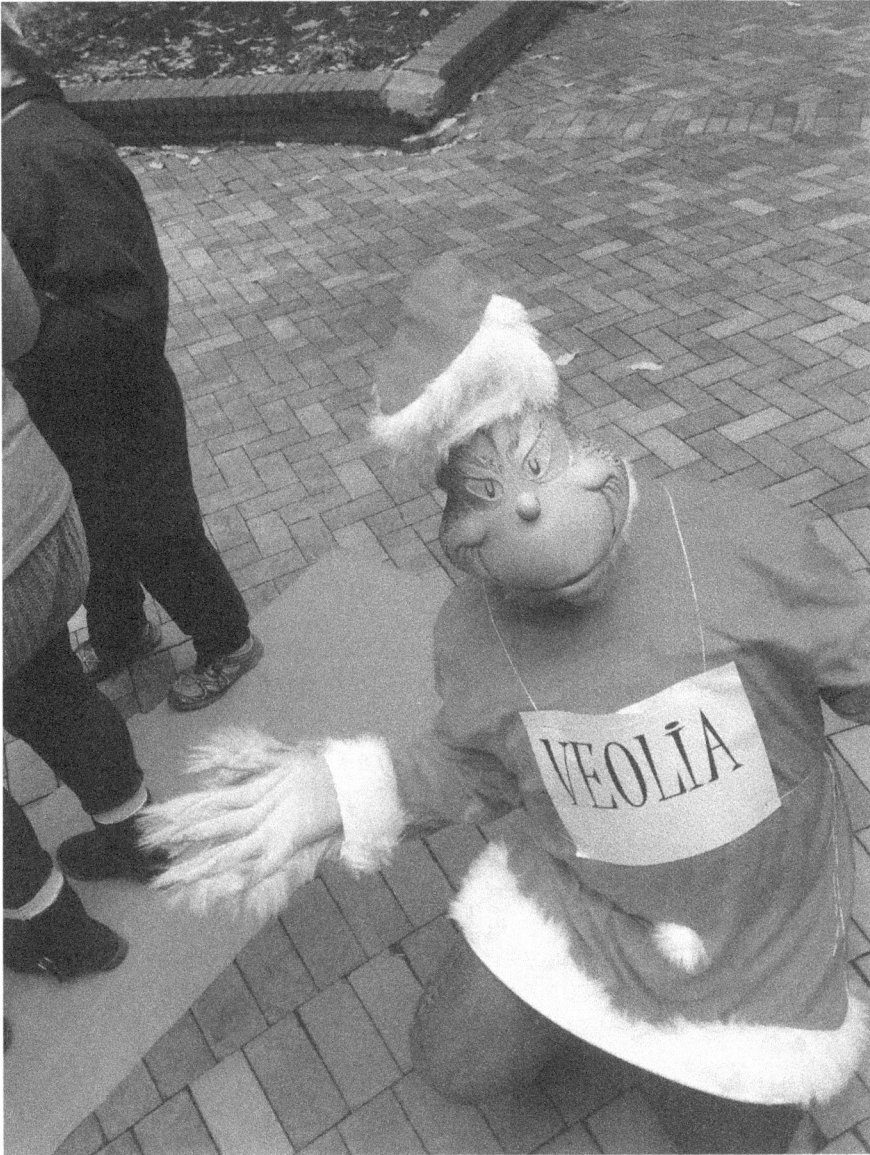

Figure 3.7 OWC Grinch action

The action drew attention to the role of a global corporation interfering with local water rights and speaks to the importance of translocal organizing (see Figures 3.7–3.10).[34]

In January 2019, at the same time as the Human Right to Water Summit in Abuja, Nigeria,[35] when the EJ organizer for the OWC campaign and three others (myself included) were in Nigeria, an announcement came out of the State Attorney General's office that he was investigating PWSA. The OWC called for Veolia's mismanagement of PWSA to also be investigated. The press release indicated that while there was blame to share (that is, PWSA is also implicated in the mismanagement), to completely ignore the role Veolia played in the mismanagement of PWSA is both unfair and negligent (Our Water Campaign, 2019; Weinman and Weiss 2019).

On 4 April 2019, Aly Shaw (the former EJ organizer for the OWC), Jamilah Lahijuddin (OWC table member and, at the time of the event, organizer with the Hill District Consensus Group), and I were invited to present on a panel at the University of Pittsburgh with water scholar Emanuele Lobina[36] titled: "The Human Right to Water: Threats from Privatization in Pittsburgh and the World." Lobina discussed the forces shaping today's heightened debate around access to water and how pressures to privatize water utilities impact cities worldwide. I focused mainly on the struggles around energy and water in Brazil and connected that struggle to the experience with the OWC in Nigeria (detailed in Chapter 6). Aly focused more explicitly on talking about Veolia and how Veolia linked the efforts in Pittsburgh with Nigeria. Finally, Jamilah focused on the organizing work the OWC had done in Pittsburgh to keep the water public. This event illustrates translocal learning and resistance by linking

Join us in Whoville to tell the private company who ruined our water that we're not going to let their greed win:

On Monday, we will be announcing a formal complaint against private water corporation Veolia for its role in the city's lead crisis and mismanagement of Pittsburgh Water and Sewer Authority (PWSA) to District Attorney Zappala.

The event will include a Grinch-inspired skit complete with 'townspeople,' a Grinch costume, Grinch-inspired carols and 'Investigate Veolia' posters "Grinch" themed for the holiday season.

This is the latest escalation in the years-long call from residents and the Our Water Campaign to expose those responsible for the elevated lead levels and keep Pittsburgh water in the public's hands.

Join us in Whoville to tell Veolia we're not going to let them steal our public water!
..

Figure 3.8 OWC FB event description

counter-hegemonic struggles against privatization and the right to water across various locals while still focusing on local organizing. It shows how activists engage with the state and markets to fight for participatory, democratic, and more horizontal governance structures, among other things (Banerjee, 2018: 812).

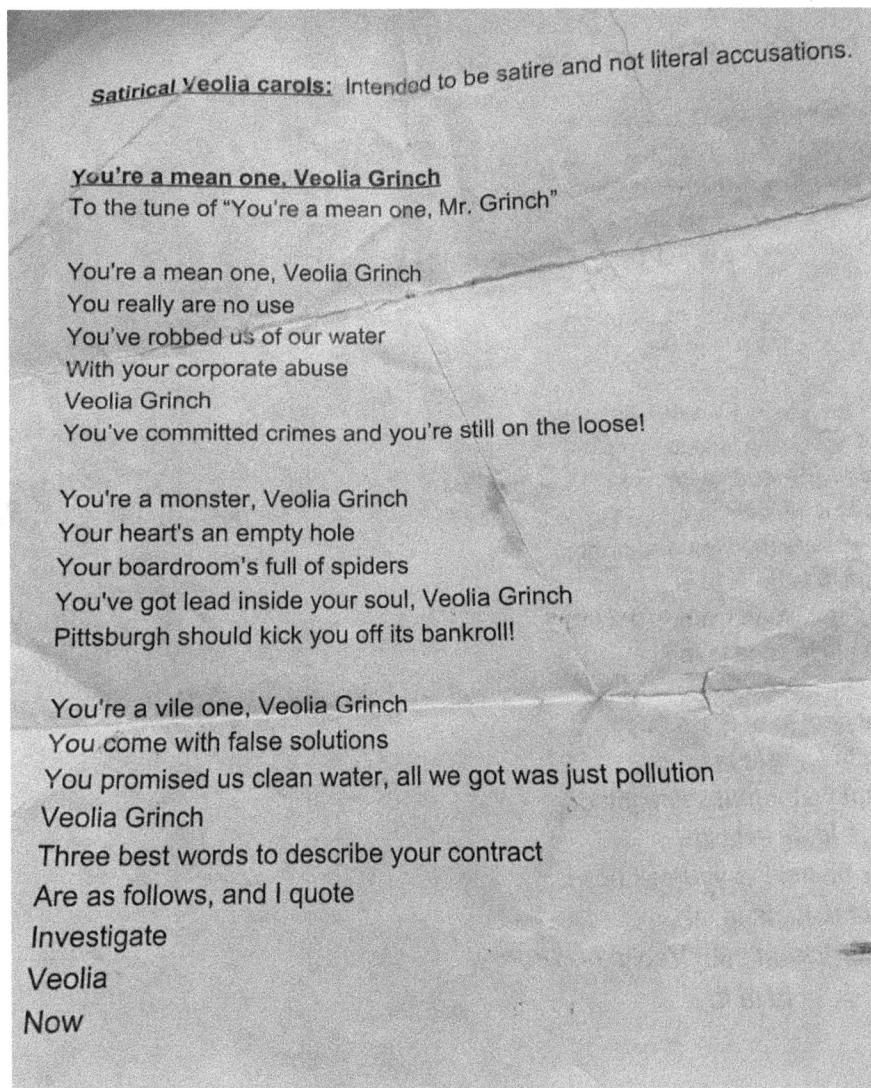

<u>Satirical Veolia carols:</u> Intended to be satire and not literal accusations.

You're a mean one, Veolia Grinch
To the tune of "You're a mean one, Mr. Grinch"

You're a mean one, Veolia Grinch
You really are no use
You've robbed us of our water
With your corporate abuse
Veolia Grinch
You've committed crimes and you're still on the loose!

You're a monster, Veolia Grinch
Your heart's an empty hole
Your boardroom's full of spiders
You've got lead inside your soul, Veolia Grinch
Pittsburgh should kick you off its bankroll!

You're a vile one, Veolia Grinch
You come with false solutions
You promised us clean water, all we got was just pollution
Veolia Grinch
Three best words to describe your contract
Are as follows, and I quote
Investigate
Veolia
Now

Figure 3.9 Grinch action carols

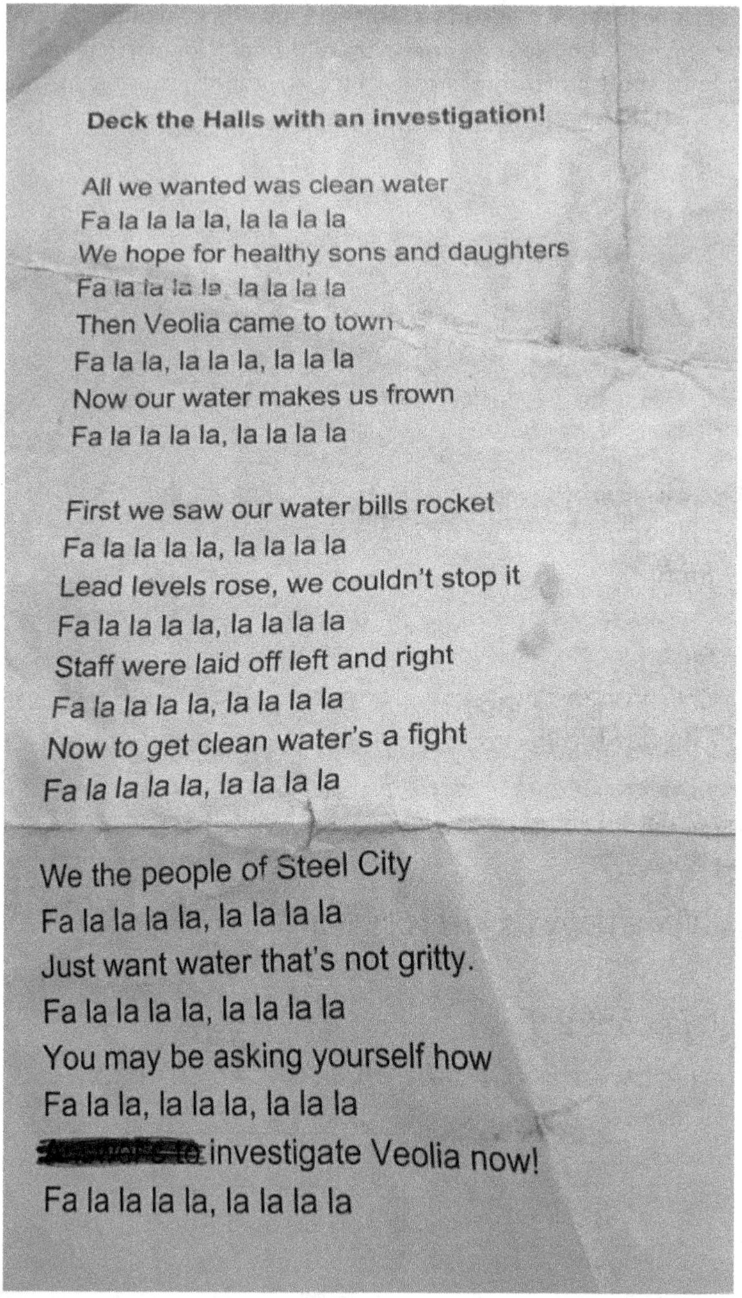

Deck the Halls with an investigation!

All we wanted was clean water
Fa la la la la, la la la la
We hope for healthy sons and daughters
Fa la la la la la, la la la la
Then Veolia came to town
Fa la la, la la la, la la la
Now our water makes us frown
Fa la la la la, la la la la

First we saw our water bills rocket
Fa la la la la, la la la la
Lead levels rose, we couldn't stop it
Fa la la la la, la la la la
Staff were laid off left and right
Fa la la la la, la la la la
Now to get clean water's a fight
Fa la la la la, la la la la

We the people of Steel City
Fa la la la la, la la la la
Just want water that's not gritty.
Fa la la la la, la la la la
You may be asking yourself how
Fa la la, la la la, la la la
~~investigate~~ investigate Veolia now!
Fa la la la la, la la la la

Figure 3.10 Grinch action carols

On 5 March 2019, Aly and I shared with the OWC what we had learned about water and environmental issues in Nigeria after the summit. This was another space to connect the local and global, and focus on how movements are fighting for the right to water and against corporate control of water (see Chapter 6). Figure 3.11 is from a Facebook post during the Summit that the OWC shared, asserting solidarity in the fight against privatization with Nigeria. This understanding is critical because companies seeking to privatize water operate locally, nationally, and internationally. In 2019, PA House Bill 751 (which would allow the state to sue public water authorities like PWSA) sought to open up privatization in Pennsylvania. The bill passed both Houses and was signed into law by the governor on 2 July 2019.[37]

Pennsylvania is now a place where private water companies are seeking more control. One of their tactics is working to buy up smaller water and sewage systems. This happened in small municipalities surrounding Pittsburgh, including Mckeesport and Clairton (Fieldnotes, 2 April 2019). Pennsylvania American Water acquired the wastewater system of Mckeesport in 2017 (Pennsylvania American Water, 2019). Other Allegheny County municipalities have already sold, or are in the process of selling, their sewage systems (Carr, 2021). There have been, however, recent victories against capital's attempt to control water. For example, residents in Bucks County, Pennsylvania, successfully opposed the privatization of their water system, and the water authority announced in September 2022 that the deal was off (DiFelice, 2022). This is why actions such as the pledge against water privatization are essential; they provide a public platform to hold public

Figure 3.11 OWC social media post

officials to their commitment to fighting against privatization and for public water. These campaigns promote transparency, educate residents on topics essential to democratic governance, and fill an information vacuum left by declining local independent media.

Conclusion

This chapter has demonstrated how the belief that water is a human right guided the organizing in Pittsburgh. David Harvey writes about how the idea of human rights in the US is often based on an individual, rather than a collective, notion of the term that can, in fact, further fuel neoliberalism.[38] This logic exacerbates the threats to collective rights and the public utilities designed to provide them, as this case shows. So, how do we elevate the collective? Harvey argues that we do this by organizing for public spaces and public goods (Harvey, 2012: 72–3) and that the "Right to the City" is a collective right and not a right to something that already exists but the right to create something different; to demand rights (Harvey, 2012: 137–8). An alternative to the form of globalization we have currently will arise from fighting for the commons and uniting into a movement with global solidarities (Harvey, 2012: 114; Machado, 2016). Right to water organizing demonstrates this alternative. Clearly, water is a critical part of the struggle for the commons; indeed, Harvey notes organizing around water – and specifically the Cochabamba, Bolivia, struggle – is an example of fighting for this "right to the city" (Harvey, 2012: 141).

Organizing for the right to water in Pittsburgh is an example of political, not simply pragmatic, drivers of remunicipalization (see Chapters 1 and 2), which serves as a counterexample to what previous research has argued to be true in the United States context (McDonald, 2018). The Pittsburgh case illustrates how privatization posed real and direct threats to people's health and living costs. The solution that emerged was to keep the water a public good managed by (local) government and to fight against corporate predation.

The OWC created clear messaging around a complex combination of processes. It connected the need for equity (affordability/ratepayer protections) and water quality/environmental sustainability (lead line replacements, switching back to proven corrosion control, and advocating for a stormwater fee) with the importance of maintaining public water and the vision that water ought to be accessible to all. The OWC engaged with utilities and public officials to institute and increase mechanisms for funding to make infrastructure improvements (such as lead line replacements). It also asserted the failings of public–private partnerships and articulated a vision of public water centered on transparency, equity, and new forms of governance. The OWC's organizing made space for opponents of privatization within the government to speak out, when otherwise they might have succumbed to the pressure (from within and outside the government) to privatize. Building relationships across diverse actors and changing ways of thinking (or at least changing positions) on critical issues – such as water privatization – mattered.

The OWC worked to create more transparent and democratic governance by showing public officials what needed to be done and organizing to make sure public utilities serve public needs. In this process of organizing to defend their health and well-being, residents also learned how city government works and how to push for more functional and responsive local government. Movement pressure can often generate responses from public officials aimed to look good – for example, creating study groups/task forces, Blue Ribbon Panels, etc. – and resident concerns are being heard and progress is happening. Still, these are typically ambiguous or contingent in terms of their impacts on the initial goal, highlighting the importance of continued advocacy and pressure on the part of movements. The fact that Pittsburgh's lead problem came on the heels of the Flint crisis (and the significant international attention to that crisis) likely mattered. This is apparent in the OWC's messaging of "Not Another Flint" and public officials' responses – they did not want another Flint and negative national attention. In this sense, the larger national and global context is significant.

The Pittsburgh struggle has been highlighted in various news outlets and progressive think tanks, including in a case study on economic democracy produced by Demos in 2022 entitled *Water as a Public Good: Pittsburgh's Our Water Campaign*. This is critical as it highlights the needs to communicate how successful struggles mobilized; while the exact strategy might not be able to be replicated in all locales, there is much that can be learned and applied, and more work to be done. As the Demos report notes:

> It should go without saying that water and other basic goods are essential to life – and thus to economic well-being. Clean, affordable water is a prerequisite for employment, safe housing, and school attendance.[6] Yet, in low-income, mostly Black and brown communities across the country, water infrastructure is undermined by economic inequality and systemic racism. (2022: 1)

This relates to how right to water movements are about more than water and are examples of challenging hegemonic thinking. Just as transnational corporations work globally, movements resisting privatization do the same: their struggles are locally focused, and organizing occurs at the local level, but these struggles are linked to more extensive national and global processes. Translocal activism is about people engaging with the state and markets, and fighting for participatory, democratic, and more horizontal governance structures, as well as the ideas of more communal notions of property rights, rights to livelihood, and social justice (Banerjee, 2018: 812). Activists engage in struggle on multiple levels – the realm of ideas and hegemony, and policies and practices. I return to this point in Chapters 4–6.

Notes

1 Introduced in Chapter 2.
2 See also Chapter 1 for discussion about how conflicts around water are in many ways a fight between two logics: capitalists forces that argue that they have the "right" to profit from the privatization of water, and people and movements who counter that water ought to be a human right and not something from which to profit.
3 The coalition changed the name to Our Water, Our Rivers at the end of a 2018 planning retreat, merging it with another campaign of Pittsburgh United (the organization that "houses" the coalition), the Clean Rivers Campaign (CRC), which addressed sewage, stormwater, and green infrastructure issues (See Schroering and Staggenborg, 2021). This decision relates to arguments I have heard from other activists – initially in Brazil – that drinking water and sanitation issues are interrelated. In January 2020, the coalition opted to return to the name "Our Water Campaign" (still keeping the campaigns merged), noting that the language of "our" water conveyed the idea that all of the water system issues are interrelated.
4 Marcela González Rivas and I have a 2021 article published in *Utilities Policy* that focuses on and explores this point in detail (González Rivas and Schroering, 2021). Chapter 6 is also focused on this argument.
5 See Chapter 2 for discussion of PPPs and Veolia.
6 Veolia continues to publicly refute any wrongdoing, including creating a website called "www.veoliapwsatruth.com."
7 On average, water privatization leads to a job loss rate of 34 per cent, along with serious disruptions in service quality (Food and Water Watch, 2009).
8 It is also important to note that in 2018, PWSA was placed under the oversight of the Pennsylvania Public Utility Commission to come into compliance with various problems, including billing issues and lead in the water. In early 2019, a coalition including Pittsburgh United, secured a settlement requiring PWSA to spend approximately $50 million in order to rectify the high levels of lead in drinking water (See ITPI, 2021).
9 The CRC had advocated for – and saw implemented – a CAP at PWSA as well as at ALCOSAN, the regional sewer authority.
10 The CRC and OWC merged, in order to better connect issues of drinking water and sanitation for a "one water approach." This decision aligns with the argument made by MAB, as well as the interviews I conducted with other water

activists and water and sanitation union leaders in Brazil, and what was articulated at the Summit in Nigeria (discussed in Chapter 6): water and sanitation are connected and need to be viewed as such.

11 See also Shields (2019).

12 The BRP was comprised of the following individuals: Fred Brown (President and CEO Homewood Children's Village); Jared Cohon (President Emeritus and University Professor of Civil and Environmental Engineering and Engineering and Public Policy Carnegie Mellon University); Michelle Naccarati-Chapkis (Executive Director Women for a Healthy Environment); Mark Stulga, Vice President (Commercial and Industrial Lending WesBanco Bank); and Alex Thomson (President and Chair of the Business Law Practice Group, Houston Harbaugh, P.C.). It also included the following employees of the City of Pittsburgh: Kevin Acklin (Chief of Staff Office of the Mayor); Jennifer Presutti (Director, Office of Management and Budget); and Lourdes Sanchez-Ridge (Solicitor) (Blue Ribbon Panel, 2017).

13 For all events and actions, the EJ organizer for the campaign would ask table members to commit to a number of people to bring.

14 As noted in the previous chapter, Veolia was also involved in the Flint crisis. I also discuss global resistance against Veolia in Chapter 6.

15 The contract with Veolia was a P3 and Veolia stopped pursuing this form of PPP in the US citing the Pittsburgh public relations disaster as the main reason. I discuss this in Chapters 2 and 6.

16 See discussion in Chapter 2 around water as a commons, public good, commodity, or right.

17 This response of "neutralizing resistance" on the part of hegemonic powers/authorities makes it challenging to study movements and their outcomes (Smith, Plummer, and Hughes, 2017).

18 Which is now known as Essential Utilities (ITPI, 2021).

19 Another euphemism that suggests the fight over hegemonic framing of the conflict is important. When water activists in Brazil would ask me about the struggle in Pittsburgh, I would share this story with them and they would laugh and point out the contradictions in the use of the term "peoples."

20 In organizing lingo, "target" refers to the public official/person who has the authority to implement the demanded change/solution.

21 This person used the word "asking" but their point was that Peoples Gas (and those within government supporting the plan) were counting on movements to be intimidated and not fight back.

22 Further, as noted above, one of the people leading this effort at Peoples, was the chief of staff to the Pittsburgh mayor for four years. Just six months after leaving this position, he took a role in charge of acquisitions at Peoples Gas (Shoemaker, 2018a).

23 And while seemingly archived on the Way Back Machine, the screen captures will not open.

24 The beginning of year 2020 planning retreat for OWC showed that the top goal for everyone was to ensure that water and sewer systems remain or become publicly owned and democratically managed. At this time, it looked like the

Aqua deal was on track to be approved by the PUC (it later was) to acquire Peoples Gas. And the point was made of the need to continue to monitor and stay vigilant, because it did seem to be a part of a "clear play to privatize everything" (Fieldnotes, 7 January 2020). Discussion was also around the need to start focusing on another publicly owned (but not democratically) managed utility in the county.

25 Ultimately, PWSA created a more equitable rate structure that protects low-income ratepayers, and has replaced thousands of public and private lead service lines, paid for partially with a grant and low-interest loan from the state government (City of Pittsburgh, 2020).

26 PWSA has replaced over half of the lead lines as of June 2021 and is on track to complete all replacements before 2026 (Fleming, 2021). PWSA also switched to orthophosphate in 2019 for corrosion control, which helped to ameliorate the lead being released into the system while in the process of replacing lead lines. By 2020, PWSA was back in compliance with the Lead and Copper rule, with lead levels below allowable levels (PWSA, 2022a).

27 This also points to how the point of "decision" is not necessarily the point of "success" for movements and highlights the importance of continued engagement and that impact may take time to see.

28 At that time using the name "Our Water, Our Rivers," which was the CRC and OWC combined, mentioned earlier.

29 First introduced in 2016.

30 See www.un.org/waterforlifedecade/human_right_to_water.shtml

31 There are no permanent low-income customer assistance programs at the federal level (see Orbach et al., 2022). H.R. 3293, the Low-Income Water Customer Assistance Programs Act of 2021, was a bipartisan bill introduced that would have provided a permanent low-income customer assistance program at the federal level. Unfortunately, it did not receive a vote (see govtrack. us for status of bills in the United States Congress).

32 These dynamics are discussed in more detail in subsequent chapters.

33 For more about Flint and Veolia, see Chapter 2.

34 To watch a video of the action, see here:
www.facebook.com/watch/live/?v=760837687436048&ref=watch_permalink

35 The OWC participation in the Summit is discussed in detail in Chapter 6.

36 Lobina is a researcher who works with Public Services International, a group that was also an important part of the Nigeria Summit, discussed in Chapter 9.

37 See here: www.legis.state.pa.us/cfdocs/billinfo/bill_history.cfm?syear=2019& sind=0&body=H&type=B&bn=751

38 See Chapter 1 for more about property and individual rights.

4

Water and energy are not commodities: resistance and knowledge production in Brazil's Movement of People Affected by Dams

"Mulheres, água e energia não são mercadorias!"[1] assert members of the Brazilian popular social movement Movimento dos Atingidos por Barragens (MAB or Movement of People Affected by Dams).[2] When I began this research, two key questions framed my inquiry: 1) Does water serve as a transformative issue that impels people to organize for democratic and public control of resources? 2) Do activists see their efforts as an isolated local struggle, or as connected to a broader national and global network of activists; and what might this mean for both movement mobilization and outcomes? Throughout my early fieldwork in Brazil during the (Northern Hemisphere) summer of 2018, I became attentive to how militantes of MAB framed their efforts as a fight against intersecting systems of oppression, the idea of social movements as sites of knowledge production, and why it matters in both understanding and organizing against the commodification of water.

MAB's struggle is led by and for those directly affected by dam projects and it is part of a larger "alter-globalization" (also referred to as counter-hegemonic globalization or globalization from below) fight to construct a world where there is global cooperation and interaction, guided by visions of human rights, labor rights, environmental rights, and cultural and national sovereignty. Alter-globalization today symbolizes the various grassroots movements that fight against oppressive structures such as capitalism, colonialism, patriarchy (Appadurai, 2000; Bakker, 2007; Brand and Makal, 2022; Falk, 1993 and 1999; Piper and Ulin, 2004), and white supremacy.[3] As discussed in detail in Chapter 1, numerous scholars have examined social movements as critical sites for the construction of knowledge, issuing calls for knowledge to be produced with and by communities themselves (Collins, 2015; Conway, 2006 and 2017; Escobar, 2008; Falcón, 2016; Icaza and Vásquez, 2013; Melucci, 1996; Mohanty, 2003a, 2003b; Rivera-Cusicanqui and Aillón-Soria, 2015; Vieira, 2015; Watkins, 2018; Zibechi, 2017).). Yet despite decades of critique and introspection, social science research too often remains colonial, imperial, and rife with epistemic exclusions (Bejarano et al., 2019; Go, 2020).

In this chapter, I explore how MAB is an example of "social thought of the periphery" (Connell, 2007a: 380) and how it matters in the global struggle for water. Guided by the question of how we might build a "new language for theorizing" (Connell, 2007a: 383), this chapter focuses on MAB's fight for the right to water, how it relates to other counter-hegemonic struggles, and what social movement theory might learn from movements that engage in praxis, while also producing theory and published research.

Formally founded in 1991 as a national autonomous movement for the rights of people affected by dam projects, MAB coalesced out of struggles dating back to the 1980s located in proximity to Brazilian dams. Today, MAB leads the fight against removing families from their homes and opposes the privatization of water, rivers, and natural resources – resources upon which communities depend for their livelihood (see Chapter 2). The movement seeks to resist current energy policy and articulate alternatives (Hess, 2018; Klein, 2015; Schroering, 2019a). Their motto is "water and energy are not commodities." MAB articulates its fight as overarching the following areas: human rights, energy, water, dams, and the Amazon, and asserts that their fight is an international one (MAB, n.d.). MAB works in partnership with other social movements, unions, and non-profits. However, the actual organization is of communities in proximity to, and affected by, current or intended dam projects. MAB leaders said they could not give me an exact number of how many individuals this represents, but they are currently organizing in over a hundred communities located in all but three Brazilian states (Fieldnotes, summer 2018). In Brazil, all corporations that construct, own, and operate dams are part of an extensive network of mineral companies, electric companies, and other forms of corporate power.

MAB argues that all resources should fall under the sovereignty and control of the *povo* (people) and that they should not be used for private gain. MAB uses the idea of human rights in its organizing and connects the human right to water to a broader struggle for rights. This concept of "rights" is not a top-down legalistic one, but rather it refers to the idea of a collective right that articulates the conception that water is not a commodity but an essential source for the production and reproduction of human and non-human life.[4] MAB's work is connected to the fight for climate justice: many people assume that dams are "clean" energy but this is based on misinformation, as discussed in Chapter 2. MAB frequently participates in actions with both the Movimento dos Trabalhadores Rurais Sem Terra (Landless Workers' Movement or MST), Movimento dos Pequenos Agricultores (Small Farmers' Movement or MPA), and the transnational social movement La Vía Campesina (The Peasants' Way or LVC), of which MAB, MPA, and the MST are members; MAB is connected to various other social movements, unions, and human rights organizations nationally and globally (Fieldnotes, 2018; Plataforma Operáia e Camponesa da Energia, 2014).

Knowledge production, power, and agency

In response to the question, "why is a movement of people affected by dams a part of a food sovereignty movement?," the short answer is the following: when dams are built, they displace people – peasant communities and Indigenous communities in particular – from their land and in turn their livelihood. We cannot examine the impact of dams without understanding how dams alter relationships to land. LVC and all of its members, including MAB, counter the dismissive notion of peasants and, instead, asserts peoples' natural rights to self-determination as well as the right to employ both humanistic and legally-grounded objections to expulsions masked as "progress" capitalist globalization. LVC is important as a Global South-led global movement focused on dismantling various and intersecting forms of oppression. Its existence and work speaks to the importance of peasant movements as producers of knowledge (Barbosa, 2016; Bringel and Vieira, 2016; Holt-Giménez, 2006; Icaza and Vásquez, 2013; Markoff, 2007; Rosset et al., 2021).

When we look to some of the most successful social movements today, they come in the form of agrarian reform efforts. Martınez-Torres and Rosset argue that LVC is considered to be one of the most important transnational social movements and is more successful than the international environmental, labor, or women's movements, because of the ability "to build a structured, representative, and legitimate movement, with a common identity, that links social struggles on five continents" (2010: 150). LVC, in contrast to other transnational networks, possesses a unique "peer group" structure that defies the "colonial patterns" too often reflected in the organizational design wherein groups from the North dominate those from the South (see Chapter 1). Samir Amin points to the critical importance of peasant movements, noting that without food sovereignty, there is no hope of political sovereignty (2022: 53). He writes: "The organization of peasant movements is, in this sense, absolutely irreplaceable" (Amin 2022: 69).

LVC challenges hegemonic structures within its organization. One way in which this is visible is in how LVC has placed a heavy emphasis on gender parity and its internal structure works to ensure that women are in leadership positions. Notably, other groups and movements – including those who are a part of LVC – learn from LVC's model. Martinez-Torres and Rosset (2010: 167) suggest that because of LVC's efforts, some member organizations, such as the MST in Brazil, have changed their own internal structure to address gender parity (Wright and Wolford, 2003: 256). Women members from LVC convened a women's assembly at the CLOC conference[5] that took place in 1997 in Brasilia, demanding that women would occupy 50 per cent of the leadership representation. At the Third International Conference of LVC held in 2000 in Bangalore, this declaration was adopted (Martínez-Torres and Rosset, 2010: 159). At the Fifth Conference of LVC held in Maputo Mozambique in 2008, the movement issued a statement acknowledging that women continue to face economic, physical, cultural, and social violence stemming from entrenched power differences wherein men continue to hold more power than women. Recognizing that gendered power imbalances are present in the communities that comprise LVC, and are also present within the organization itself, the 2008 LVC statement below asserts that this reality is an injustice, as well as a limit to growing the strength of the organization:

> We recognize the intimate relationships between capitalism, patriarchy, machismo and neo-liberalism, in detriment to the women peasants and farmers of the world. All of us together, women and men of La Vía Campesina, make a responsible commitment to build new and better human relationships among us, as a necessary part of the construction of the new societies to which we aspire. For this reason during this Fifth Conference we decided to break the silence on these issues, and are launching the World Campaign 'For an End to Violence Against Women'. We commit ourselves anew, with greater strength, to the goal of achieving that complex but necessary true gender parity in all spaces and organs of debate, discussion, analysis and decision making in La Vía Campesina and to strengthen the exchange, coordination and solidarity among the women of our regions. (Martinez-Torres and Rosset, 2010: 167; Vía Campesina. 2008)

Like many of LVC's member groups, MAB works to construct and strengthen networks both nationally and globally, as well as build collaborations with a broad range of groups. MAB has a focused and intentional effort to bring women, youth, and other historically marginalized people into leadership, and they articulate the importance of not replicating hierarchical structures (including patriarchy and heterosexism) within their internal structure. The focus of this chapter, however, is on what MAB can teach us about movement knowledge production. The MST – an agrarian peasants rights' movement with whom MAB works closely and from which some MAB members have come – has its own press, Expressão Popular, that produces and publishes books. This alone demonstrates that MAB and other popular social movements are producers of knowledge, not simply movements to be studied by researchers (I return to this in more detail in the following chapter). Of course, this is not a novel assertion (as I discuss at length in Chapter 1). Even still, the dominant narrative that persists – especially within academic circles in the United States – is the idea that social movement scholars ought to remain outside, impartial observers, analyzing whether and how movements fail or succeed. In fact, social movement scholarship may even be taken more seriously if we say a movement has failed. This raises the following questions: what is the role of scholars in shifting the system we have to alternatives that remedy the problems we see? How can movement scholars embrace the socially transformative projects of social movements?

What we in the Global North – especially those engaged as scholars and participants in social movements – can learn from Global South-led movements such as MAB is twofold: 1) that movements do not need to be the object of scholarly analysis, but rather have something to teach the academy at large; and 2) that the challenge and goal should be to see how our work as scholars can be in solidarity and collaboration with movements to advance the creation of worlds of alter-globalization. My use of the broad term "academy" here is intentional, especially as I participate in interdisciplinary work that spans well beyond social movement studies and the discipline of sociology. My work with MAB has shown me the important role that scholars have played and can play in social movements, specifically in terms of creating space for thinking and analysis, and to uplift and strengthen the struggle and provide legitimacy to social movement goals. This relates to what Tarlau (2014) writes, citing Bevington and Dixon, on movement-relevant theory scholarship which "seeks to draw out useful information from a variety of contexts and translate it into a form that is more readily applicable by movements to new situations – i.e. theory (p. 189)" (2005: 721). Choudry writes that "much of the theory produced by participants in social movements may not be recognizable to conventional social movement studies since it is produced by activists" (2015: 128; also see Chapter 1).

Scholars and the university can play a part in creating spaces for critical learning, and as more feminist, anti-colonial, anti-racist, and Global South scholars become connected globally, more transformative knowledge production and praxis are happening. Yet, what I have learned is that spaces where this occurs are rare; and the academy writ large and social movement studies in the United States specifically, are most often seen by movement practitioners as *not* doing this and not being interested in hearing these critiques. Since the start of this larger project, I have been in a continuous process of learning about the gaps in my own (colonial) education with significant epistemic exclusions. With this in mind, I want to note that in Figure 4.1, I outline some of what academia might learn from movements, illustrating why this is needed and what I observe that MAB can teach. I do not claim that what I outline here is something new or my own unique observation. I think about this table in the context of four areas: framing the struggle, leadership, revolutionary memory, and international solidarity, each of which I discuss in turn.

	Why it is needed	How MAB does it
Asking new questions	Academia encourages normal science, incremental questions.	Imagining new futures; options previously not thought possible.
Asking normative questions	Academia encourages leaving social justice outside.	Imagining new futures; options we had not thought possible based on first-hand knowledge and experience.
Linking questions/struggles	Academia encourages specialization at the expense of linking struggles.	Organizing and solidarity work across movements including at the local, national, and global level.
Building collaborative knowledge networks	Academia (especially in the United States) encourages competition, building individual profiles.	Solidarity work across movements plus empowering marginalized groups; fostering collaborative/bottom-up leadership.
Making positionality visible	Academia strips us of our identities; the unexamined norms are therefore colonial/ patriarchal/capitalist and center whiteness; problem of methodological nationalism.	Making identities and histories (individual, national, and world) of oppression central
Drawing on learned histories	Academia encourages innovation, finding something new; at the expense of learning from the past; methodological nationalism.	Focus on knowing/learning from history(ies); memories of resistance.
Guiding cultural narratives	Research encouraged to be esoteric/uninspiring/ apolitical.	Use of storytelling; cultural work; consciousness-raising.
Broadening audience/movement	Research produced by and for "experts" only; objective and "apolitical."	Consciousness work plus organizing across movements/international solidarity work.

Figure 4.1 Movements as producers of knowledge

Framing the counter-hegemonic struggle
for a new world

Brazil's MAB emphasizes that their work is not only to resist the current exploitative system but to create a new way of living and being that respects and honors human rights. MAB moves beyond criticism of the current system and offers a vision of what could be – of alter-globalization. MAB points to capitalism as the problem and argues that the right to water is inextricably linked with the right to land, energy, food, education, safety from violence, self-determination, and sovereignty. MAB's fight focuses on rights and the idea of the collective – rather than profits and the individual – at the center of how society should be structured. It is a radical politics that aligns well with what Gianpaolo Baiocchi describes as "popular sovereignty" – both a theory of democracy and a "transformative political project" (2018: 95). It is about the imagination and construction of alternatives to the world as it is. The path there is not yet built; it is being made.[6]

People in MAB see their work as a struggle for basic rights, including food, water, and land, which they cannot separate from the right to exist and livelihood. As one woman, Fatima, who is a part of organizing her neighborhood in Belém (and has been involved in struggles for racial and social justice for decades), put it: "It is a fight for the right to live"[7] (Personal interview, summer 2018). It is a fight for access to water, sanitation, education, transportation, and healthcare. It is the right to be free from police violence because of the color of your skin and to have the right to a quality of life. For the most part, people did not become involved because of the question of water – although some did. Most leaders in MAB are *atingidos* whose life or that of their families have been affected by dams. Some were previously involved in other social movements, including the MST. Most are engaged in the struggle for justice for those affected by dams and against the privatization of water and see their work as a part of the larger struggle for the rights of workers, the poor, women, and the marginalized (Fieldnotes, summer 2018).

Fatima's words resonate with what Maria,[8] who worked for CDDH,[9] told me: "to be poor is always to be a problem to the police. If you are poor and Black and live in the street, the police will likely assassinate you" (Fieldnotes, summer 2018). As Carla de Carvalho, executive coordinator of CDDH, put it, the objective of their work is to "serve life" – every person deserves the same rights and access to services. She hopes that someday the city will not need the center because there will be justice and a new city. Right now, she argued, people do not have a right to the city – because it is all about tourism and capital (Personal interview, summer 2018).

One striking aspect of MAB is how it frames its work: MAB uses stories to tell its story.[10] For example, the account of Nicinha – an atingida murdered in January 2016 for protesting a dam in her community – is an important one to MAB (Fieldnotes, summer 2018). Nicinha's story is connected to the phrase: "Women, water, and energy are not commodities,"[11] a counter-hegemonic, anti-capitalist, and anti-patriarchal assertion. MAB's efforts are neither specifically urban nor rural: the fight for access to water is for everyone, everywhere, in the countryside and the city. In this sense, "We are all affected [by dams]."[12] One of the powerful things I have observed about MAB is its focus on "o campo e a cidade" – that is, both the rural and urban matter, and the issues facing both are interrelated. MAB works with the MST; they also work with urban movements (which I touch on in the following chapter). Raúl Zibechi has written that the MST in Brazil takes a more top-down organizing approach whereas the new urban movements for housing rights take a more horizontal approach. Zibechi sees that "An alliance between Brazil's two main emancipatory movements – rural and urban – would most likely lead to a qualitative leap in Latin America's anti-systemic struggles" (2014: 291). I posit that social movements in Brazil are working to form powerful alliances with each other, and that this divide is indeed transforming and diminishing.

The discussion of Nicinha (see Figure 4.2) and the importance of stories – narratives – brings to mind the importance of mística. Abdurazack Karriem (2009) has written on this as it relates to the MST. Karriem explains that in the MST theory informs practice, and practice informs theory. At the beginning of the formation of the MST, Karriem argues that liberation theologians served the role of the "organic intellectual" by raising consciousness, operating within the "cultural realm of common sense or the folklore of the landless." Catholic values of suffering and redemption form the MST "mística," with most meetings starting with a play that utilizes folklore and acknowledges historical figures in the fight for justice (Karriem 2009: 319). They accomplished this by creating their own symbolism – a flag, song, poetry, or theatre – displayed and used at movement gatherings. I observe this same process in MAB.

The use of mística operates as a mechanism of economic, political, and cultural organization. It is a part of the fight against cultural hegemony – Antonio Gramsci's notion that dominant ideas, assumptions, and stereotypes of how the world ought to be can hold great power over people, affecting their daily experiences and consciousness (Gramsci, 2000; Moore, 1996: 127). This concept applies to the work of MAB, which has constructed an alternate way of viewing social, economic, cultural, and environmental relationships. In so doing, MAB is fighting against deeply held assumptions about land rights, control of resources, and economy.

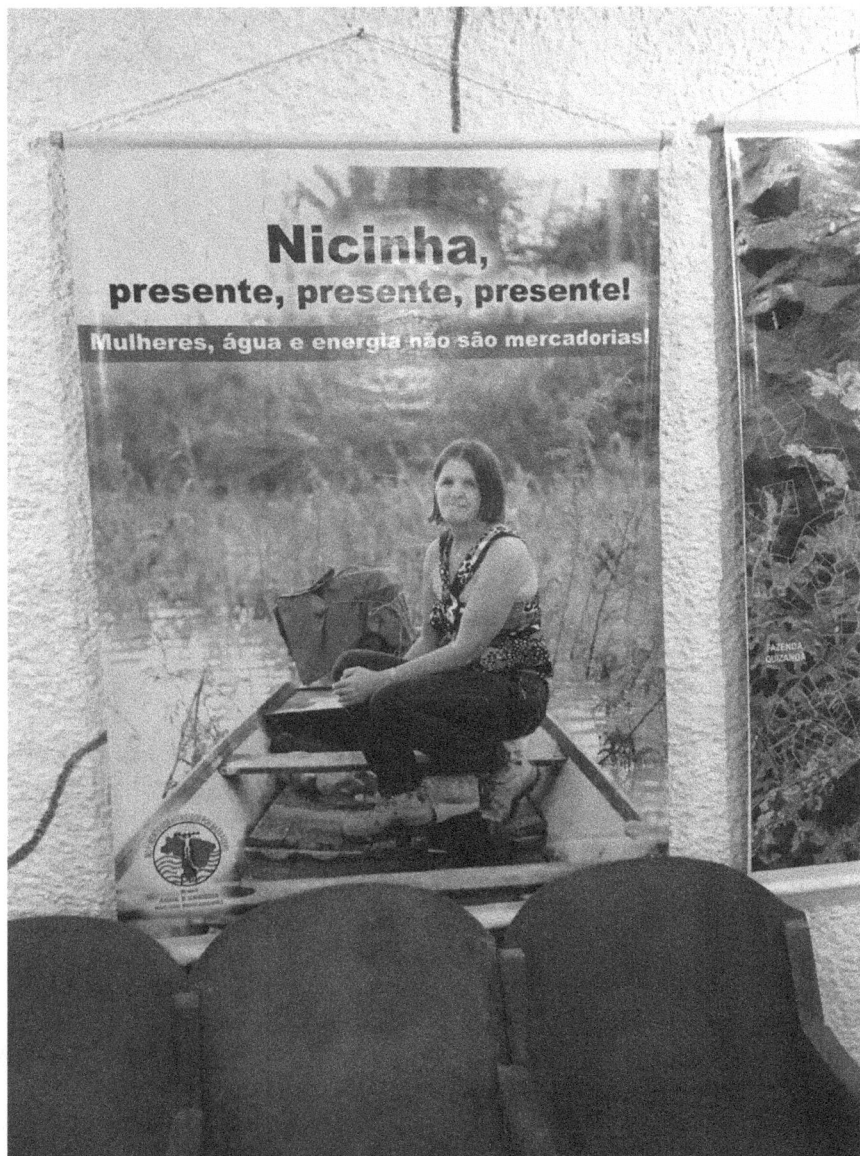

Figure 4.2 Poster of Nicinha

During the evaluation of a weekend-long training for new militantes, one of the participants stated that there needed to be "mais mística" in it (Fieldnotes, summer 2018). This feedback struck me because, as an outsider, I found the story-telling vehicle to be quite present and compelling. Yet, participants saw that there could have been more of it. This critique speaks to the idea that MAB's struggle is not just about fighting the "system" but about consciousness/cultural work. The inclusion and focus on mística is present in ways I am not familiar with in the US movement spaces.[13]

Leadership

Many pamphlets produced by MAB contain questions for discussion and debate (MAB, 2018). A standard format includes reading material together, answering questions, and having a group discussion using those questions in training sessions. MAB has adopted this strategy as an important way of building literacy and leadership: both in the sense of actual literacy and literacy regarding knowledge of past and present resistance and movement-building. I observed that this format comes out of the legacy of liberation theology and CEBs (base communities).[14] This history was also referred to by MAB leaders during my fieldwork.

A recurrent theme I observed was the importance of women, youth, and children,[15] to the movement. As one MAB militant, Yara, in São Paulo, told me: MAB's model is one woman, one man, and one youth (under thirty) in leadership. Once members turn thirty, they are expected to take their skills and help organize somewhere else while opening up the space for someone new (Personal interview and Fieldnotes, summer 2018). Through my work with MAB, I have had many conversations with young MAB militantes about this and observed that these aspects of MAB's vision (such as gender parity in leadership and the critical role of young people in growing the movement) are constantly put into practice. MAB also works with other popular social movements, including Brazil's popular youth movement, Levante Popular Juventude. One of the things that I noted was the vibrancy of the movement and the inclusion and active leadership of young people in its efforts. There is a deep and intentional focus on pedagogy and leadership development, specifically focused on including women, youth, and children.

A fundamental part of MAB's pedagogy is focused on connecting historical systems of oppression and resistance to the present and examining how various forms of oppression and injustice are connected. That is, the murder of a person because they are queer or trans is related to the dispossession of a peasant farmer from their land because of a dam project. The death of a woman from intimate partner violence is associated with the child that dies from a lack of clean drinking water. This is why it is a "Popular fight."[16] At the core of this fight is the understanding that capitalism feeds systems of exploitation because it requires dispossession and exploitation to function. To build a world where LGBTQ+ people are respected, where women are safe, where children do not die from lack of calories or polluted water, and where people are not driven from their homelands, requires that the capitalist system itself be changed.[17]

I observed this while attending the Formação de Militantes do MAB – a training[18] focused on the history of struggle around the construction of dams that took place in a rural community located a few hours outside of Rio de Janeiro. In answer to the question "why do we study this?" posed by one of the leaders of the Formação de Militantes do MAB, the answer was: "We cannot do anything without energy. The same thing with water – we cannot do anything without water."[19] This is what makes water a right – you cannot exist without it (Fieldnotes, summer 2018). A fight for water rights is, at its core, a fight against commodifying life, human or otherwise. A man who had spent his life farming and who was discussing the changes he had seen, including the absence of waterfalls due to the construction of dams, put it this way: "We need to respect the limits of the river."[20] Following his statement, another person raised the point that the root of the problem is that nature and people have been privatized. Capitalism does not observe limits; it creates problems and then tries to create a "sustainable" solution, which is not possible because capitalism is inherently at odds with the idea that life has intrinsic, non-monetary value (Fieldnotes, summer 2018).

This relates to liberation theologian Leonardo Boff's analysis of the connectedness of social and environmental injustice. Liberation theology and ecology have in common that: "they start from two bleeding wounds." The former is the wound of poverty and the latter, the wound of methodical assault of the Earth. As such, he viewed that the two discourses ought to be discussed in tandem – because, ultimately, both stem from the same root cause, which is, as Boff articulated it: "a prevailing system of accumulation and social organization," which means some people have many resources, while others have nothing (Boff, 1997: 110–11).

While MAB's analysis points to capitalism as the root of injustice and environmental degradation, my work within MAB reflects a repeated theme of the importance of empowering those historically excluded from the political process. By extension, then, fighting oppression in all forms within the broader socio-political, economic system also means confronting internal/organizational forms of oppression. As one woman, Cleidiane – a member of MAB in Belém – told me, there is a lot of intentionality around empowering women to organize and lead in all parts of coordinating the movement because historically, they have been subject to machismo, patriarchy, and violation of their rights. There has been, she said, an "Invisibility of their [women] rights"[21] (Personal interview, summer 2018). Another member of MAB's coordinating committee disclosed to me the depths of this commitment, delineating MAB's long-term vision and strategic plan with goals laid out for the next five years, twelve years, and up, until 2070 (Personal interview, summer 2018). Within MAB there is an emphasis on the idea that knowledge production is a collective and iterative process that is critical to articulating an alternative way of organizing life. Cleidiane also affirmed the following regarding the participation of women in the movement:

> We have always had the participation of women in MAB ... Organization of women and youth strengthens the organization of the movement as a whole, whether at the base or at a distance because women are the main subjects in this process of building the movement in all regions of Brazil. It is the women who run the base community groups. It is the women who organize the meetings there in the community, the women who are in charge of the mobilizations, the women who are coordinating the movement, understand?[22] (Personal interview, summer 2018)

One of the foci of social movement studies is outcomes (Amenta, Andrews, and Caren, 2018; Piven, 2006; Staggenborg and Lecomte, 2009; Wood et al., 2017). MAB's efforts are ongoing, and while long-term outcomes are always impossible to predict, one tangible result of their work today involves the empowerment of historically disenfranchised and politically excluded individuals to become leaders. Their trainings seek to articulate how a "new path" (or alter-globalizations) is a process of education and growth, where people learn through the format of lectures, conversations, and discussions. Empowerment informs the core of MAB's organizing work in hundreds of communities and hundreds of spaces of learning. As I reflected in my fieldnotes after my second day with MAB:

> I flipped over the pamphlet "Em Defensa Da Petrobras e do Brasil" [about energy policy and sovereignty in Brazil], and on the back are nine questions for debate in a communal study session like the idea of base communities ... I recognize that this format comes out of the base community/liberation theology tradition ... which is something that Rodrigo[23] [a MAB militant I had interviewed earlier in the day] in particular discussed ... and it is absolutely a strategy for building leadership, for raising consciousness and empowering people ... which is another theme Yara, in particular, talked about in the context of women, children, and other historically disenfranchised groups ... they have a long strategy/process and pedagogy for empowering and creating space for people to speak out and lead in their communities. The format even of these pamphlets is very similar to the format of the ones I researched [for my master's thesis on the role of liberation theology in environmental social movements in Brazil] that were produced by the Catholic church in previous decades ... Gabriel had a lot of questions of me about the US and what is learned from/how movements take heed from the Black Panthers and Civil Rights Movement. (Fieldnotes, 15 June 2018)

In the next section, I detail more about how liberation theology informs MAB's pedagogy. Chapter 5 provides more examples of what this focus on liberatory education and empowerment looks like in practice. Overall, this focus on leadership leads to other significant lessons learned, which I discuss in turn.

Revolutionary memory

MAB fights against the idea that human life is a commodity. Participants believe that since water is essential for life, when it is commodified, life itself is commodified. This point is demonstrated in MAB's motto, "water and energy are not commodities!" MAB articulates a model of leadership built by and for the people historically excluded from hegemonic structures: the poor, the peasants, the workers, the women, the LGBTQ+ community, and the youth.

In the left-hand corner of a bulletin board in the MAB headquarters (pictured below) in Rio de Janeiro, is a poster for a book titled *Arpilleras Bordando a Resistência* (2018). This book has also been adapted into a film of the same name,[24] produced by MAB:[25] Arpilleras is the term used for the colorful pictures made in many parts of Latin America by appliquéing scraps of fabric onto a hessian backing. During the Pinochet dictatorship in Chile, this medium became politically significant since working-class women used arpilleras to depict the reality of life under military rule. In the Arpilleras project, MAB followed this model to chronicle the struggle in Brazil against human rights violations. Over 16 different human rights violations[26] are time and again chronicled during and after the construction of dams. The book also includes pages explaining the history of this artform in Chile and contains works produced by women affected by dam projects (*Arpilleras Bordando a Resistência*, 2018). Numerous MAB leaders also raised the importance of the Arpilleras project with me in interviews and conversations (Fieldnotes, summer 2018). While focused on the Brazilian struggle of those affected by dams, this book also details conflicts in a dozen other countries, thereby depicting the translocal aspect of the struggle. It is a global fight against oppression and for human rights. But in drawing on the example and history of arpilleras, this project also illustrates the importance of revolutionary memory in comprehending the past (see Figures 4.3 and 4.4).

MAB emphasizes education and understanding of how historical processes inform present-day struggles. Their model speaks to the importance of Marxist theory, liberation theology, and a liberatory model of education (based on the work of Paulo Freire) that also informs the broader social movement community in the country, to which MAB is connected.

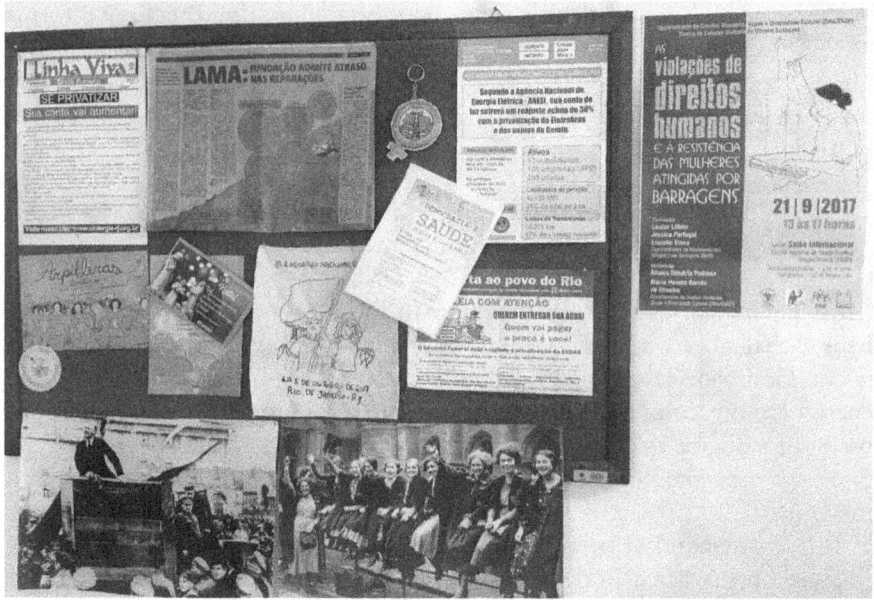

Figure 4.3 Bulletin board in MAB office in Rio de Janeiro. Note the poster for Arpilleras on the left-hand side

Figure 4.4 Inside the book, detailing the various dam projects from which Atingidas contributed art to the project

In her book, *Occupying Schools, Occupying Land* (2019), Rebecca Tarlau writes about how liberation theology and the formation of base communities were deeply informed by Paulo Freire's work as well as Marxist and socialist thought (Tarlau, 2019: 40 and 52). Tarlau writes of the MST and its Florestan Fernandes National School (ENFF) in Guaranema, São Paulo: "The ENFF is one of the MST's political training schools (*escolas da formação*), founded in 2005 to support the internal training and political education of MST activists and other social movement leaders across Brazil and Latin America" (2019: 112).[27] My observation of MAB's education model aligns with Tarlau's discussions of the MST. Tarlau writes:

> Freire offered MST activists a concrete set of pedagogies to employ in their classrooms, such as the incorporation of generative themes based on students' reality, problem posing, dialogue, and praxis – connecting theory and practice. Freirean theory also helped local activists understand that social change was not only possible but also ethically necessary. Furthermore, Freire taught the movement that education is never neutral; it is always either actively maintaining or transforming the status quo. (2019: 51)

After an informal conversation with Yara in June 2018, where we discussed the importance of pedagogy to MAB and MAB's connections to the MST, LVC, and other social movements, I wrote the following in my fieldnotes:

> In response to a question that I asked about MAB's structure and focus on gender parity, etc., and from where that came, Yara shared with me how MAB's structure change didn't come as a top-down process from the MST or LVC so much as it was the collective effort of knowledge production between movements. She noted, however, that it was formalized in LVC's structure before the MST and MAB. I continue to be inspired by the organization and dedication to creating an alternative society and vision … very intentional about empowering people to think and participate in the process … and the question of how MAB is connected to La Via or the MST is really a no brainer. They all – and many other social movements like MPA – work together very closely. They build and share knowledge together. And they fight together. This is also true with the work to make sure that women are in leadership … also in their youth committee … and in the LGBTQ committee. The goal is to empower those previously disempowered to become leaders.

In addition to the Formação de Militantes do MAB, I attended a morning-long training led by professors and movement leaders on the history of the fight for land in the state of Rio de Janeiro. This extension project training was held in Cachoeiras de Macacu and was made possible by the collaboration of several universities, the municipal government, and MAB. The project's objectives included calling attention to the importance of memory in the fight for land and the contribution of memory to the work of MAB in organizing the resistance of farmers threatened by a dam construction project on the Guapiaçu river. The project also serves to provide university students and community members with an opportunity to participate in developing pedagogical activities for use with school-age children (Fieldnotes, summer 2018; Material Didático para as Oficinas do Projeto de Extensão, 2018). In this training (and in the Formação de Militantes), the starting point was the legacy of colonialism and appropriation of resources. I was invited to join the breakout group for creating a syllabus for high school students on the history of land reform. Figure 4.5 shows what we made. At this point, I was early in my fieldwork process, navigating my role and opting to primarily engage only when called upon, serve as a notetaker, or answer direct questions posed to me about life – and organizing and activism – in the United States. Later, as I describe in Chapter 5, this would change.

Another example of the importance that MAB places on teaching the history of resistance struggles occurred in the first few moments of the Formação de Militantes training. For the "icebreaker," we were all blindfolded as some of the leaders read a poem by Hailton Mangabeira, "40 Horas na Memória," about Paulo Freire and how we remember his work for literacy, consciousness-raising, and creating a more liberatory world. One by one, someone removed our blindfolds.[28] A facilitator then put us into groups named after historical figures and leaders of resistance. In addition to Nicinha and Paulo Freire, I noted the inclusion of Zé Pureza, a Brazilian leader of land reform and a sociologist, and Zumbi (Zumbi dos Palmares), a quilombola leader and symbol of Afro-Brazilian resistance against slavery. I learned more about the significance of these groups on the last night when there was an interactive mística activity organized for the purpose of naming this class of militantes.[29] Ultimately, the class was named in honor of Nicinha. This exercise demonstrated the importance of pedagogy, history, and collaborative learning, and was conducted using an interactive model designed to engage people. In his writing on the MST, Miguel Carter detailed the movement's focus on education and "raising popular consciousness" of its members, using both the pedagogy of Paulo Freire and its own materials (2011: 201). By building collective power through "mobilization capacity, multifaceted but flexible organization, strategic creativity, quest for financial independence, resourceful allies, investment in popular education, and mystique and discipline [religion/Catholic liberation theology]," the MST has created spaces and mechanisms for people to become engaged in changing policies and transforming their country (Carter 2011: 198). This same emphasis is present in MAB.

In trainings drawing heavily on Paulo Freire's (1968) *Pedagogy of the Oppressed*, MAB focuses on collaborative learning and literacy. The model

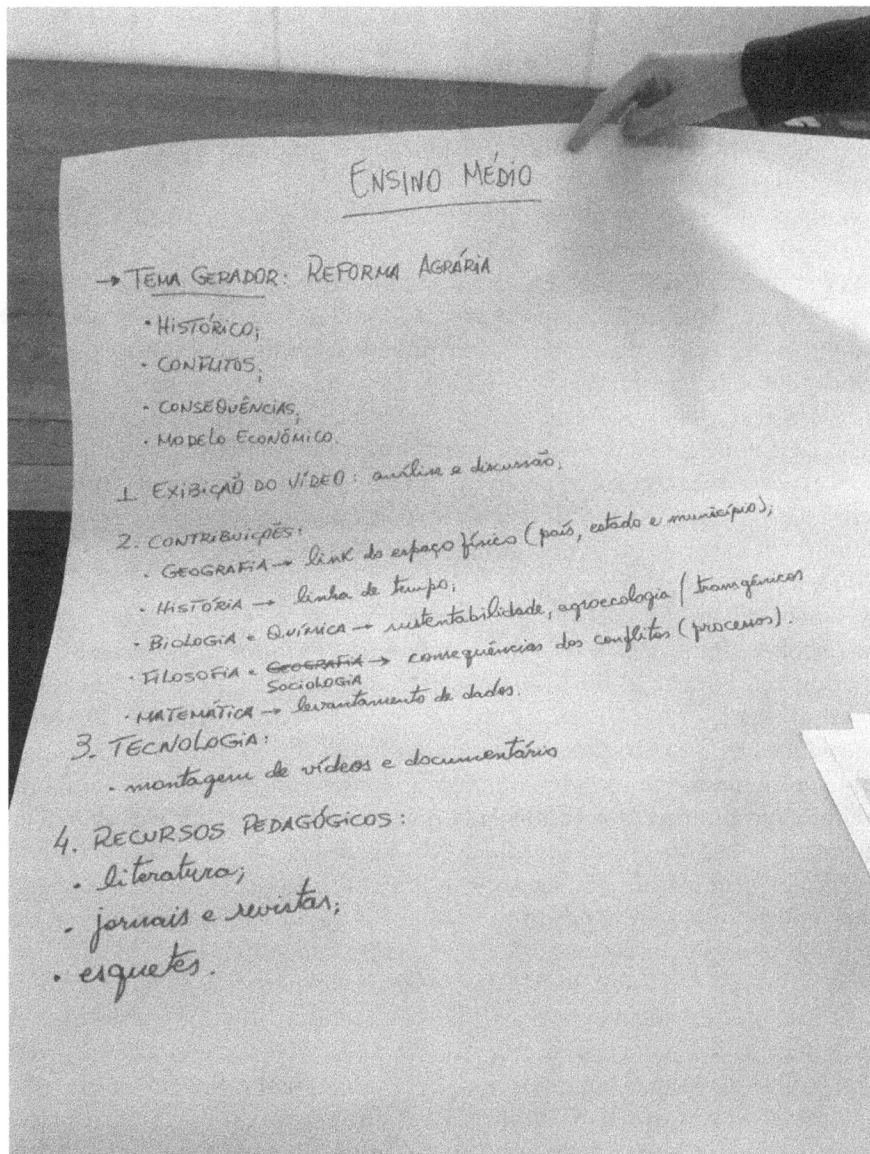

Figure 4.5 Breakout group summary poster, the general theme of how
to teach agrarian reform in high school

they use of small break-out groups where people take turns reading pas-
sages helps people learn to read. There is an intentional effort to fight
against interlocking systems of oppression: classism, racism, heterosexism,
and patriarchy, as these are viewed as interlinked with the root cause of

capitalism (Fieldnotes, summer 2018). Or, as a MAB leader put it: "It is a global fight; a fight for humanity"[30] (Personal interview, summer 2018).

International resistance and solidarity

Finally, I observed the importance to MAB of the history and victory of the Cochabamba, Bolivia, struggle – one of the most striking and successful examples of resistance to water privatization in recent history. Over eight days in April 2000, an estimated 100,000 Bolivian citizens mobilized, taking to the streets to protest water privatization. In addition to forming blockades that cut off access to the highway and occupying the city center, activists also took over Aguas del Tunari's offices and refused to move until their demands had been met. The mobilizations ultimately culminated with concessions from the government and the corporation Aguas del Tunari (a subsidiary of Suez, one of the largest corporations involved in water privatization)[31] (Dangl, 2014: 306; Muehlebach, 2023: 29–30; Olivera and Lewis, 2004: 37–9).

Oscar Olivera (one of the principal leaders of the resistance in Bolivia) has spoken at the MAB national conference (Fieldnotes, summer 2018). During the Formação de Militantes training, MAB showed an animated short film called *Abuela Grillo* detailing the Cochabamba struggle. The film, introduced by a MAB leader, explains that while the content is made accessible to children, the message remains universal and profound. The film is about appropriating water from camponeses in Bolivia, and it was shown as an example of hope. After the film, a MAB leader made the point that a few years ago, people from Bolivia came to Brazil and talked to MAB; it is where they got the sign that hangs in the room: "Without water, there will be no chichi, there will be no cachaça"[32] (Fieldnotes, summer 2018). The Bolivian activists also gifted a tree to MAB as a sign of solidarity (see Figure 4.6).

There are important lessons to be gleaned from the mobilization and resistance in Bolivia and how that story remains vital to the Brazilian struggle. Bolivia illustrates the importance of transnational solidarity in the fight against water privatization – both as a learning network for tactics and strategies but also as an example of hope and inspiration, and successful resistance to hegemony. Indeed, MAB is a formal member of LVC – a "peasant internationalism," which I introduced earlier in the chapter. As also noted earlier, MAB works closely with other members of LVC such as the MST and MPA. Leaders from MPA (The Small Farmer's Movement) attended the last day of the training to share their stories and struggles, and to discuss the importance of solidarity and working together (see Figure 4.7). This relates to what a MPA leader in São Paulo told me a couple of weeks earlier in an

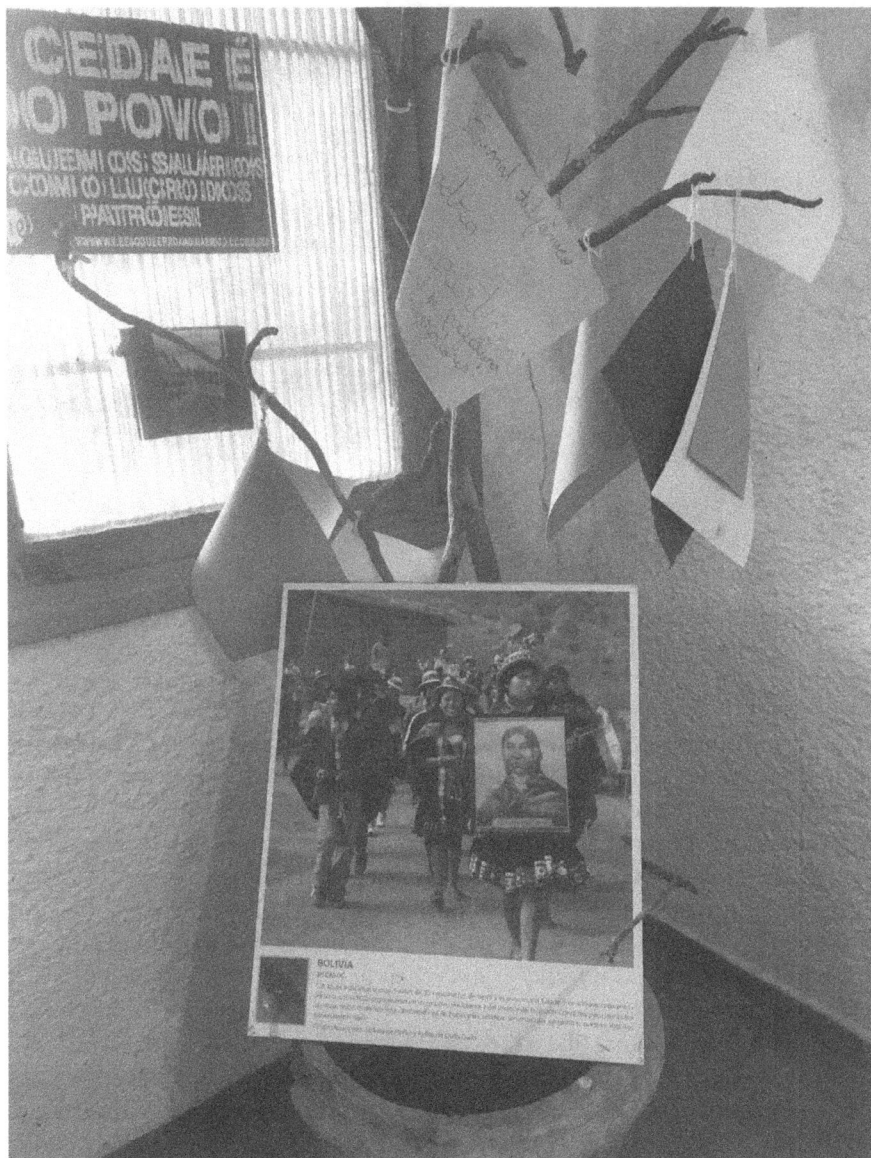

Figure 4.6 A gift to MAB from Bolivian activists

interview: "MAB is fighting for water ... MPA is too. If you do not have water, you do not have anything"[33] (Personal interview, summer 2018).

During the training, a MAB leader conducted a session on the history of energy production in Brazil and how it is situated within the larger global

Figure 4.7 MAB on the final day of a training (note MPA flag as well!)

economy. Patricio[34] said: "What's the point of neoliberalism? [It's] Not just about producing but speculating. This is why the price per megawatt of electricity can be so high – it's speculation."[35] He then showed a graph to illustrate how the profit is exorbitantly higher than the cost of production. Another graph illustrated how energy production changes based on rainfall, as well as where/when the world needs energy. The high energy prices in Brazil are expressed in a common statement by MAB: "The price of light is robbery."[36] Another person at this point pointed to a map of US energy and said, "where Caitlin lives,"[37] and then asked me, "How many months are below zero [Celsius] in Pennsylvania?"[38] I answered, saying it depended, but at least five months. She asked me this to illustrate how places in cold climates need more energy during more months, and that this has an impact elsewhere in the world, including Brazil. Someone else chimed in about how this is why MAB's struggle is an international fight – because so many countries are enmeshed with and desire Brazil's resources.

Just as capital is connected, so too must be the resistance. Solidarity alliances are crucial because they demonstrate the strength of peasant movements. These alliances relate to a large body of literature within social movement scholarship around network and micromoblizations (including McAdam, 1986; Snow et al., 1986). The term "solidarity" is the one used most frequently amongst the movement actors themselves, and so I choose to use that word here.[39] As discussed in Chapter 1, peasants have not become "obscure," even as, to draw on Philip McMichael's (2008: 37) language, "the narrative of capitalist modernity" has seen the peasantry as something outdated that would disappear with progress and development. LVC and all of its members, including MAB (and MPA and MST), counter the disparaging idea of peasants being encapsulated as historical relics and assert instead peoples' natural rights to self-determination as well as their rights to both humanistic and legal objections to expulsions masked as "progress" in the form of capitalist globalization. LVC is essential as a Global South-led transnational movement focusing on fighting various and intersecting forms of oppression. These alliances also speak to a broader literature, noted in Chapter 1, that highlights the importance of peasant movements as a site of constructing globalizations from below and of Global South peasant-led movements as producers of knowledge (Amin, 2022; Barbosa, 2016; Bringel and Vieira, 2016; Holt-Giménez, 2006; Markoff, 2007; Rosset et al., 2021; Rosset and Altieri, 2017; Vieira, 2011).

Moreover, numerous Brazilian academics have conducted research and dissertations and theses on the work of MAB – yet their work remains relatively unknown in the United States.[40] Knowledge production flows not just from movement to scholars, but from Southern scholars to Northern scholars as well. In an interview with two university professors in Belém do Para, I was encouraged by their acknowledgment that the work I am doing around water is critical. They simultaneously urged, as an equal imperative, the need to form a network of researchers to share information, noting how obtaining information on the activities of corporations (and governments) related to the privatization of water is difficult since there is little transparency and there are few mechanisms to access data[41] (Personal interviews, summer 2018).

A common point articulated to me in various ways by MAB and others fighting for the right to water was that the fight against commodifying water and in defense of life is "a local, national, and international fight"[42] (Personal interviews and Fieldnotes, summer 2018). As one woman who works with CDDH, Franciela,[43] responded when I asked if she saw her work as part of a local, national, or international struggle:

> I see it as an international fight. I'll explain why. Today, we are here in the center. We deal with the issue of territory; we deal with the issue of LGBT rights; we deal with the issue of street populations. But, we are always connected by a network, right? For example, in Brazil, there are networks of human rights centers, right? We see MAB ... we see the struggles of people in Salvador. So, everyone can be just one movement that specifically deals with other issues, but we are always interconnected. We are always looking to strengthen each other, right? Seeking experiences with each other so that

we can contribute to our struggle as well. So, we live connected through a network, you know? Unfortunately, the defenders, the defenders of rights, they really suffer persecution, understand? Are murdered ... that's why we always have to strengthen it [the network], right? The defense of defenders, the defense of those people that we want to protect, understand? So, we are always connected. We have the question of FAMA, right? Which is the World Water Forum that we [CDDH] were at. So, we are always together and strengthening each other. (Personal interview, summer 2018)[44]

In line with Franciela's comments, MAB integrantes[45] also discussed the importance of the Fórum Alternativo Mundial da Água (FAMA or World Alternative Forum on Water) as pivotal for building the national and international aspects of the movement. Held in Brasilia in spring 2018 as an alternative to the Fórum Mundial da Água (FMA or World Forum on Water), FAMA was created in opposition to FMA, which had been overrun by corporate interests seeking to privatize and control water (see Figure 4.8). As

Figure 4.8 FAMA poster on the desk of a union leader in Belém

those involved in FAMA refer to it, FMA is the "forum of corporations" (Central Única dos Trabalhadores de São Paulo, 2017; and Fieldnotes, summer 2018). FAMA was the people's forum, bringing together nearly seven thousand people.

MAB, together with 36 other bodies, also drafted a document at the end of FAMA affirming that water is a right and for the people, not a commodity. They asserted:

> The document reaffirms the fight against any privatization and the establishment of private water ownership. FAMA defends water as a common good, that is, it must be controlled and be at the service of the people, reinforcing the motto of the meeting: "Water is a right, not a commodity." (Fórum Alternative Mundial da Água, 2018)[46]

In many of the informal conversations I had beyond the interviews conducted, I was asked questions about the struggle against privatizing water in the United States; some people suggested that perhaps the US water rights movements could learn from MAB. I shared my own organizing history with people, which served to build trust and rapport. After my first interview with Yara and Gabriel, they asked me why I wanted to do research in Brazil. They also asked (knowing I was engaged in water organizing in my own city) if they could ask me questions about the water struggle in the United States. Thus, after I interviewed them, they interviewed me.[47] Yara, told me that she (and MAB) wanted to connect and learn from one another (Personal interview, summer 2018).[48] In June 2018, during a two-plus hour drive to a MAB training in the state of Rio while riding in a car with several MAB militants and supporters of MAB, I was asked a question by Alexandra,[49] a chemistry professor at a university in Rio. Alexandra wanted to know if movements in the US talk about water as a right, not a commodity. I said that it was discussed as a right in the OWC, but that in other places it was not, and that using rights language around water in the US, while not ubiquitous, seemed to be gaining more prominence. I shared with her (and many others at various points in time) about the struggle against water privatization in Pittsburgh and about how social movements organize in the United States. These reflections strengthened my own understanding of the Pittsburgh fight and its position within the broader struggle for water and against the present socio-economic system.[50]

Near the end of the 2018 trip, I interviewed Robert, a MAB militant living in Belém, Brazil, who was also working on a graduate degree in Geography. Near the end of the interview, he asked me: "What type of theory do you use?" I started responding to him, and thus began a conversation about shared theorists (including David Harvey) and the importance of Global South knowledge production. He also made the point that knowledge production is unequal and that there is not just the problem of the US dominating the realm, but also within Brazil between the South of the country and the North (where he is from). He also asked me: "Are you going to publish in Portuguese?" making the point that it was important for people who do not read English to be able to read what I write about them. I answered honestly, explaining that I would like to but that I was not sure, and that my first priority would have to be in English since I needed to write my PhD dissertation. I will return to this point in the next chapter.

At a moment in history when right-wing governments are coming to power – including in Brazil – the struggle to create and maintain alterglobalizations becomes even more challenging. Many of these challenges were articulated to me in all my interviews (and many informal conversations and participation in events) during my research trip in 2019. Vítor,[51] who had a history of work in government, unions, and social movements, spoke of the increased threats against social movements, the challenge of engaging people politically, and the Bolsonaro administration's rollback of environmental progress. I took an hour and a half bus ride from the city of São Paulo to Campinas to speak with him and, after meeting me at the bus station, we went to a bakery/coffeehouse where I interviewed him. He told me:

> Speeding up the pace that could represent water privatization in Brazil, today we are facing a dismantling of the environmental arena, dismantling of social participation, dismantling of social control, and the introduction of privatizing measures that significantly facilitate deforestation and loss of areas of protection [that] are environmentally protected or socially protected ... [there is] a very strong action to dismantle the environmental protections, and the people appointed to these positions even have a certain similarity with Trump when he took office.[52] (Personal interview, 21 June 2019)

Vítor also spoke of the importance of needing to strengthen social movements and bring them together; he noted the importance of MAB specifically as a movement and also that "more international cooperation" is required.

Situated within a global context dominated by multinational corporations (a topic to which I return in Chapter 6), this international coordination becomes even more critical. During an interview with two MAB militants in São Paulo in 2019, I was told about the "informal" and "diplomatic" discussions that took place at the FMA the previous year, and the presence of both multinational water privatization firms and the bottled water industry, these firms' connections to certain Brazilian politicians, and their interest in exploiting and exporting Brazil's vast freshwater supply. The militantes also talked about the presence of United States-based companies who have holdings in Brazilian hydroelectric energy and the dam crimes of Brumadinho and Mariana (discussed in Chapter 1). They told me:

> today what we have is increasing intensification of privatization advances, and with the government today, the hand of this extreme military right, and a private sector of the Brazilian bourgeoisie, an even more violent apparatus. So, for example, we had a comrade, Dilma, murdered, and also the [dam collapses/crimes of private companies] Brumadinho and Mariana.[53] (Personal interview, summer 2019)

MAB and other movements are indeed continuing to resist, and the work continues – even amidst the onslaught of rollbacks on human rights and environmental protections (MAB, 2019a; Schroering, 2019a).

Conclusion

The phrase "knowledge is power" is well-known. However, during my time working as a community organizer, this phrase became increasingly troubling for me. The point was made by many with whom I worked that knowledge does not equal power; that power is a) organized money or b) a large number of organized people; and that power is, simply put, the ability to help or to hurt. The counterargument could be: "But knowledge[54] is necessary to build people power!" Over time, I became less insistent and accepted that knowledge might not be power. My work at that time centered around the idea of turning out thousands of people to a large annual public action, and I still believe that organized people power might be our best hope of changing this broken world. But if knowledge is not power, then why work in academia? The relationship between knowledge and power is dialectical and, as sociologists (or academics in general), we must wrestle with these questions. Knowledge is key – it is about understanding how power operates and what is going on "behind closed doors." It is knowledge about how politicians and political and economic systems function. It is understanding that even with an "ally" political figure, nothing changes without popular mobilization and organization.

Academics strive to pursue "objective and sound research." I am not suggesting that we jettison rigorous and precise methodological strategies. Indeed, the goal of this work is to produce conscientious research and theory. However, to borrow from the field of political ecology, the idea that the knowledge that scholars have can even plausibly be apolitical is inherently political in itself (Robbins, 2012: 18). Arturo Escobar and Susan Paulson provide a relevant framework for thinking about these hybrid identities as well. They question if the world can:

be redefined and reconstructed from the perspective of the multiple cultural, economic, and ecological practices that continue to exist among its many communities? This is above all a political question, but one that entails serious epistemological, cultural, and ecological considerations. It speaks of the utopia of reconstructing the world in an ecologically sustainable, socially just, and culturally pluralistic manner. (2005: 274)

It is critical to recognize the many powerful examples of resistance and resilience. If we look to the current discourses within social movements, we see an alternative to the present. This resistance and articulation of "alter-globalizations" (Bakker, 2007) is what I discussed above. MAB's resistance to the privatization of water and energy *and* its articulation of a new path is an example of Diálogo de Saberes (DS),[55] which comes out of a long tradition in Latin America and within La Vía Campesina (see Collado, Montiel, and Ferré, 2011; Ghiso, 2000; Grajales, 2010; Rossett and Martinez-Torres, 2013). In simplified terms, DS refers to dialogue between different people and groups, bringing together different ways of knowing; this is including, and especially focused on, knowledge from Indigenous and peasant ways of knowing. Rosset and Martinez-Torres define DS as the following:

A collective construction of emergent meaning based on dialog between people with different historically specific experiences, knowledges, and ways of knowing, particularly when faced with new collective challenges in a changing world. Such dialog is based on exchange among differences and on collective reflection, often leading to emergent re-contextualization and re-signification of knowledges and meanings related to histories, traditions, territorialities, experiences, knowledges, processes and actions. The new collective understandings, meanings and knowledges may form the basis for collective actions of resistance and construction of new processes. (2013: 4)[56]

People are exercising sovereignty and reclaiming their land, water, labor, and communities and moving beyond capitalist, colonialist, patriarchal, and Western logics.

Knowledge and power are related and, too often, sociology (specifically US-based) still fails to incorporate voices – knowledge – from the periphery. The sociology of knowledge matters because it relates to perspective; ideas do not emerge out of nowhere. Connell speaks of Derrida's notion of "erasure" and how the term means an overwriting, rather than obliteration, of experiences. As Connell (2007a: 368) states, "where" matters because "where" is related to voice, experience, and perspective. She argues that while many sociological theories and texts are openly critical of neoliberal globalization, they do "not challenge the way that knowledge of the social is constituted" (2007a: 378). This is in large part due to the reality that literature "*almost never* cites non-metropolitan thinkers and *almost never* builds on social theory formulated outside the metropole" (2007a: 379).[57] Amidst the various global crises faced by humanity at the present moment – including the unfolding turmoil of viewing water as a commodity rather than a human right – it is imperative to consider Connell's call for a "new language for theorizing," and to work to decolonize how we think, research, and write about movements. To do this also means engaging with and learning from movements on the ground – with "social thought from the periphery" (2007a: 383).

Power matters, especially thinking about it in the context of theory building. The focus on abstraction in theory-building is problematic. As Sankaran Krishna explains, he deliberately uses the term discourse over theory as, "The use of discourse is intended to inflect theory, discipline, or any social narrative with considerations of power" (2001: 421). Thus, "discourse" connotes the power relationships at play in a way that "theory" does not. In addition to power, discourse forces attention to praxis – what people in counter-hegemonic movements are doing. While an essential and significant component of activist research must include the co-production of knowledge between scholars and social movements, another critical aspect is for scholars (especially those in the North) to pay attention to and learn from praxis – what movements are already producing. MAB (and the various other social movements with which they partner) would be an example of discourse – one that too often is, to return to Connell (2007a), overwritten (though not obliterated).

In my research, I have observed the importance of knowledge production and how this is a critical piece of the work accomplished by MAB. What capitalism does well is to use culture to make us think that this system is in our interest and to reduce exposure to counter-hegemonic ideas (Sklair, 1997: 530). Hegemony works by controlling knowledge and the production of knowledge. One alternative to the logic of capitalism is the logic of collective rights. As discussed in Chapter 1, rights language is imperfect, and the term elicits various ideas and definitions. It can, however, represent a clear and succinct alternative to the language of profit (Rajagapol, 2006; Smith, 2017b). Many movements today (especially from the Global South) use rights language in a way that challenges individualistic, legalistic, colonial, and Western notions of the term and that also move beyond the focus on human rights to include the rights of nature, and the idea of buen vivir (good living). Buen vivir, a term that originated in South America, sees that true development and progress can only come from community. It also elevates culture, diversity, and an eco-centric ethic (Gudynas, 2015; Zimmerer, 2015).[58] MAB uses the idea of the right to water to construct a narrative where capitalist ideals of profit are not the ones that guide how we structure society.

My work with MAB – and also in Pittsburgh – shows that water activists use the phrase "right to water," but *do not* use it to describe a top-down legal process.[59] A powerful and important example of this discourse of rights comes from social movements fighting for them, as I have demonstrated here through the case of MAB. A site of knowledge production, MAB is also an organizing presence creating a different framework for life; it is an example of alter-globalizations. I argue that conceptions of rights as collective versus individual challenges hegemonic institutions – including the global primacy of states, and of private property, including the privatization of land. Social movements such as MAB (and the larger LVC to which it is connected) are pushing for something different: to elevate the collective and the right for all people to have access to land and water. This is similar to what James Holston (2009) calls "insurgent citizenship" where people on the peripheries are demanding to have their rights recognized, including the right to have access to land.

Amin (2022) discusses how Karl Kautsky wrote in *The Agrarian Question* that the peasantry would disappear as a result of capitalist expansion. But, as Amin writes,

> While this was true (for 80 per cent) of the other capitalist countries (the Triad: 20 per cent of the world population), it is not the case for the 'rest of the world' (80 per cent of the population). History has shown that not only has capitalism not solved this question for the 80 per cent of the world population, but that, as it pursues it expansion, it cannot resolve it. (1988 [1899]: 65)

Global South-led peasant movements around the world are organizing and resisting. Peasants have not become "obscure." To the contrary, agrarian reform movements (which revolve around the resource of land and challenge the capitalist idea that the land/commons ought to be enclosed) are standing up for the right to their culture and way of life. As McMichael (2008: 38) relates, quoting a peasant leader from Mexico:

> a campesino comes from the countryside. There have always been campesinos. What did not exist before were investors, industrialists, political parties, etc. Campesinos have always existed and they will always exist. They will never be abolished.

In this chapter, using empirical examples, MAB's standpoint offers crucial insights into the operation of systems of power and strategies of resistance. Purely technocratic approaches to solving water problems are destined to fail if they do not account for both the lived and theoretical knowledge produced and articulated by the people most impacted. Further, underlying systemic realities that cause struggles around water must be acknowledged by all – the problem is not solely one of scarcity versus abundance. This points to the need for a reorganization of social relations. MAB centers its struggle around the idea of water (and energy and education) as a commons rather than a commodity. This relates to my argument in Chapter 1: this project is not just about water, as conflicts and struggles for water are also system struggles that push for change of social and economic orders. This counter-hegemonic work is also about knowledge and imagination – a different world from the one in which we currently live cannot be realized if we do not understand the processes that shape the current one, or if we cannot imagine a different one. This is one of the ways in which I argue that knowledge is flowing from the South to the North.

As MAB argues, solidarity between movements and across national borders is increasingly important. A critical component of this, I contend, is to learn about, from, and with Global South-led movements, who are producing theory and living it out in praxis. In the next chapter, I explore the implications of this mode of knowledge production. I show that the *what* and *how* of my study (i.e., the questions I ask and methodologies I choose) cannot be separated from the *who* and *why*. Taking a collaborative and solidarity-based approach to knowledge directly shapes the theories and methods of analysis. As I show, this enables the production of insights in real time on how to organize for the right to water, especially in terms of the role of popular education and political formation, as well as the necessity of alliances and collaborations that transcend national borders. As MAB says, "A luta continua!"[60]

Notes

1 "Women, water and energy are not commodities!"
2 This chapter builds on a previously published paper (see Schroering, 2019a).
3 Also see Chapter 1.
4 See Chapter 2 for more discussion about rights.
5 CLOC stands for the Coordinadora Latinoamericana de Organizaciones del Campo (Latin American Coordination of Rural Organizations), one of the forebears of LVC.
6 MAB's location in the Global South also matters for how it can frame its struggle in more explicitly counter-hegemonic terms than movements typically do in the United States. I return to this point in the conclusion of this book.
7 É uma luta para direito morar.
8 A pseudonym.
9 Center for the Defense of Human Rights (Centro de Defesa dos Direitos Humanos de Petrópolis or CDDH), an organization founded by liberation theologian Leonardo Boff and committed to furthering environmental justice and human rights.

10 Others, including Francesca Polletta, have examined the importance of story-telling in movements (Polletta, 2009) as well as the role of emotions (Goodwin, Jasper and Polletta, 2000; Gould, 2009).

11 Mulheres, água e energia não são mercadorias.

12 Todos somos atingidos.

13 I discuss MAB's use of mística more in the next chapter.

14 Alongside mística and liberation theology, Base Ecclesial Communities (CEBs or base communities) were important to the history of a progressive Catholicism and popular resistance and mobilization against oppressive structures, and inform the praxis of popular social movements, including MAB, today. Comprised of fifteen to twenty families who gathered once or twice a week for Bible study and reflection, these communities also served as vehicles for oppressed people to mobilize against injustice. CEBs in Latin America took different forms in different places. In Brazil, they became an important place to have political discussions: a space demonstrating the 'liberation' theorized in liberation theology. Given the political context of the time – when a repressive military regime that took control in 1964 – CEBs became particularly important as a place where discussions could transpire (Wright and Wolford, 2003: 6).

15 Centering children's needs can also be a counter-hegemonic strategy (Smith, 2021). I return to this in the next chapter.

16 luta popular.

17 I return to this discussion in the next chapter. A great deal of the history of socialist movements from the late nineteenth century until relatively recently has involved side lining or postponing some forms of oppression to avoid distracting from the class struggle against capitalism; in this sense, I argue that MAB's theorizing them as connected matters.

18 This was the third step (out of four or five steps total, which varies based on circumstances) of this particular training.

19 A gente faz nada sem energia. Mesma coisa com agua–gente faz nada sem agua.

20 a gente precisa respeitar o limite do rio.

21 invisibilidade de seus direitos.

22 Sempre teve a participação das mulheres no MAB desde sempre … Organização das mulheres e jovens mais nós fortalece o conjunto da organização do movimento seja na base seja na distância, por que são as mulheres as principais sujeitos nesse processo de construção do Movimento em todas as regiões do Brasil. As mulheres que correm nos grupos de Base. São as mulheres que organiza a reunião lá na comunidade, são as mulheres que estão à frente das mobilizações as mulheres que estão na coordenação do movimento, né?

23 A pseudonym.

24 Available here with English subtitles: www.youtube.com/watch?v=PEu-AATb3TU

25 Arpilleras embroidering resistance.

26 In 2010, the Council for the Defense of Human Rights (CDDPH) conducted a study that found that rights are violated in all stages of dam construction and

operation. These included the right to information and participation; right to work and to a decent standard of living; right to adequate housing; right to improvement of living conditions; and right to full compensation for losses. See here: https://mab.org.br/2010/11/24/conselho-defesa-dos-direitos-da-pessoa-humana-cddph-reconhece-exist-ncia-um-padr-viola-es-do/. MAB also has called particular attention of the need to recognize the violation of rights of Indigenous people, traditional communities, and women.

27 In the next chapter I discuss my own visit to the ENFF school, organized for me by a MAB leader.

28 During this weekend-long training, we were also asked to turn in cell phones, which served the purpose of encouraging people to be present with each other and the information.

29 Like most of the popular education conducted by MAB, formation classes are ongoing, and typically structured in a format that repeats with new cohorts.

30 É uma luta global; uma luta pela humanidade.

31 Suez is now a part of Veolia, adding another layer of connection between these struggles, as discussed in Chapters 2, 3, and 6.

32 sin agua, no hay chichi, no hay cachaça.

33 O MAB está lutando pela água ... o MPA também. Se você não tem água, você não tem nada.

34 A pseudonym.

35 Qual é o significado do neoliberalismo? Não apenas sobre produção, mas especulação. É por isso que o preço por megawatt de eletricidade pode ser tão alto – é especulação.

36 O preço da luz é o roubo.

37 Onde mora Caitlin.

38 Quantos meses são abaixo de 0 na Pensilvânia?

39 It also relates to the discussion of translocal struggles, introduced in Chapter 1, discussed in Chapter 3, and which I will return to in Chapters 5, 6, and 7.

40 Many of these are housed in the MAB headquarters in São Paulo and I had hoped to spend more time there reading the work to cite and include it here. Covid disrupted this plan.

41 I would note that I don't think this is necessarily unique to Brazil, although there are more resources available, in general, to researchers in the United States to track down information.

42 uma luta local, nacional, e internacional.

43 A pseudonym.

44 Eu vejo como uma luta internacional. Vou te explicar por quê. Hoje, nos estamos aqui no centro. A gente lida com a questão do território, a gente lida com a questão dos direitos LGBT, lida com a questão da populacao da rua. Mas, a gente está sempre ligado por uma rede, né? Por exemplo, no Brasil, existem redes de centores de Direitos Humanos, ne? A gente vê a pessoal do MAB em mina e em minais, a gente vê a questão do pessoal em Salvador. Então assim, todo mundo eles podem ser só um, só movimentos que lidam especificamente com outras questões, mas a gente está sempre interligado. A gente tá sempre

buscando fortalecer um ao outro, né? Buscando experiências um com outro por que a gente possa contribuir a nossa luta também. Então a gente vive ligada através de rede mesmo, sabe? Infelizmente, os defensores, os defensores de direitos, eles sofrem mesmo sofrem perseguições, né? São assassinados … por isso que a gente tem que estar sempre fortalecendo isso, né? A defesa de defensores a defesa daquelas pessoas que a gente quer proteger, entendeu? Então a gente vive sempre ligada. A gente tem a questão da FAMA né? Que é Fórum Mundial das Aguas que a gente tava lá, então a gente tá sempre junto e fortalecendo o outro.

45 In my half a dozen interviews with sanitation and water union leaders, whom I interviewed in 2018, all also noted the importance of FAMA as a place of connection and building resistance to privatization.

46 O documento reafirma a luta contra qualquer privatização e o estabelecimento de propriedade privada da água. O FAMA defende a água como um bem comum, ou seja, que deve ser controlado e estar a serviço do povo, reforçando o lema do encontro: "Água é direito, não mercadoria" (Fórum Alternative Mundial da Água, 2018).

47 In 2021, over a Zoom interview with Gabriel for his own research project, we chatted about the possibility – sometime in the future – of writing a paper together. In August 2022, Gabriel invited me to give a talk about the Pittsburgh struggle for a course for graduate students in Education as part of a postgraduate course offered through the municipal government of São Paulo, Brazil. I shared the (virtual) space with two other guest lecturers from MAB. A condensed and written version of our presentations will be included in a co-authored chapter (between the three of us and Gabriel) in the book of the semester's speakers, and has now been published (Schroering et al., 2023).

48 One significant piece of this is my ongoing work with MAB and others from the United States who comprise the US Solidarity Committee for MAB.

49 A pseudonym.

50 These conversations also informed my understanding of how future organizing in Pittsburgh unfolded, including my subsequent experience in Nigeria, detailed in Chapter 6.

51 A pseudonym.

52 O acelerar o andamento que pode representar a privatização da água no Brasil, hoje nós estamos enfrentando um desmonte da arena ambiental, desmonte da participação social, desmonte do controle social e a introdução de medidas privatizantes e que facilitam no significativamente o desmatamento e perda de áreas de proteção sejam ambientalmente protegidas ou socialmente protegidas … então a uma ação muito forte do desmonte da área ambiental e as pessoas indicadas para esses cargos tem até uma certa similaridade com Trump quando assumiu.

53 Hoje a nossa o que temos cada vez mais se intensifica o avanços privatizações contudo o governo hoje a mão desse extrema direita militares e um setor privatista da burguesia brasileira, eles são aparato mais violento. Então, por exemplo,

a gente teve a assasinata a companheira Dilma ... e também os [rompimentos de barragens / crimes de empresas privadas] Brumadinho e Mariana.

54 This perhaps provokes another question: knowledge of what? How money has come to translate into power (or how to organize in order to counter that), are the forms of knowledge I am thinking about here.

55 In an earlier draft of this chapter, I utilized Boaventura de Sousa Santos "monocultures of knowledge," "sociology of absences," and "sociology of emergences." As noted in another footnote in Chapter 1, during the editing of this chapter, the news broke of his sexual misconduct; further, more stories came forth that many of his concepts, including the ones I mention in this note, were built on the idea of Diálogo de Saberes (DS). I made the decision to reference and build on that work instead. I acknowledge that my attempt at doing this is also incomplete and that the concept builds on the work of many.

56 The idea of prefigurative politics, where people create and model the future society they would like to see at a micro level (Törnberg, 2021), is applicable here as well.

57 Connell's argument also raises another query: by assuming that we as scholars can operate outside the social settings we study, we fail to ask whether and how our positionality – including our position within the university industrial complex or "edu-factory" (The Undercommoning Collective, 2016) – impacts the communities we study.

58 Ecuador and Bolivia's new constitutions were drafted with this concept in mind (Gudynas, 2015).

59 For an important discussion on this, see Farhana Sultana and Alex Loftus' (2012) edited volume, *The Right to Water: Politics, Governance, and Social Structure*. Also see my discussion of individual versus collective rights, and the work of Janet Dine, noted in Chapter 2.

60 The struggle continues! This assertion is used by MAB to draw attention to the long history of struggles, and that the work continues. Specifically, the phrase comes out of the Mozambique independence struggle, and is used by MAB and other movements in Brazil, but also around the world.

5

Collaborative knowledge production and the right to water: solidarity and translocal learning networks

In 2017, I met Rob Robinson, a founding member of the US Solidarity Committee for MAB, who had been invited to the University of Pittsburgh to give a talk on housing justice, and to visit with graduate students. Upon learning of my background in organizing, current work, interest in water justice, and past experience in Brazil and hope to return there, he asked me: "Do you know MAB?" While quite familiar with the MST and LVC, I told him that I did not know MAB. Fast forward a few months, and Rob had put me in touch with Yara and Alexania, two of his comrades in MAB. From 12 June to 19 July 2018, I resided in various regions of Brazil where I conducted 24 semi-structured interviews with members of MAB and partner movements. During this first research trip, however, I did not just conduct interviews. I was also invited into other spaces that amounted to more than 140 hours of participant observation and, through this process, began to think earnestly about and examine what "coresearch" is and what it means specifically for me, both as an activist and organizer, but also as a white queer cis woman from the United States.

The previous chapter concluded with the statement used by MAB (and other popular social movements and revolutionary social movements) "A luta continua!" I examined, using empirical examples, how the standpoint offered by Global South actors provides important insights into the operation of systems of power and strategies of resistance. This chapter builds on the previous by focusing on the following question: how could the study of social movements be transformed, utilizing methodologies other than theoretically based analysis that is produced exclusively inside the university and within the Global North, and what might this mean for organizing for the right to water? This chapter examines the potentials of using categories of analysis that emerge beyond the academy and Global North university. It is both methodological and analytical, where I examine knowledge production and, specifically, how MAB's work is grounded in theory (Marx, Gramsci, Fernandes, Freire, liberation theology, and many others) and praxis, and is led by many young people who are adding to, critiquing, and changing theory, and in so doing building a national (and translocal) movement for the right to water. In addition to the *production* of knowledge, the focus is also on the *exchange* of knowledge, and my positionality in that process, which makes this chapter in part autoethnographic. In turn, this chapter also provides insight on the main questions of this book: 1) How are global social movements communicating and organizing around water and other basic rights? 2) How are movements engaging with and learning from each other, and is the "West to the rest" paradigm subverted in these interactions?

I returned to Brazil for seven weeks during the summer of 2019 to conduct more fieldwork. Amidst a general strike and the political upheaval brought by Bolsonaro's administration, there were palpable differences in the summer of 2019 compared to just a year earlier, which I will touch on throughout the chapter. On 29 June 2019, Yara arranged for someone to bring me to the ENFF school (introduced in the previous chapter) for a visit. The ENFF, created and run by the MST, is grounded in building a popular movement for agrarian reform in Brazil, while also noting the importance of internationalizing the fight. As someone from the MST noted during my visit: "It's not a school for the MST. It is a school for all the people of Latin America … for ancestors, for peasants … a school for the people – the international working class." The emphasis is on access to education (with an extensive library, and courses) and knowledge that historically has not been accessible to peasants and the working class. Their concept, as stated in the presentation (I participated in a "tour" with Friends of the MST), is that "organizing workers and studying are not opposed to each other." There is a moment to fight and a moment to study. The school is named after Florestan Fernandes, a Marxist sociologist who saw the process of social transformation as intertwined with education. A prolific writer, he wrote an article in 1986 titled, "Para o sociólogo, não existe neutralidade possível: o intelectual deve optar entre o compromisso com os exploradores ou com os explorados" which means, "For the sociologist, there is no possible neutrality: the intellectual must choose between a commitment to the exploiters or to the exploited."

Upon returning to the United States in August 2019, I had a conversation with Rob as we walked through the streets of New York City, where I was visiting for a sociology conference. He mentioned the work of the US Solidarity Committee for MAB, and that he was going to talk with others about my joining. The committee agreed that I could join and, since September 2019, I have been a part of this solidarity committee, which remains a place for those of us in the US and in Brazil to maintain connections with each other, share updates from our respective struggles and countries, strategize, and have a sense of solidarity, even amidst the Covid-19 pandemic. It was also through this work that I was invited to return to Brazil in early 2020 (before the pandemic was something those of us in Brazil or the United States were really paying attention to) to commemorate with others from around the world the one-year anniversary of the Brumadinho dam collapse. In addition to the 10 days of activities associated with this, I remained in Brazil to participate in the second part of the Course on Energy, which is a two-year, four-part course that is a partnership between MAB and the Universidade Federal do Rio de Janeiro (Federal University of Rio de Janeiro or UFRJ).[1] It brings together more than 70 people from 21 organizations, social movements, and unions from five countries across the Americas. The goal is to make the university more accessible to workers and the public and, in the process, strengthen the struggle for the human right to water and fight against the privatization of resources and education. From 15 to 26 July 2019, I attended the first 10-day part of this course, held at UFRJ, which I will discuss later in this chapter.

Amita Baviskar, whose book *In the Belly of the River* (2004 [1995]: 4) guided my praxis and interest in research for 15 years, writes,

> While positivist scholars assume that inquiry can and ought to be value-free, I work with the explicit recognition that research is inherently a process guided by the values of the inquirer, values that manifest themselves in the formulation of the research agenda, and in the choice of theory and methodology.

Baviskar also discusses how participant observation places the researcher into a position of being both "inside" and making sense of that "inside" reality with the "outside" (2004 [1995]: 8). Drawing on Paulo Freire, she asserts how "At its best, besides articulating people's lived concerns, fears and aspirations, critical research could act as a catalyst for ideological reflection and action" (Baviskar, 2004: 8). When I first read Baviskar's book, I had no idea that over a decade later I would also be conducting research on conflicting ideas of development and mega dam projects, albeit on a different continent than where Baviskar's research took place. Baviskar's work, however, has greatly informed my own scholarship and praxis.

In 2019, in between my second and third fieldwork trip to Brazil, I read Marina Sitrin's book *Everyday Revolutions: Horizontalism and Autonomy in Argentina*, in which she writes:

> In the years since completing the books in 2005 and 2006, I have continued to spend time in Argentina and relate with the many movements. As things changed, challenges grew, and new paths to surpass them were experimented with, I continued to do interviews, again imagining another oral history. However, after many conversations with compañeros about what might be most useful, I made the difficult decision to write more of a reflective and analytical book instead, relying on what people had said and what I had observed,

but using my voice as the motor and refractor. This book is a result of that process. It is also a product of what was my dissertation, although from the beginning my relationship to Argentina has been one of militancy and that of another movement actor from another place, not as an academic doing field-work or research on an "other." (2012: xv)

The words of Sitrin, a sociologist doing work in Latin America, in the same century as my own, have served both as reassurance and as guide. While there are numerous examples of politically committed academics from all continents, Sitrin's frank assertion of her commitment, and of giving herself permission to use her own voice in her writing, inspires my own work. In what follows, it is not just MAB that serves as my object of analysis; I am, as well, in the sense that I am discussing what I have learned from MAB, my positionality in that exchange, and what that might mean both in terms of knowledge production and organizing around the idea that water is a commons and not a commodity. In the sections that follow, I discuss how MAB uses the idea of human rights in its organizing, and how the human right to water is connected to a broader struggle for rights. Next, I turn to the focus and importance of both sovereignty and international solidarity in MAB's work, followed by an examination of how MAB's anti-systemic fight is not just focused on economic structures, but also dismantling other oppressive systems, such as patriarchy and racism. Finally, I look at the role of popular education in MAB's struggle, and its importance in political formation and organizing.

Human rights from below: what MAB means and why it matters

During my first research trip in 2018, members of MAB connected me with various partners of theirs who work on related issues around the right to water and sanitation in social movements, unions, and also government. One of these interviews was with someone in the Human Rights Commission in Belém, Pará, Brazil. After wandering around the government building, clearly lost, and asking multiple people for directions, I finally stumbled into my destination. I had thought there was some sort of confusion as people kept pointing me toward the parking garage. Finally, a frustrated man walked me into the garage and to a door that said above it "Comissão dos Direitos Humanos." Yes – it was in fact in the parking garage. Edison,[2] my interviewee, reflected how the human rights abuses in Belém are terrible (he argued the worst in the country) and that this is especially true if you are poor, Black, or live in the periphery of the city. Children die every day, he lamented. And if you ask most people if they want water privatized, he said, they will say no. But, he said, most people won't join the fight. Old methods of mobilizing don't work, he pondered, so what do we do? He said that he hopes my work can be a part of figuring that out. I told him that I noticed the office was in the garage. He started laughing and said, "It's good you noticed." I asked why and he said, "I don't know but ... you saw it!" Then he went on to say how the other divisions have nice large offices inside the actual building. He said that the concept of human rights here is to prevent people from a criminal attack, not to provide social or economic rights that are so desperately needed (Personal interview, summer 2018).

This relates to what one of my interviewees, Franciela, who works with CDDH (introduced in the previous chapter) said when describing her work related to housing and land rights for people. She said how she learned that when housing rights are violated, you find all other types of rights have also been violated:

> all other rights have already been violated ... including the right to basic sani-
> tation and the right to water, you know? The right to human dignity even for
> people, do you understand? They usually live in peripheral areas, they usually
> suffer from security issues, they suffer and are criminalized and marginalized.
> So, when you have the right to housing, all the other rights too, they come
> together, so you end up very much fighting for everything in these communi-
> ties.[3] (Personal interview, summer 2018)

After my interview with Edison, I wrote the following in my fieldnotes:

> Corporations in collusion with corrupt governments work everywhere with
> the same goal: to make profits. Profits over people. And the struggle of organ-
> izing the people to say no to this is a hard one. As Edison said, it is a long
> hard fight. But we have to continue. I am convinced that the concept of human
> rights must be at the core of my work. But I am less convinced that the idea
> that we can use institutions to implement human rights is the way to go. Direct
> action and targeting the decision makers is the only way, I think.

Describing its fights and origins, MAB provides the following description on its website:

> MAB's history was formed out of the denial of a number of rights to the
> affected populations – peasants who already come from a more humble condi-
> tion, and face difficulty in accessing the justice system. According to the report
> of the National Human Rights Council, in the construction and operation of
> dams in Brazil, at least 16 rights are systematically violated. (MAB, n.d.)[4]

MAB's fight is for water as a commons and for people affected by dam projects; it is also inextricably linked to a broader counter-hegemonic strug-gle for dignity, livelihood, and the creation of a socio-economic political system that does not look like the present one. In June 2019, Gabriel invited me to attend a day-long training with him organized by one of the home-less worker's movements in São Paulo (organized by the União Nacional de Moradia Popular on 15 June 2019). His role in the meeting was to hold a break-out group on energy and the price of gas. Speakers asserted that there is a *right* to occupy vacant buildings, especially amidst a reality where rent is exorbitant. The role of education and learning in creating this right to the city was also emphasized, connecting the idea of the right to the city, to the right to education, which also has broader implications for knowledge production. I observe how this understanding of the intersections of rights and the indivisibility of them is counter-hegemonic. It also reflects knowl-edge about how power works – i.e., Western thinking and policy processes compartmentalize economic and social rights, and separate types of rights as well as individual from collective rights (Rajagapol, 2006), which only serves to benefit those in and with power.

One of the training facilitators handed out a thick packet to everyone, which included a book, and asserted: "It is important to study and analyze" and said that it is a "very important document." I asked Gabriel about the book,[5] which detailed histories and presents of urban development and housing policies in the city. I asked who had funded the copies to give out to the dozens of participants. The answer: if a researcher conducts research at a public university using public funds, they must give away copies of that book. I think that this point brings new meaning to the discussion about the right to the city, accessibility, knowledge production, and open-access publishing that we are also having conversations about here in the United States (Bartling and Friesike, 2014; Go, 2020; Ren and Montgomery, 2015; Stacey, 2007; The Undercommoning Collective, 2016). The importance of Paulo Freire and his teachings is also illustrated in this example, which I will return to later in the chapter. At the end of the day, everyone (including me) received a certificate of completion for participation (see Figure 5.1).

A speaker at the training asserted the importance of countering the dis-course from the Right, and the idea that we must challenge the dominant narrative and create the narrative we want and have a right to live into. Another aspect of creating this narrative is visible in the importance and use of mística, which I also discussed in Chapter 4. Mística is imbued with values of suffering and redemption, and most meetings/events of MAB (and other popular movements in Brazil) commence with 5–15 minutes of a sort of play, music, other art that utilizes folklore and acknowledges his-torical figures in the fight for justice (see Karriem, 2009) for a discussion of this examining the MST). It is used as a tool for imagining and creating the world that could be; a world where life is valued over profit, and one with radically different social and economic relations than the one in which we currently live. At "breaks" each attendee had been given four pages of

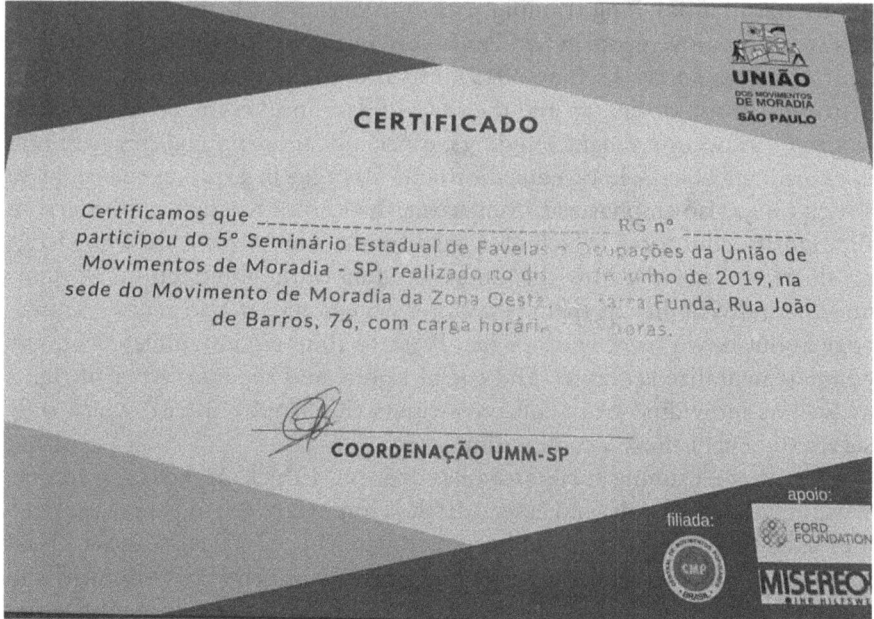

Figure 5.1 União Nacional de Moradia popular training certificate

poems and songs, which we read and sang together. One, called "I cannot breathe"[6] proclaimed, "I cannot breathe, I can no longer swim, the earth is dying."[7] Three main things stood out to me at this housing movement meeting: 1) the comradely manner in which different popular movements interact with, organize with, and support each other;[8] 2) the analysis that the right to water, the right to land, and the right to housing are all inextricably connected and must be fought for in tandem; 3) the connection between the academy and social movements.

I detailed in Chapter 2 how on 25 January 2019, the worst human-caused environmental crime in Brazil's history occurred (Costa, 2021; Stropasolas, 2020) when a dam – owned by the transnational Brazil-based mining company Vale – collapsed in Córrego do Feijão in Brumadinho, Minas Gerais, Brazil. For MAB, and many others affected by the fallout of this collapse, where 272 lives were lost and hundreds of thousands are adversely affected from the socioenvironmental damage caused, this was not an accident, but rather a crime: Vale knew something like this could happen (Schroering, 2019c). As part of the one-year commemoration[9] of this crime, MAB organized a five-day march beginning 20 January 2020 in Belo Horizonte and ending on the 25 January in Córrego do Feijão with a memorial service (see Figures 5.2–5.4). The march brought together 350 people from around

Brazil (and 17 people from around the world), to commemorate the lives lost and to demand that Vale be held accountable for its actions. On the previous day, 24 January, participants gathered for an international seminar organized by MAB titled: "Profit Does Not Value Life! One Year of Vale's Crime in Brumadinho." At this seminar, as the deluge of rain continued

Figure 5.2 "Brumadinho: 1 year of impunity," Belo Horizonte

Figure 5.3 25 January 2020 commemoration

outside, making hearing difficult at times, famed liberation theologian and supporter of MAB, Leonardo Boff,[10] spoke.

In his speech, Boff asserted that letting people starve is a sin, and that "everyone has the right to land; everyone has the right to education;

Figure 5.4 "We are all affected," 25 January 2020

everyone has the right to culture; we all need security and have the right to housing – these are common and basic rights."[11] This argument is akin to the discourse articulated at the housing rights training I had attended months earlier. Boff also noted that "we don't get this world by voting – we need participatory democracy"[12] and noted MAB and the MST as examples of this (see Schroering, 2020a).

At the end of this seminar on 24 January, all of the international participants were asked to come to the front and stand up. We were each given a rose, by members of MAB from the community, and words were spoken about the importance of international solidarity in bringing justice to the Brumadinho atingidos and atingidas, and in creating the world that we want. The moment was tender, emotional, powerful, and felt like a more horizontal power dynamic being led by the grassroots of the people impacted by this crime. It also spoke to how MAB sees its fight as an international one:

> More than 800,000 dams have already been built on the planet, their reservoirs have flooded some 1 million square meters (1% of the planet's surface). At the same time, the number of people displaced by dams in the past 20 years is estimated at more than 40 million people. Most of them are indigenous and tribal populations. In all cases, the same consequences happen over time: the degradation of forests, drastic reduction of fishing, emission of gases that contribute to the greenhouse effect and global warming, risks of earthquakes, climate change, death of streams of water. Not to mention, the indebtedness of the economies of poor nations like Brazil due to gigantic loans for the construction of these huge and very expensive works. For these reasons, MAB's commitment and fundamental value is to the fight for internationalism and the relationship with the different experiences of the fight against dams in the world, through international meetings of affected people, and in Latin America in particular through the Movement of People Affected by Dams (MAR). (MAB, n.d.)[13]

I turn now to further examine how MAB's fight is an international one.

The fight for sovereignty and the necessity of international solidarity

I arrived in Belo Horizonte on 19 January 2020. On my cab ride to where I would be staying, it started pouring with rain and traffic came to a standstill. The driver said he could go a different route (down a hill) but said that the roads can flood, and it can quickly become extremely dangerous, so it was better to stay put for a while. I said I trusted his judgement and that we should stay stopped. I watched out the car window over the course of thirty minutes the street below us (the possible detour) turned from a road into a river. The ferocity of the water, and the speed with which it rose, sweeping downstream anything in its path, made me reflect on Washington Boulevard in Pittsburgh, Pennsylvania, my home at the time and where I was also engaged in water justice work, where people have died from flooding. As

I watched the water rise, and objects, trash, then a part of a door off one of the buildings get taken rapidly downstream, I thought about how all of those homes were totally flooded with water (and dirt and sewage) on the first floor. The driver told me that people die during these floods. I thought about how climate change will only make these things worse. I thought about how the poor (usually, for sure there are exceptions) live in the low-lying areas that are prone to flooding, with no resources to escape. While rain and floods might be "natural" disasters, most of the time the impacts of flooding are not felt equally, and socio-economic and geopolitical structures shapes who is and who is not impacted.

I thought about the fragility of life. I was safe and privileged above in the car. As quickly as the rain had come, the deluge stopped, and traffic slowly resumed. But when we did start to get moving again, the trip was a little precarious, due to all of the flooding. Eventually (and just as it started pouring again), I made it safely to where all of us international invitees (and many from MAB) were staying (a training school run by one of the major unions). I share this experience because it showed me the power and ferocity of water in the region; and it gave me more context to understanding the area's struggles with flooding and water, and both the similarities and dissimilarities with struggles closer to home.

For the first time, Rob Robinson and I found ourselves in Brazil together at this International Seminar. During one of the final days there, we discussed how incredibly innovative, inspiring, practical, and revolutionary MAB's work is – yet no one knows about it in the United States. What might be learned if we did, we pondered to each other? I also spent a lot of time reflecting on all the linkages and solidarities forming and being built through this convergence for me, and for everyone participating, with both new and long-established collaborations between academics, researchers, and social movements. (Most of the other international guests were also affected by dam projects in their respective countries, which included Colombia, Venezuela, Guatemala, Spain, France, Italy, Basque Country, Turkey, Balkans, United States, Mexico, Canada, and Chile.)

Water justice and human rights scholar Farhana Sultana contends that it is critical to pay attention to how water justice is linked to other issues of justice, and she calls for the need to democratize water policy and governance so that multiple voices can be included and heard in the discussion (2018: 489). One helpful framework for thinking about this is the idea of translocality, introduced in earlier chapters.

As Banerjee defines it:

The prefix 'trans' refers to the ability of translocal engagements to 'both transcend territorial locality and change the local spaces from which they emerge'

(Banerjee, 2011: 331). Communities inhabiting these spaces interact with particular configurations of market, state and civil society actors and form relationships with local activists, community groups, domestic and international NGOs, and political parties. (2018: 811)

A part of translocality is also the existence of "translocal learning networks" (discussed previously in Chapter 3 and continued in Chapter 6), where citizens connect and learn from each other (Banerjee, 2011 and 2018) "across locales and across national contexts as they confront some of the same corporate entities that threaten local livelihoods" (Manski and Smith, 2019: 8). Translocality, in the context of water justice is also relevant, as one concern of the universalizing call of the "human right to water" is that locally specific practices could be lost if the universal call is effective (Bakker, 2007). What the translocal framework does is allow for local (and Indigenous and decolonializing) frameworks, while still linking activism to larger state and market processes, and creates networks where people are learning from and sharing with each other, even though every case is different (Banerjee, 2018; Schroering, 2021a). In their article, "Environmental Justice Movements in Globalising Networks: A Critical Discussion on Social Resistance Against Large Dams," Shah et al. discusses the translocal dimensions global dam struggles, writing:

> Their translocal mobilisation has made it possible to make the voices of affected people heard in the international spheres that support the defense of human rights and environmental protection, such as Friends of the Earth, Amnesty International, and MAB. Despite earlier disappointments with national and global 'outside support agents', these experiences have taught them how to fight their battles and who to actively involve and or not, rather than simply and passively 'being involved' by supralocal outsiders. (2019: 1019)

Breno Bringel and Flávia Braga Vieira (2016) also speak to this translocal dimension of peasant movements, examining Brazil's MST specifically and asserting that if:

> we look at the increasingly close relationship between the local and the global, perhaps one of the most interesting features of contemporary internationalism is the fact that some of the most internationalised movements are also those more territorialised. In other words, movements that are very localised, but not localist. (paragraph 2)

This argument resonates with my observations of MAB's struggle, which while very much a movement fighting for national sovereignty, also has – as one of its core pillars – the importance of international solidarity. Translocalism is important because it destabilizes existing categories and identities (including the concepts of statehood and citizenship)

Figure 5.5 March through Belo Horizonte

and reinforces similarities in experiences through which solidarity can be built. MAB, and the international convergence to commemorate the one-year anniversary of Brumadinho, is an example of a translocal learning network.

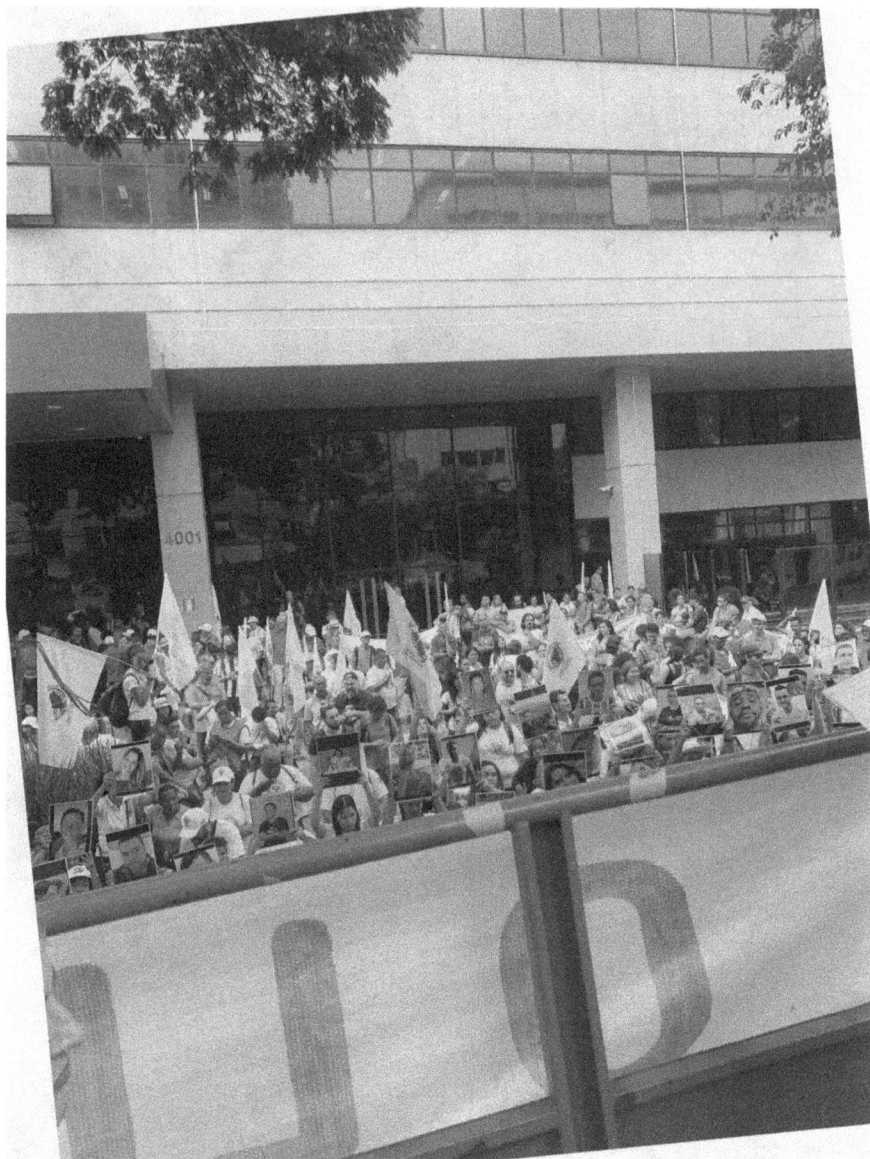

Figure 5.6 Belo Horizonte, people hold up photos of loved ones lost in Vale crime

On 20 January 2020, more than 350 people marched through a mid-dle/upper-middle-class neighborhood of Belo Horizonte chanting: "It was not an accident, Vale killed the river, killed the fish, killed the people" and "Vale destroys, the people build."[14] See Figures 5.5 and 5.6. I reflect that participating in this international seminar (which also included days of meetings between the international partners planning and strategizing for how to build the movement, which I was included in) marked a shift in my relationship with MAB and my role in international solidarity both as someone fighting for water justice and as a researcher. I will share two key examples of what this has meant for my work.

The first relates to information production, exchange, and translation. I had a conversation with Rob Robinson and Kelvim (a member of MAB's communications team) who asked if I would be able to occasionally do some translating work for MAB because the MAB leaders who do translation work are always overextended. I said that yes, I would be honored to do that and, since that conversation, I have done this in various formal and informal ways. A few months later, during a US Solidarity for MAB video call, I was also asked by Kelvim and three other MAB militantes if I could write a short piece (in Portuguese and in English) about the dam collapse that happened in March 2020 in Michigan. They emphasized the point that knowledge exchange needed to go both ways: not just me translating and sharing work of MAB to a US or English-speaking audience, but to share what was happening in the US with MAB. And so, out of this exchange I wrote my first Portuguese language short article (Schroering, 2020b). In other words, my praxis shifted from 2018 when first asked by a MAB militant (see Chapter 4) if I would write in Portuguese – and answering I hoped to, but first I would have to write the PhD dissertation – to this moment in 2020 when I did so (before completing my dissertation).

The second example of how my praxis and my methodological approach has shifted is illustrated in the following scenario. After my time in Brumadinho, I returned to São Paulo for a few days before heading to Rio for the second part of the Course on Energy. Dani (of MAB who also works to coordinate the course) asked me if I could come to the Secretariat (headquarters) to have a conversation with her. When I arrived for our meeting, she noted that I had been invited six months earlier to participate in the course as an observer, but that now I was here again, and attending the second part, did I intend/was I able, she asked, to commit to all four parts? Dani asked me about what I wanted to get out of the course. She said that they had invited me to participate in the first part as an observer but that, if I planned on continuing with all four steps, they would like me to officially matriculate and to transform my role from one of "observer" to "participant" who would produce a piece of work about the water privatization landscape in the United States.[15]

I said that capacity wise I could not write a completely different paper, but that of course the content from the course would be a part of my dissertation, and I could revise (and translate into Portuguese) a chapter of my dissertation to fit with the scope of the course. We talked about how I could use a part of my dissertation – the part that overviewed the water situation in the United States – as my paper, and I agreed. I shared that I had assumed MAB would not want me to "formally" participate in the course and she replied "No, the opposite," explaining that the knowledge I could share from my perspective about the United States would be valuable. This exchange also reminds me of a conversation I had in June 2019 with Bira, a MAB militant, who said to me: "We are interested to hear and read what you have to say about MAB; and your analysis and perspective of our work."

These exchanges (and many others) served as critical moments for me, and helped me in a very tangible way to connect my militancy and my scholarship. I do not know of an equivalent course that exists anywhere else, and certainly not in the United States. It has helped affirm for me that neutrality is also a political choice, and one that I am not interested in making. It relates back to the quote I shared earlier from Fernandes (1986) regarding the impossibility of being a "neutral" sociologist; you are committed to the exploiters or the exploited.

As I navigated the challenges and tensions of finishing my PhD, the professors who participated in and taught classes for the course set the examples that militancy can be part of your work and gave me the energy to continue doing my own work. The course also deepened my understanding of the historical and current realities of the political-economic system – capitalism – in which we live. In June 2019, during my second research trip, while attending an overnight training led by MAB before the first part of the Course on Energy, various people suggested that I should participate more and ask questions in the trainings. My tendency had been to stay quiet, unless I was called on, or during more informal conversations outside of the official training. They told me that they wanted to know what I was thinking and wanted me to share experiences/differences/similarities with things in my country. This would make it more of an exchange of knowledge. These interactions also informed my understanding of my own role and place, and the impossibility of separating my scholarship from my activism. Following Freire – whose pedagogy and example grounds much of MAB's approach to education – "neutral" education does not exist (Freire, 2018 [1968], 1985). For me, this also means that neutral theory, methods, and knowledge production also do not exist.

My participation in the first part of MAB's Course on Energy as an invited "observer" also highlighted these challenges, contradictions, and possibilities for anti-imperial, anti-colonial, militant co-research. Held between 15 and 26 July 2019, this first etapa[16] of the course had modules on each of the following areas: capitalism, nature, and scarcity; the State and classes in modern society; energy and industrialization in the modern world; methodology of scientific work; basic principles of political economy; and then a detailed process of evaluation to close out the course.

On the first day, the participants who had already arrived (around 40 of the original 70) engaged in an opening exercise where we introduced ourselves and responded in a word or short phrase what the term "sovereignty" meant to each of us. Responses included: "distribution of wealth," "autonomy," "respect for indigenous people and nature," "people power," "liberty," and "education." I said: "a world without imperialism." This exercise and opening each day with mística (which different people planned each day) kept the deep dive into history and theory that the course required we all take, grounded in praxis and the "so what" of the course.

Flávia Braga Vieira, a sociology professor at the Federal Rural University of Rio de Janeiro who helps to organize the course, has been engaged with MAB for 20 years. On the first day she noted that the point of the course is to create a space to collectively construct a popular movement: to help popular movements and specifically MAB. This was the fifth term of the course (each term spans two years). It began as a conversation in 2008 around the need for a course for militant formation. Flávia noted the challenges of designing a course meant both for people who have gone to college and those who have not. She also noted the shifting political and social environment, and how now, under the government of Bolsonaro, it was a much less comfortable political environment for the course than even three years earlier (when the fourth term of the course began) due to increased social movement repression. One of the pivotal coordinators of the Course and MAB militant discussed how the object of this course is to take technical information and use it to fight for sovereignty. On this first day the point was made that the intention of the course is to be a part of constructing new possibilities and to create a better world for the working class and for all, and how this is a collective process we are constructing, made easier when we each do our part. Revolution is a process.

Participating in the course were people from all regions of Brazil, plus Cuba, Venezuela, Colombia, and two other people (not academics) from the United States. Previous terms of the course have included people from other Latin American countries in addition to those listed here, and this is an intentional structure of the course: in addition to creating a space for reciprocal knowledge production, it is intended to be a place to "internationalize the struggle" and build international solidarity. During the second day of the course, the lecturing professor detailed histories of colonialism and imperialism and brought the conversation to the present day with Bolsonaro as president. He noted that Bolsonaro was not the central problem – he's a big one, but the central problem is the larger system. Bolsonaro was a political representation of this political program (which also relates to what Boff said six months later – noted earlier in this chapter – about how voting alone will not solve the crises of our time). After discussing Brazilian history and colonialism/imperialism, the professor noted how the impeachment of Dilma Rousseff in 2016, succeeded by the right leaning Michel Temer, and then ultimately the election of Jair Bolsonaro in 2018, constituted an institutional (versus military) coup. He compared it to a dictatorship and discussed the appropriation of resources through privatization. He also discussed the current turn (in Brazil and elsewhere) toward fascism and argued that it is a reflection of the fact that a lot of people are profoundly frustrated by the neoliberal system (Fieldnotes, 16 July 2019).

Six months later, we reconvened for the second step of the course from 4 to 15 February 2020. This part had sections on the history of energy in Brazil; imperialism and other theories about world capitalism; the state and revolutions; and history of environmental issues and its institutional apparatus. For me, this second part of the course was quite different than the first portion of the course, and many individual conversations, as well as the collective discourse, confirmed that others shared my impression. The petroleum workers with Petrobras[17] were on a strike (the course had petroleum workers participating in it who could not attend due to the strike), the city of Rio was in a water crisis, and the Bolsonaro administration had now had six more months of cracking down on social movements, which made everyone slightly less hopeful. In a material and lived daily reality, the water situation provided significant challenges: the previously potable drinking water was no longer safe (despite the city insisting it was), as many learned after getting sick from drinking it, and simply obtaining a large enough quantity of bottled water to supply such a large number of people (during the hot Rio summer) was a challenge that took a few days to resolve, compounded by the city-wide bottled water shortage caused by the water crisis (Phillips, 2020).[18]

Instead of ten plus hour days in lectures (like during the first part), the structure of the course was rearranged to include experiential learning and allow participation in the Petrobras workers' strike. For several days during the course, we spent some or all of the day down at the strike, sometimes having our lectures under one of the tents (see Figure 5.7). During one of these, the professor stated that petroleum is a central commodity in our capitalist economy; he also noted that we have food and bottled water in the strike camp but cannot drink the water back at the university gym where we were housed. He remarked how big business dominates Brazilian agriculture, and that this – the water and food crisis – is also related to petroleum, who controls it, and the strike. The wealth concentration and control are

Figure 5.7 Photos from the Front of Petrobras, Rio de Janeiro, during strike

not sustainable, he contended, and Brazil is still on the periphery of capitalism, with borders created for imperialism.

On the one side, there are trillions and trillions of dollars controlled by the core; and on the other is the periphery, controlled by the force of workers and the possibility of emancipation. He noted that this force was yet small, and so part of the task of the striking workers and those there in support of them was to educate the workers inside the Petrobras building. "It is important to not just support but build a movement," he said. His lecture was followed by striking workers who spoke of the importance of consolidating worker power and for the bosses inside to see everyone out here. At the end, Dani (with MAB) also made a point to draw attention to the three people present from the United States and that while the center of imperialism (an international form of capitalism) is the United States, not everyone from there agrees with those policies, and that the presence of those from the center of the empire is also critical to this international fight.

In reflecting about these experiences, I found myself thinking of all the enormous challenges faced by MAB and other popular movements, and the long road ahead between the present reality and the envisioned one: a world where life is placed ahead of profits, and where the planet's resources are not exploited for the benefit of a few. Water and energy are rights, as MAB argues, and I agree. But what does that mean? Farhana Sultana and Alex Loftus (2012: 10) discuss how the language of rights can be coopting:

> We are all for the right to water – from the vendor selling from his tanker to the thirsty activist seeking radical change. Lacking specificity, the right to water loses its conceptual weight: it becomes a floating signifier devoid of any political content. Like 'sustainable development' and many other fuzzy concepts that have gone before, the right to water is emptied of any real meaning. If all concur it is a good thing it loses its ability to disrupt contemporary water governance which has persistently reproduced inequities.

One of MAB's refrains is that "Water is not a commodity!" which I think works well to provide a concrete statement of what is meant by water as a right in the context of popular social movements using that phrase: it means it is not a commodity. This clarification is important because, without it, those who seek to trade water on Wall Street (which began in December 2020) (Yale Environment, 2020) can argue that by opening the market up to water, the "right" to water can be realized. MAB's struggle is articulated clearly as an anti-capitalist one. But the struggle spans beyond one of class. As Sultana and Loftus (2012: 9) note, class intersects with gender (and race, caste, dis/ability, etc.) and "water crises can exacerbate socially constructed differences and power relations." They continue by noting how scholarship has "argued that multiple, situated, and place-based struggles thus can link and contribute to transnational movements (Harcourt and Escobar, 2005; cf. Mohanty, 2003), where difference and diversity are constitutive of the broader calls of equality in the right to water" (Sultana and Loftus, 2012: 9).

This discussion relates to a conversation I had with a young woman and MAB militant in June 2019. I asked her how she got involved in the movement, and she told me that MAB has organized her community, where most people have been adversely affected by dam projects. I commented on how MAB appeared very "young" (in terms of age of participants) and asked for her thoughts on this. She said that she thinks MAB's focus on incorporating and making an opening for LGBTQ+ people and for women has contributed to its youth. She said that the MST and other movements are also focused on this, but that from her perspective they also have more ingrained/internalized prejudice. In her opinion, MAB has less. There is space for women and LGBTQ+ people in leadership, so it draws in more young people who want that. Later, I reflected in my fieldnotes the following:

> MAB is articulating a very anti-capitalist vision of a new world ... but what MAB wants is something new. Not just communism – though I think pretty much everyone identifies as a communist or socialist, if forced to put themselves into a typology – but the idea of intersectionality is also at the core. Patriarchy, heteronormativity, racism ... those have got to be dismantled. (Fieldnotes, 26 June 2019)

This relates to a point made during one of the lectures of the second part of the Course on Energy: Racism, patriarchy, and machismo all existed before capitalism but gained strength and serve as pillars to support the system of capitalism (Fieldnotes, 9 February 2020). MAB is attuned to the ways in which hegemony shapes social relations, and a part of its counter-hegemonic work to dismantle oppressive structures is to re-imagine and construct new forms of relationships – which relates to the discussion in Chapter 4 on how LVC and many of its member movements, including MAB, have changed their internal structure to focus on gender parity, and focus on combating patriarchy, heterosexism, and racism within.

Constructing an anti-systemic struggle

During my second trip to Brazil, I was given a pamphlet produced by MAB entitled, "Our fight is for life, Enough of Impunity!"[19] which detailed the struggles of four women important to MAB's struggle: Dilma,[20] Nicinha, Berta, and Marielle. Dilma and Nichina were two women atingidas who were murdered in their fights against dam projects in their communities. Berta was a Honduran environmentalist who also engaged in dam struggles and was murdered. Marielle Franco, a Black, bisexual, socialist city-councilwoman (with Brazil's Socialism and Liberty Party) in Rio was killed in March 2018 (BBC News, 2020). Marielle has been a recent galvanizing figure in Brazil. I share this because I think that it shows how MAB's struggle is one that spans beyond its own fight, and beyond the fight against water privatization. MAB's struggle is part of a larger journey. As the pamphlet states, "Dilma, Nicinha, Berta, and Marielle were fundamental in the construction of popular organizations and were faithful workers for the harvest and deserve our recognition"[21] (MAB, 2019a: 6). In a world that too often ignores the stories, achievements, and struggles of women, and specifically women from the Global South, Black women, and queer women, this statement is important.

I was invited to attend a women's seminar organized by MAB in Brasilia on 25 June 2019 called "In defense of life, Affected Women in the fight for rights."[22] Approximately 95 per cent of the seminar participants were women, mostly from MAB but also some other popular social movements. The day commenced with a statement that it was not just a fight for the working class in Brazil but an international fight, a fight against capitalism, a fight against a system created 300 years ago, and was structured for men. During introductions, I experienced another formative moment in my experience with my role as researcher and outsider, attempting to conduct anti-colonial research. As is customary in MAB gatherings, the day started with everyone going around and introducing themselves. When it was my turn, I said I was from the US, a doctoral student in sociology studying transnational right to water movements. My statement was met with concerned looks and I sat, feeling slightly uncomfortable, as the introductions wrapped up. After all of the 70+ people had introduced themselves, one of the coordinating committee members I knew said to the room: "We are all here ... not just from Brazil but have a comrade from the US and you don't need to worry. You can trust her. She's a comrade." Then people who knew me – some of whom I had not seen since the year before – started laughing and vigorously waving at me from around the room. This seemed to ease the concern and the day carried on.

The tightly packed day consisted of back-to-back speakers and panels, some of which focused on the details of how women and children are disproportionately impacted by mega hydro-dam projects. One speaker noted that women are more affected by crisis, because men traditionally do not do the labor of caring, women's rights are criminalized, and the media is silent about the impacts of mega dam projects. All of the speakers emphasized how capitalism is interconnected with the above-named problems.

As one panelist asserted: "A capitalist society has rules – non-negotiable rules" that are about limitless accumulation of wealth and human bodies serve as large repositories of labor. The system, we were instructed, cannot be transformed within the law because the justice system is inherently built to be conservative and to maintain the status quo, including structures of gender, race, and class. She argued that the justice system is not thinking about "interseccionalidades" (intersectionalities), inequality, and systemic injustice. The system criminalizes Black people, poor people, and sex workers; and machismo continues to cause femicide. As one speaker put it, it is a "capitalist, patriarchal, racist, heterosexist system"[23] and the anti-capitalist fight is more than just a socialist/communist society: "it is about designing a new world, not about rigid visions"[24] (Fieldnotes, 25 June 2019).

After the day-long seminar, MAB organized an interfaith candlelight service and action to remember the victims of Brumadinho and others who have died in the struggle for a more just world (see Figure 5.8). This action used mística, which served as powerful, embodied art and theatre that tells

Figure 5.8 Brasilia MAB Action

a real story and asks participants to put themselves into a state of saying "todos somos atingidas." We are all Dilma, Nicinha, Berta, Marielle. We recited: "Nicinha, presente, presente, presente; Dilma, presente, presente, presente; Berta, presente, presente, presente; Marielle, presente, presente, presente!" (Fieldnotes, 25 June 2019). To lift up these women, and especially Marielle, relates to the earlier story I shared about MAB's commitment to fighting sexism and "lgbtfobia." Brazil struggles with fighting against deeply ingrained patriarchy, homophobia, and transphobia; it is the deadliest country in the world for trans people (Lopez, 2020).

In 2018, after attending a house meeting of residents organizing for housing rights in Belém, I observed that the host, Fatima, also had a sign in her house for Marielle. She shared during the meeting that getting other neighbors organized is challenging and she talked about the growth of

Pentecostal churches (one or more on every block). I later asked Robert, the MAB leader (introduced in the previous chapter) who had brought me to the gathering, about this. He said that there are two major organizing forces in the basin neighborhoods: Pentecostals and drug dealers. It presents a challenge for MAB to organize, he shared. One of the struggles he noted, is that MAB talks about empowering women and the LGBTQ+ community – and the Pentecostals here are very conservative and promote "family values" (Fieldnotes, 14 July 2018). While I lack space to go into detail here, I wish to note this point: just like in the United States, or anywhere else, it is important not to make broad stroke generalizations. There are Pentecostal pastors, churches, and individuals actively involved in MAB. Further, while many Pentecostals in Brazil are quite conservative, there are also factions that identify strongly as environmentalists, and also women and LGBTQ+ led Pentecostal churches. The statement made to me, however, also relates to the history of liberation theology and base communities (noted in last chapter) rooted in Catholicism that historically has played a significant role in Brazil's popular movements, and how those demographics are shifting.

In the vein of organizing base communities, what I observe is that MAB meets people where they are, and from there expands the conversation about creating a world where there might be dignity and rights for all. For example, I attended a two-day long community training entitled "Popular Education, Rights, and Social Participation: Embroidering the Health of Women Affected by Dams" in a rural community in the state of Rio which is threatened by a new mega dam project (see Figure 5.9).

Approximately twenty women from the community (in addition to children and MAB members) attended and I observed that the training was basically sex education; it was grounded in the community's health needs as part of a multi-series course. The women participating in it were embroidering arpilleras (tapestries) as part of the larger MAB project on "Mulheres bordando a resistência" (women embroidering resistance), which I discuss in the previous chapter (Fieldnotes, 3 July 2019).[25] As during other trainings to which MAB invited me, I participated in activities and discussions. While this training was not directly related to water at all (and a few people noted this, somewhat apologetically, to me), it served as an important part of my participation with MAB. First, it helped me better understand how MAB's work is one of base building: of organizing a community around resistance to a proposed dam project by beginning with building relationships. Second, it was useful in my own navigation of my role and place.

As an example, during the second day, one of the MAB leaders pulled me aside and said that she hoped I would speak more; that people were curious to hear my perspectives, and that this would especially be true in the

Figure 5.9 Arpilleras

coming weeks when I participated in the Course on Energy. Navigating how much to say, and when to say it, was a challenge, especially because I was understanding my role in terms of a) an outsider from the United States, and b) a researcher socialized to compartmentalize my professional from my personal identities. However, day by day, interaction by interaction, I became more comfortable and adept at navigating this. It relates back to how I saw myself similarly to how Marina Sitrin described herself as more a movement actor from another space, rather than just an academic. It was appropriate, I think, for me to remain quieter and to take my lead for how to engage based on invitation. A full year had passed since I was first in this exact space, with many of the same people, playing with babies who were now toddlers.

I noticed a shift in how people interacted with me: I had come back, not just visited once and left. There was a process of knowledge exchange: me answering questions about what the landscape of energy and water production looked like in the United States, how social movements organized, why I was interested in water, why I was in Brazil, and the dominance of non-profits (versus social movements) in the United States. Sometimes these interactions occurred at the larger group level, but more often they happened during conversations with a few people over meals or in the evenings. On the last day, as the discussion veered more into water and energy privatization and dams, one of the MAB participants, Amanda[26] – with whom I had spent many hours in long car rides, and who had helped arrange for my Rio lodging at Raizes do Brasil – run by the partner social movement MPA, said: "This is a global fight, and Caitlin will bring this [fight and information] back to the United States ... she is also staying here in Brazil longer to participate in MAB's Course on Energy" (Fieldnotes, 4 July 2019).

The importance of popular education

Larissa Souza Pinheiro (2016: 94) writes about (drawing on Freire) MAB's focus on popular education in the following:

> Popular education is a model of education that valorizes the history, culture, and customs of a people. It aims to train its students beyond a logic of the market accumulating for a critical reading of their social, political and economic realities in order to accumulate for the construction of a more just and egalitarian society.[27]

Paulo Freire is an important figure in the world, in Brazil, and in MAB for liberatory educational models. A popular quote of his (seen on t-shirts and elsewhere) asserts, "When education is not liberatory, the dream of the oppressed is to be the oppressor." In the United States, a lot of us who attempt to do activist-based research spend time discussing how we make our work "accessible." This means various things, including the literal ability to obtain a published piece of work (which is why open-access online publishing is so critical). But usually imbedded in the idea of "accessibility," is also an understanding that the work be not too "academic": that is more simply written, more empirically grounded, and less theoretically based. There are strong arguments for why this should be done. My work with MAB, however, has also made me ponder in what ways this approach is perhaps itself elitist. What happens if we flip the script to say that theory should be collectively understood, created, and utilized instead of eliminated? Here I think is where the powerful combination of Marxist thought, the work of Paulo Freire, the history of liberation theology, and the active praxis of Brazil's popular movements (and specifically MAB) is instructive.

It relates to Marina Sitrin's work and observations on revolutionary social movements in Argentina. Sitrin discusses the idea of "horizontalidad" and how to create new forms of power not from the state, but by organizing together. She writes: "It is not about asking for power, it is about creating a different power. It is not about asking liberal democracy to be democratic, but rather about creating real democracy" (Sitrin, 2012: xiv). One of Sitrin's goals is to rethink "the meaning of revolution" (2012: 7). Sitrin also writes, referring to her experiences with revolutionary movements in Argentina: "In all of my years of militancy I have never experienced such high-level theoretical discussions, all based in the day-to-day experiences of social movements" (2012: 12). This quote applies to my observations of MAB – although I would add that while lived experiences guide everything, people also talk about and read theory. This relates to my discussion in the previous chapter of how popular social movements in Brazil, such as MAB, produce and publish books. At the MAB headquarters in São Paulo, there is a library of books and theses – many of which have been written by leaders of MAB who completed a graduate degree (many MAB militantes conduct research, including through the Course on Energy, as a way to increase education and produce knowledge for the movement).[28] On 2023's World Water Day (23 March), Dalila Calisto, a coordinator of MAB, launched her book *Mercantilização da água: análise da privatização do saneamento de Teresina (PI).*[29] As Rob Robinson said to me, "There is nothing like it [MAB] … I try to explain to people here and then say, you just have to go see it for yourself" (Fieldnotes, August 2019).

In a pamphlet produced after the disaster of Brumadinho, titled: "O Lucro Não Vale a Vida: Análise do MAB Sobre O Crime da Vale em Brumadinho/MG,"[30] there is a well-researched and clearly articulated summation and analysis of what happened. This work was written by the coordinating committee of MAB and is thoroughly cited (MAB, 2019b). As another example, a pamphlet detailing the movement's struggle discusses how, through a process of drawing on lived histories and experiences as well as researching policy recommendations, MAB "wrote a proposal for a National Policy of Rights for those Affected by Dams (PNAB)" so that rights might be formally acknowledged and new violations from dam projects stopped. The pamphlet asserts: "In 2014, we had our first victory of this new phase of struggles, with the promulgation of Decree number 51.595/2014 of the state of Rio Grande do Sul, which creates the state policy of the Affected in this state, but the struggle for the national policy continues" (Scalabrin and Fernandes Maso, 2015: 6). MAB's model of popular education, then, is also focused on political formation, and policy.

It is also aimed at children and youth. I attended a day-long course on popular education and environmental health directed at high school age participants (15–19 year olds). This was the third course in a four-part (each held on a Saturday) long series held in a rural area in the state of Rio. This particular day detailed the history of resistance for the land in the region. I was invited (and expected) to participate in and was placed in a small group to create our own *mística* or act out one of the stories of resistance about which we had just learned (Fieldnotes, 13 July 2019). MAB organizes courses such as these in the various communities where they are doing organizing work.

Childhood education is an important focus of MAB's work. At all meetings, trainings, and other gatherings there is childcare available, with trained early childhood educators. It's not simply day care: children are enriched with various educational, cultural, and artistic activities. This emphasis translates into knowledge production. As one example, MAB Rio produced an illustrated children's book, *Contando Histórias da Terra e das Águas* (Telling Histories of the Land and the Waters) in collaboration with extension project Memórias das Lutas pela Terra in the State of Rio de Janeiro (this is the same extension program discussed in Chapter 4). The book chronicles the lives of four children – Margarida, Hiroki, Vitória, and Francisco – who, in a fun and animated manner, tell the history of the municipality of Cachoeiras de Macacu, including its historical struggles for land and water (Ribeiro et al., 2020).

This is another example of the value that MAB places on theory, research, and knowledge, and the idea that knowledge ought to be accessible to all – theory and scientific reports are important but are not just to be consumed and distilled within the ivory tower; they are not the only forms of learning and knowledge production. Popular education includes children, youth, adults, and elders,[31] and brings together lived experiences with formalized partnerships with professors and universities for various educational programs and activities, all coalesced around the idea that this serves as a critical component of building a new society, and of organized resistance.

MAB's Course on Energy, described in more detail in the previous section, is a part of this larger vision. For each of the four parts of the course (spanning over two years), everyone is in a base community of six to nine people. As a group, you work together on collective homework and writing projects (often until 12/1 a.m.); have rotating assignments for cleaning the shared sleeping, eating, and learning spaces; preparing coffee, breakfast, and snacks; and organizing the daily *mística* and other tasks. These groups rotate for each part of the course, so that everyone is in four different small groups during the duration of the two-year term.

It is intended to build relationships and community, as well as create discipline, order, and structure.[32] Everyone spends seven to ten hours a day in an academic learning environment, and then spends the additional waking hours learning together through communal living and studying. There is bonding and learning that happens when you sleep in a tent in a gymnasium for 10 plus nights; there is solidarity built in taking freezing cold showers; and there is solidarity in being the group assigned to make breakfast at 6 a.m. after only a few hours of sleep. There is hope in realizing that despite the very disparate backgrounds and countries we come from, everyone believes that together a different world can be created and is being created in the present.[150]

During one of the virtual meetings of the Course on Energy[33] in August 2020, one of the members of the MAB coordinating committee introduced the session by noting that "it's good to see everyone, especially the international people: this is an international fight we have."[34] He noted the Black Lives Matter movement in the United States, the global Covid-19 pandemic, and said that "we are in a rich historical moment right now ... it's very hard, but we have never seen a moment like this ... and this could open opportunities, windows ... popular education is very important now. We are working to construct a more just, fraternal society. We have to strengthen our strategies right now."[35] He went on to argue that a clear direction is needed to do this, a clear plan to construct and organize the strategy. Questions of race and gender, how to work with unions, leftist movements – all of this is important: "Political formation has three parts: the fight, the organization, and the formation/training."[36] He also noted how organizing protects us – protects each other. Without organizing, "you aren't going to transform anything"[37] he said, asserting that "popular education is an act of love."[38] He talked about how we are at the end of a world system cycle and in a moment of transformation, and that the objective of the fight is to give power to the workers: "Nothing is predetermined. Everything can be transformed"[39] (Fieldnotes, 29 August 2020).

This point of transformation was also noted by an integrante of Levante Juventude,[40] Luisa,[41] during an online event on 15 September 2020 titled "MAB AO VIVO | A necessária participação popular na luta pela água."[42] She talked about how there is a huge challenge in front of us, and that the inequality, lack of water, and lack of proper sewage treatment, is racist. The fight is one for dignity. When we care for each other, she said, "we transform our reality."[43] Silas, a MAB militant speaking on this panel (and involved in writing the aforementioned children's book) noted the need to do more popular education, including around environmental concerns, "Because the powers that be will keep fighting to privatize ... and the people will keep fighting because water is a right, sanitation is a right!"[44,45]

Conclusion

"The people united will never be defeated!"[46] MAB has much to teach regarding how to construct a fight against the commodification of water in terms of the need to build people power, and the role of popular education and knowledge production in this process. There is a deep understanding of the importance of liberatory education and consciousness-raising – it is counter-hegemonic work that is critical to creating the conditions for change. In this sense, MAB's focus is as much about process as outcomes – which is also an example of counter-hegemonic logics, including the history of Diálogo de Saberes, discussed in the previous chapter.

What then are the implications of co-research and collaborative knowledge production? There is no universal answer to this. Dynamics of power and privilege are always present. The question is not how I erase them (I cannot) or make completely egalitarian "co-research." A more instructive question, I think, is how might learning be reciprocal and how do I conduct myself in a way that is serving to be a part of a path to collective liberation, rather than extractive? And this is where, for me, I understand my actions as a process of communication, exchange, and learning. There is also a place to leverage my privilege, when invited and called upon to do so. For example, I have written (alone and co-authored) op-eds about MAB's struggle and the global fight against commodifying water, given invited talks, done some translation work, and have other popular writing projects (individual and with MAB) in the process. In addition to examples of knowledge exchange discussed in the chapter, since the Covid-19 pandemic (and with it, so many changes, including the Course on Energy moving to a virtual format for the third portion), there have been opportunities to continue my research and to continue the process of learning and knowledge exchange.

In February 2020, I had a conversation with a water and sanitation union leader in São Paulo, Anderson, who I had previously interviewed. While talking about the increasingly dire state of the world and trend toward fascism, I reflected on social movements and spaces of alter-globalization that I saw gaining strength. He said to me: "The revolution will start in São Paulo." In this same conversation, another union worker asked about my research, and my intent behind it. He said that to him, as a worker, my research sounds interesting and really important – and, too often, academic research doesn't seem to have any real-life applications. I have reflected a lot about this statement. My decision to enter into academia and my choice of research topic has always been grounded in my own lived experiences and hope that my research could have real-life applications.

When I began thinking more actively about anti-colonial research and co-research methodologies, I had an idea that "co-research" meant co-writing and publishing. And that is a form that it takes, but it might not always be that way – because co-writing does require labor and that labor might not be a good use of co-conspirators' time (and so could also turn into an extractive process). This is not a perfect, hierarchy-less, plotted out plan of what to do, but rather a process, a navigation, built on shared solidarity and trust. But it is also built on the idea that my role as a researcher cannot be separated from my politics. As Sitrin said of her own work, and which resonates profoundly for my own experience, her relationship to her research was "one of militancy and that of another movement actor from another place, not as an academic doing fieldwork or research on an 'other' " (2012: xv).

In July 2022 – a year and a half after we should have gathered for the fourth and final part of the Course – participants gathered in a municipality on the outskirts of the city of Rio for the final portion of the course and graduation.[47] The pandemic presented enormous challenges and as we endured the third stage online – not everyone was able to complete it and/ or attend the last stage in person. Still, the last stage in July 2022 provided the chance to be face-to-face with each other, to hug, to eat our meals together, and to stay up until dawn some days talking. During these more informal times, I also learned as much – or more – as I did in the classroom. It also strengthened my hope that, despite all that is unjust in this world, we can build a new path. Our studies and our research must transform us. To think otherwise is to hide behind the idea that the researcher is a neutral entity. As Paulo Freire said, and people repeated at various moments during the course: "Education does not transform the World. Education changes People. People change the world."[48] And people don't change as individuals, but as individuals as part of the collective. One of the beautiful things that I not only learned but felt in my whole being was the deep culture of care that MAB practices. Receiving that care, and also giving it and sharing it, is something that I treasure in my heart. The fact that we chose to name our term after Marielle Franco is also poignant. We are among the many seeds that continue the work. At our graduation at UFRJ,[49] one of the speakers remarked that the room we sat in was the room where Marielle launched her political campaign. That was an incredibly moving moment. The banner we made hung in the room above the table with the lecturers said: "The time has arrived to listen to the Marias, Mahins, Marielles, Malês."[50]

As MAB describes itself on its website, it is a national, autonomous movement based on collective participation regardless of skin color, gender, sexual orientation, religion, political party, or education level. MAB organizes people affected by dams (before, during, and after the construction of them). Their "struggle is nourished by the deep feeling of love for the people and love of life." In my work with MAB, I observe four main things: first, how MAB uses the idea of human rights in its organizing, and how the human right to water is connected to a broader struggle for rights. This concept of "rights" is not a top-down legalistic one, but rather it refers to the idea of a collective right that articulates the conception that water is not a commodity but an essential source for the production and reproduction of human and non-human life. The "right to water" is a struggle against water accumulation for profit. Second, the importance of both sovereignty and international solidarity in MAB's work. Third, how MAB's anti-systemic fight is focused on economic structures, and also dismantling other oppressive systems, such as patriarchy and racism. Fourth, the role of popular education in MAB's struggle, and its importance in political formation and organizing. Just as water is not a commodity, knowledge and knowledge production are not commodities.

Through my participant observation, interviews, and autoethnographic reflection, this chapter looked at how social identities, understandings of interests, and inter-connections that enable direct communication across local spheres are key to producing transnational struggle for the right to water, that is also interconnected with a broader struggle to redefine and reshape what globalization looks like and to create a world that honors people's rights and dignity. This chapter provided a "backstage" look at how some of these narratives and struggles are being produced. Ultimately, I see this as part of a larger translocal struggle for the right to water, and I turn to this discussion now.

Notes

1 See Appendix A for more details.
2 A pseudonym.
3 todos os outros direitos delas já foram violados … o direito ao saneamento básico e o direito a água, né? O direito à dignidade humana mesmo dessas pessoas, entendeu? Geralmente, elas moram em áreas periféricas, geralmente elas sofrem com a questão de segurança, elas sofrem e são criminalizados, são marginalizados. Então quando você tem o direito à moradia [tem] todos os outros direitos também. Eles vêm juntos, então você acaba lutando muito por tudo nessas comunidades.
4 A história do MAB foi formada a partir da negação de uma série de direitos às populações atingidas – que já partem de uma condição mais humilde, campesina, de dificuldade de acesso ao sistema de justiça. Conforme o relatório do Conselho Nacional de Direitos Humanos, na construção e operação de barragens no Brasil, pelo menos, 16 direitos são sistematicamente violados.
5 The book is called *Dimensões do Intervir em Favelas: Desafios e Perspectivas* (2019) and a PDF is available online: www.causp.gov.br/wp-content/uploads/2016/03/Dimens%C3%B5es-do-intervir-em-Favelas-novo.pdf

6 Não posso respirar.
7 Não posso respirar, não posso mais nadar/ A terra tá morendo ...
8 This movement is also a part of CMP (Central de Movimentos Populares, Brasil), a broader alliance of popular social movements. Post-Bolsonaro's election there were also more alliances being made between unions, social movements, and, at times, political parties of the Left, etc.
9 Commemoration does not fully capture this; it was to mourn and honor lives lost, and to carry on the struggle and fight in their memory.
10 Referenced in Chapter 1.
11 todo mundo tem direito a terra ... todo mundo tem direito a educação ... todo mundo tem direito a cultura ... todos somos nos precisamos segurança, temos direito a habitação – são direitos comuns e basicos.
12 Which is not to say he was saying to eschew voting. I had a couple minutes to chat with him before his talk and expressed my gratitude in meeting him. His parting words to me: he told me not to vote for Trump and to vote for Bernie.
13 Mais de 800.000 represas já foram construídas no planeta, seus reservatórios inundaram algo em torno de 1 milhão de metros quadrados (1% da superfície do planeta). Ao mesmo tempo o número de deslocados por barragens nos últimos 20 anos é estimado em mais de 40 milhões de pessoas. Boa parte são populações indígenas e tribais. Em todos os casos as mesmas consequências acontecem ao longo do tempo: a degradação de florestas, redução drástica da pesca, emissão de gases que contribuem para o efeito estufa e o aquecimento global, riscos de tremores de terra, mudanças climáticas, morte dos cursos d'água. Sem falar, no endividamento das economias de nações pobres como o Brasil em função de empréstimos gigantescos para a construção destas obras enormes e caríssimas. Por estes motivos o MAB tem como compromisso e valor fundamental da luta o internacionalismo e a relação com as diferentes experiências de luta contra as barragens no mundo, através dos encontros internacionais de atingidos, e na América Latina em especial através do Movimiento de Afectados por Represas (MAR) (MAB, n.d.).
14 "Não foi accidente a Vale mata rio, mata peixe, mata gente" and "A vale destrói, o Povo constrói."
15 The structure of the course itself is a rigorous academic experience that culminates in a 40-to-50-page thesis-like research project.
16 Literally "step" and the best translation for this context is probably "course module."
17 The state-owned petroleum company that Bolsonaro sought to privatize.
18 While limitations due to space constrain for an extensive discussion of this here, it is also important to note that the politics surrounding the water contamination were complicated, especially as the water provider, CEDAE, was a publicly owned company by the state of Rio, prompting some pro-privatization factions to use it as an example for why water should be privatized, while MAB – and others – argued that the crisis was a result of disinvestment in public services made worse since Dilma Rouseff's ousting. Further, they contend, this is an intentional strategy to be able to make a case for turning the water

over to privatized interests, which in the long run would make the problem worse, not better. Unfortunately, the water services in Rio were privatized in 2021, which has resulted in (among other things), an increase in water shutoffs for poor households (Britto and Finamore, 2023).

19 A Nossa Luta É Pela Vida! Chega de Impunidade!

20 Dilma Ferreira was murdered on 22 March 2019 in the state of Pará, in the region of the Tucuruí hydroelectric dam. I visited this dam in 2008 during my first time in Brazil where I learned of some of the ongoing socioenvironmental problems caused by dams.

21 "Dilma, Nicinha, Berta e Marielle foram parte fundamental na construção de organizações populares, foram operárias fiéis da grande messe e merecem o nosso reconhecimento."

22 Em defesa da Vida, Mulheres Atingidas Na Luta por Diretos.

23 sistema capitalista, patriarcal, racista, heterossexista.

24 é sobre a criação de um novo mundo, não sobre visões rígidas.

25 MAB has also produced a film about this project, and a book.

26 A pseudonym.

27 Educação popular é um modelo de educação que valoriza a história, cultura e costumes de um povo. Ela tem como objetivo formar seus educandos para além de uma lógica de mercado acumulando para uma leitura crítica das suas realidades sociais, políticas e econômicas com fim de acumular para a construção de uma sociedade mais justa e igualitária.

28 The research produced in the Course, including from the 5th Turma, in which I participated, can be accessed via the UFRJ repository at pantheon.ufrj.br. I have also used work produced in the Course in this book.

29 *Commodification of water: analysis of privatization of sanitation in Teresina (PI)* (PI is the abbreviation for the Brazilian state of Piauí). The publication is part of a larger series called "Água, Energia e Sociedade," which is a partnership between MAB and the MST press Editora Expressão Popular (see MAB, 2023).

30 Profit Does Not Value Life: MAB's Analysis of Vale's crime in Brumadinho/MG.

31 I use this word, in this specific case, with intention. In much of what I would call the "Western" world today, "elder" or "the elderly" are considered words we shouldn't use – to use "older people" instead. But in this context, the point is that at each life stage, people bring with them their own important perspective and knowledge. We learn from and with each other. Elders have wisdom and knowledge of the land, of ways of life other than simply working for the capitalist economy.

32 A part of this means no cell phones during class – we turn them in and leave them in another room, claiming them if needed during the breaks, and at the end of the day (this is a practice followed at other MAB trainings as well).

33 For the second part of the course, my base group worked very well together, with little tension to work through. In the first group, however, there were conflicts, specifically around gender and race dynamics, and specifically with one

man in his 50s who came from a higher-up position in his union, and who held ideas around gender and race not shared by others in the group. He did not return for the second portion of the course. There were also struggles around hierarchy – MAB (and Levante Juventude, which also has participants in the Course) focused on being more intersectional, and uses a much more egalitarian approach to decision making than some participants who come from union backgrounds were used to.

33 Necessitated due to the Covid-19 pandemic.

34 é bom ver a todos, principalmente os internacionais: esta é uma luta internacional que a gente tem.

35 Estamos em um momento histórico rico agora ... é muito difícil, mas nunca vimos um momento como este ... e isso pode abrir oportunidades, janelas. A educação popular é muito importante agora. Estamos trabalhando para construir uma sociedade mais justa e fraterna. Temos que fortalecer nossas estratégias agora.

36 A formação política tem três partes: a luta, a organização e formação.

37 Você não vai transformar nada.

38 educação popular é um ato de amor.

39 Nada está predeterminado. Tudo pode ser transformado.

40 A Brazilian youth movement focused on fighting for systemic changes in Brazil, that works in solidarity with other popular movements, including MAB. More can be found on their website: https://levante.org.br/quem-somos/

41 Who was also a participant in the Course on Energy.

42 MAB Live: The Necessary Popular Participation in the Fight for Water.

43 A gente transforma nossa realidade.

44 Porque os poderes continuarão lutando para privatizar ... e as pessoas continuarão lutando porque a água é um direito, o saneamento é um direito!

45 Another panelist, representing CUT, the main national trade union in Brazil, also talked about how the fight is about finance capital, which has no limits. This relates back to Chapter 4, and MAB's analysis of what makes the present form of neoliberal capitalism different than previous eras.

46 This is a chant that was a slogan for Salvador Allende's 1970 campaign (Baiocchi, 2018: 23); it is one used by many movements today across the world, from São Paulo to Pittsburgh.

47 I also completed my paper for the course, written in Portuguese, about the struggle against water privatization in the United States.

48 This quote is widely attributed to Freire, and it is an excellent paraphrase of what he argues. However, this exact statement comes from Carlos Rodrigues Brandão, who was writing about Paulo Freire (see Brandão, 2008: 64; Carvalho, 2021).

49 See https://mab.org.br/2022/07/19/5a-turma-do-curso-de-energia-e-sociedade-no-capitalismo-contemporaneo-se-forma-na-ufrj/

50 "Chegou a vez de ouvir as Marias, Mahins, Marielles, Malês!"

6

Constructing another world: translocal solidarities and the right to water

"Water is life! Sanitation is Dignity!" asserted Laila, a member of African Women Water Sanitation and Hygiene Network, and Corporate Accountability and Public Participation Africa (CAPPA).[1] Around the world, approximately 2 billion people lack access to safe drinking water and almost 50 per cent do not have access to adequate sanitation, illustrating that the right to water and sanitation remains far from realized (Bayram, 2023). Despite numerous studies showing that privatization decreases access to safe water and increases cost, multinational companies continue to privatize water systems around the world. This chapter examines efforts to reclaim the commons of water, and how grassroots movements drive the struggle and demand the prioritization of democracy, transparency, and human rights over corporate profits in public policy.[2]

In early 2019, my involvement with Pittsburgh's OWC brought me to Nigeria for a convergence organized by Our Water, Our Right (OWOR). OWOR is a campaign of and is in partnership with CAPPA, which is connected to Corporate Accountability.[3,4] My engagement with OWC led to my participation as an invited delegate from Pittsburgh with three other Pittsburgh organizers connected to the OWC to a Water Summit in Nigeria. I was invited to attend pre and post strategy meetings of Our Water, Our Right, and I spent two weeks total in Nigeria, visiting Lagos, Ibadan, Calabar, and other towns, meeting with Nigerian environmental activists, and seeing firsthand some of the challenges around gaining socio-environmental justice. This chapter of the book focuses on that period. OWOR coalesced in 2014 when CAPPA learned "that the Lagos state government had been secretly negotiating with the World Bank to hand Lagos water resources to privatisers under a globally-discredited public–private partnership (PPP) structure" (CAPPA, 2021a). Using language similar to that of water activists elsewhere, the activists in Lagos, Nigeria, fight against the privatization of water and call for "transparency, accountability, and democratic public control in the management of public water infrastructure" (Environmental Rights Action/Friends of the Earth Nigeria, 2016: 3).

For the sake of clarity, I want to return to a note I made in Chapter 1, which is that this chapter discusses three movements that span three continents: the first is MAB in Brazil, the second is OWC in the United States, and the third is Our Water, Our Right out of Nigeria. What I argue is that these three cases actually reflect a single case of a translocal movement for the right to water, with the *National Summit on the Human Right to Water, Nigeria's Water Emergency: From Resistance to Real Solutions Against Corporate Control* held in Abuja, Nigeria, from 29 to 30 January 2019 (referred to from here forward as the "Summit"), as one specific convergence space of translocal organizing for the human right to water. Indeed, there is a growing body of literature that examines the shifting formations of transnational organizing and the need to examine the wide "*ecology* of organizations, networks, practices, and strategies" (Evans and Rodríguez-Garavito, 2018: 10) of movements. There is a convergence of campaigns/movements, with the Summit as a translocal space of encounter that shows how they flow out of and into the Summit. As Evans and Rodríguez-Garavito (2018) illustrate, it is insufficient to examine movements in isolation and as single points in time – to do so provides only a partial understanding of the larger story.

MAB was not a part of the Abuja Summit. However, members of both CAPPA (who learned I did work with MAB) and MAB (who knew I was attending the Summit) asked me to connect them, which I did.[5] I am a part of the US Solidarity Committee for MAB, and I include a discussion of MAB here because, as noted in the beginning, I see my research and organizing as interconnected, and I argue that MAB is an important part of this broader translocal fight for water justice, even as my focus in this chapter is on the Summit. I have discussed the concept of translocal activism at length in Chapters 3 and 5, and will situate it here within the context of this chapter. This study of translocal organizing and its influences on flows of knowledge and strategic learning draws from my participatory research in two organizing settings, Pittsburgh and Brazil. While I focus on a particular convergence of activists at the Human Right to Water Summit in Abuja, Nigeria, 29–30 January 2019, I understand and treat the Summit as an instance or space of translocality and intersecting learning networks that connect Pittsburgh with Nigerian and Brazilian activist networks to fight the corporate forces that are engaged in the privatization of water, through various water grabbing tactics such as bottling water and financializing water as a commodity.

This work expands the empirical foundations that can help illuminate the complex and multifaceted ways by which information and knowledge flows through transnational movement networks, thereby contributing to a learning that can disrupt prevailing power alignments and social relations. People are linking their disparate fights to win victories. The struggle is ultimately a conflict of power between *who* has a right to water. On the one hand are people and movements saying that access to water to meet basic needs is a human right. On the other hand, capitalists argue that they have the "right" to profit from the privatization of water. Too often, governments collude with private interests for capital in so-called public–private partnerships or PPPs. This is happening with water around the globe, as I will detail later. As water justice and human rights scholars Farhana Sultana and Alex Loftus explain:

> Recognizing the right to water signals that authorities can be held politically and legally accountable, enabling those who are denied water to have means to contest and struggle for water. Opportunities can be created for marginalized communities and peoples to enter into (often elitist) decision-making processes of water policies, management systems and institutions. (2012: 5)

This relates to what Jackie Smith observes of rights language: "Despite some academic critiques that have dismissed the transformative potential of human rights, I saw activists embracing this language in an emancipatory way (see Santos, 2007; Rajagapol, 2006)" (Smith, 2017b: 350).[6] This becomes even more relevant as we see an international turn toward right-wing governments, with policies that place capital control and accumulation over life (Smith, 2017b). Movements fighting for the right to water are part of a larger struggle for the right to livelihood.

As Banerjee (2011: 331) describes, there are numerous struggles across the continents against transnational corporations and governments for land, livelihood, and, I would add, water. These movements are not just local or global. Instead, they are "translocal":

> Local communities living (and dying) in so-called democratic societies but governed in very non-democratic ways that are engaged in conflicts with both the state and the market, and sometimes even with 'civil society' while also making connections with other resistance movements in different parts of the world. (Banerjee 2011: 331)

This translocal resistance relates to the processes and discussion taking place in movements for the right to water. According to Banerjee (2011, drawing on Sassen 2006), translocality captures the idea that there are "specific local spaces that are distributed across multiple nation states involving particular configurations of actors, resources, territory, authority, rights and relationships of power" (Banerjee 2011: 331). Translocality provides for new insights into understanding and analyzing change; of seeing (and participating in) movements as learning networks (Desai, 2016; Schroering, 2021a; Schroering, 2019b; Smith, 2022), as previous chapters have discussed and I will explore further here.

The Summit: a fight against corporate power

Figure 6.1 illustrates how the Summit served as a translocal space for imagining and building a different world. The Summit, co-organized by AUPCTRE (Amalgamated Union of Public Corporations, Civil Service Technical and Recreational Services Employees), Corporate Accountability, CAPPA, and Public Services International (PSI), brought over 150 people together from around the world to fight against water privatization and create solutions for public water (Weinman, 2019b).

Pittsburgh activists with the Our Water Campaign received an invitation to attend the Summit to share experiences of PPPs, and their struggles and victories to reclaim their water. When three other activists from Pittsburgh and I landed in Abuja and exited customs and immigration, a billboard advertising the Nigeria International Oil Conference (co-sponsored by Shell) greeted us (see Figure 6.2). This conference occurred at the same time as ours, with attendees staying at the same hotel. Given Shell's horrible human rights and environmental record, especially in Nigeria,[7] it was significant that we shared space with that conference. It details the competing discourses of human rights and environmental rights versus corporate profit from extraction, control, and privatization of resources.

Multiple speakers – both in person and through pre-recorded video messages – highlighted the importance of the Summit for everyone present. A video message from Representative Raúl Grijalva from Arizona noted that the fight in Lagos – where millions of people are not receiving water – is an essential struggle for justice and for human rights. He noted how privatization will not solve the problem, because corporations want to maximize profit at the expense of public health. Grijalva argued that the issue is international and climate change will only make it worse. Millions of citizens in the US do not have access to clean water, especially Indigenous communities, communities of color, poor communities, and rural communities. As Grijalva said, the story of Flint happens time and time again around the world: "It's important for you to know that you have allies." Water is a human right and government has a responsibility to ensure that right is observed, he noted.

Akinbode "Bode" Oluwafemi, Executive Director of CAPPA, chronicled the failed history of PPPs in Lagos and noted that while the city has been the site of progressive struggles, it has also become the symbol of capitalism. Lagos is "Nigeria's Big Apple" and the target of corporations. It is a megacity, and it is also mega-poor: 60 per cent of residents live in slums and in poverty. Bode stated: "The battle in Lagos is that of reckless capitalism and our common humanity … We used to joke it was not a crime to be poor … now it is." He continued, "capitalism can kill people." Summit participants also

How are transnational movements communicating and organizing around water and other basic rights?

How are movements engaging with and learning from each other, and in what ways is the "West to the rest" paradigm subverted in these interactions?

NGOs such as Corporate Accountability, and international research and advocacy institutes such as TNI and PSI

Summits, like the one detailed in this chapter

National and international movement networks

Movement actors from disparate locales brought together by Global South-led movements to share, learn, and create strategies

Learning network continues and expands

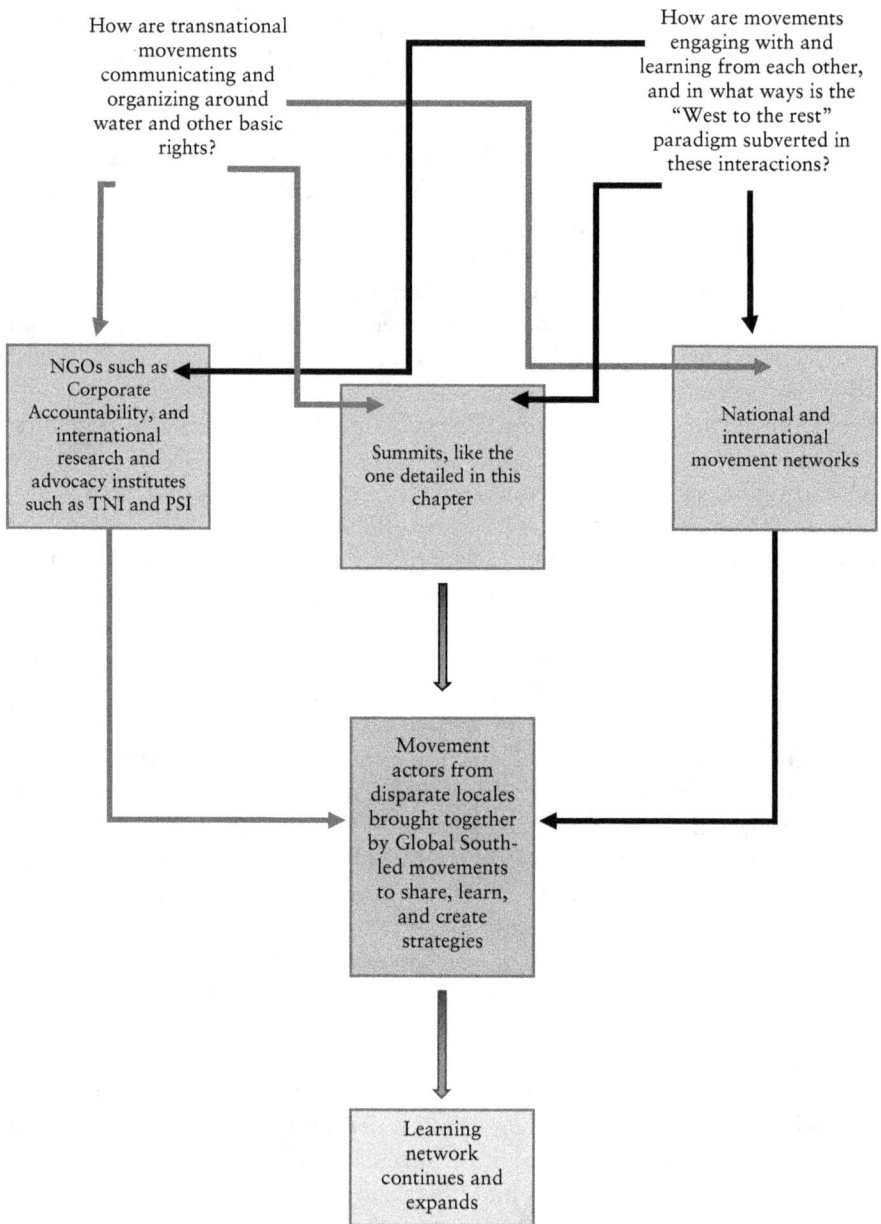

Figure 6.1 Translocal learning networks

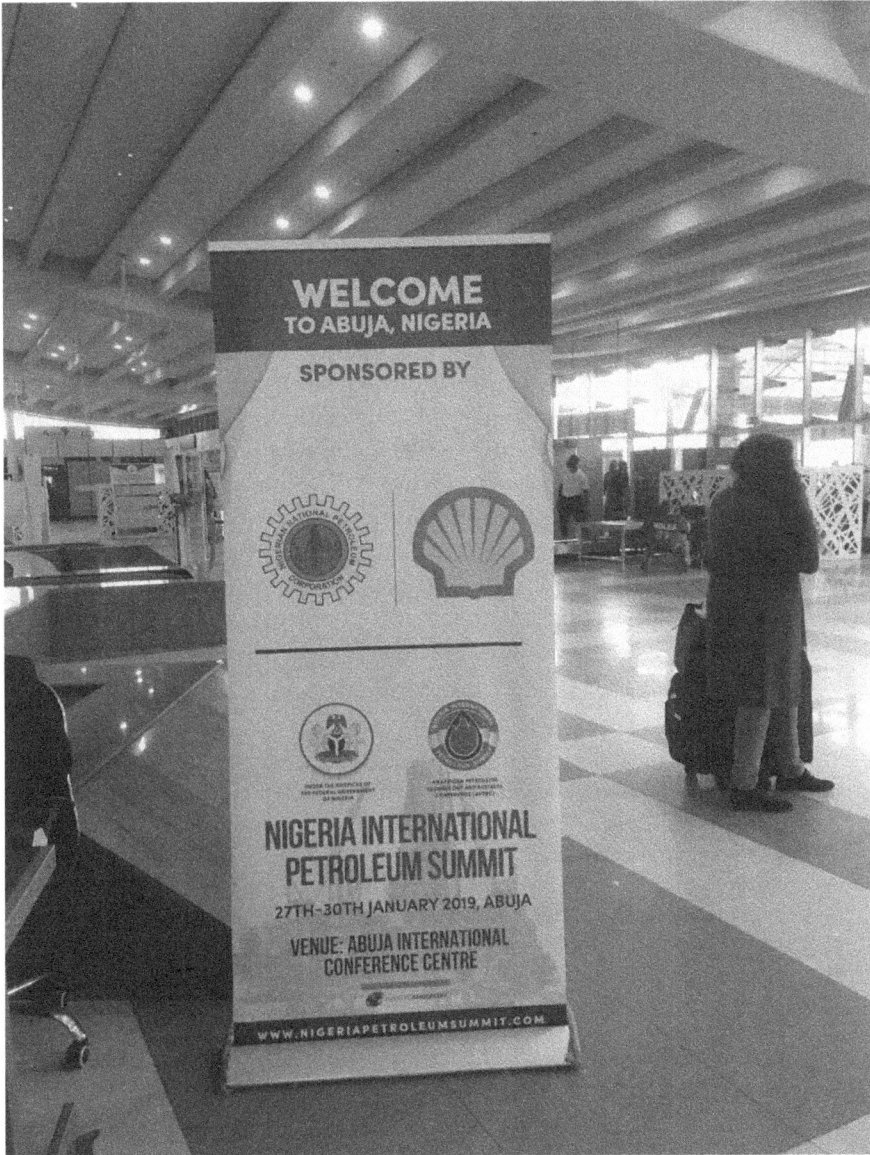

Figure 6.2 Nigeria International Petroleum Summit poster, Abuja Airport

made the point that colonialism takes a new form today via World Bank and other financial institutions pushing for PPPs (Weinman, 2019b). This point connects to the discussion in previous chapters on cultural hegemony: capitalism is not just a "given," it is a system constructed by (some) humans, and it is produced and reproduced through coercion and ideology. One way this economic paradigm is maintained is through the policies of the World Bank (Broad, 2006: 388). Robin Broad details how the World Bank actively discourages dissent. She writes that James Wolfensohn (the World Bank's president in 1996), "launched an initiative to magnify the research and dissemination role of the World Bank by transforming the institution from what was called a 'lending bank' into a 'Knowledge Bank'" (Broad, 2006: 407). Here, global capitalist hegemony is linked with knowledge; maintaining that the capitalist order requires constant reinforcement and the spreading of a certain type of knowledge and maintaining the discourse that neoliberal globalization is "good." As Broad details, in the media, the World Bank's voice is one with authority and power, and so dissenting views are not heard (2006: 408–9). Understanding this process, however, creates liberatory openings to imagine and create a different world.

Oluwafemi's statement relates to what Rob Nixon (2011) calls "slow violence," a term used to describe the suffering, disease, violence, and environmental destruction caused from toxins, climate change, war, etc., that capitalism causes (see Figure 6.3). This concept is particularly apropos for discussing the socio-environmental catastrophe being faced in Nigeria. As Nikhil Deb writes:

> Nixon's concept of slow violence offers fresh critical insights into prolonged social and environmental destruction affecting marginalized people in the Global South. Using the oil spills in the Niger Delta as an example, Nixon highlights how vulnerable populations are exploited and ravaged for profits and resources. Specifically, the people of Ogoniland in Nigeria, a micro-minority group, are gradually entangled in the all-encompassing destruction of Shell. Shell not only ravaged the native people's environment, but allowed for the continuation of Nigerian police violence and genocide to quell any resistance to progress. Nixon (2011: 105) elaborates on the injustices in the region through the standpoint of the prolific Ken Saro-Wiwa, whose work made way for "a broader estimation of the global cost" of oil production and extraction. (2021: 5)

Conference participants also discussed how these effects are intensified in the era of climate change. Indeed, as the UN Intergovernmental Panel on Climate Change (IPCC) noted in 2015, "the world has not really woken up to the reality of what we are going to face in terms of the crises as far as water is concerned" (Bhalla, 2015). Legal scholar Carmen Gonzalez asserts: "the 'slow violence' inflicted by the fossil fuel industry on racialized and poor communities throughout the world remains a central feature of contemporary capitalism" (2021: 118). This argument shows that the slow violence of extractivism (and I would extend this to thinking about water) must be addressed. Further, to address it, we have to reckon with histories of colonialism, imperialism, racial capitalism, and settler colonialism – and

Figure 6.3 Slide from Summit on Capital and the Market

how these systems continue in the present including via forms of neocolonialism, militarization, and market based "solutions" to climate change. Yet, too often when talking about climate change, it is seen as something all of humanity has caused and that affects everyone. While it does threaten the whole planet, it does not affect everyone equally, nor have we gotten to this place because of all of humanity's actions. As Nicholas Mirzoeff states in "It's Not the Anthropocene, It's the White Supremacy Scene; or, The Geological Color Line," there has been a tendency when examining the Anthropocene and its causes and effects to "turn away from understandings of race, white supremacy, colonialism, and imperialism, which undermines the possibility of a politics of resource use and allocation, also known as the commons" (2018: 125).

In other words, conflicts around water are also conflicts around larger issues of equity, power, and access, and about dismantling systems of oppression including white supremacy, patriarchy, and imperialism. As discussed in Chapters 2 and 3, one critical player in this conflict is Veolia, one of the largest corporations involved in water privatization currently on the shortlist to privatize water in Lagos, and the same company that Pittsburgh entered into a PPP with in 2012. At the Summit, Aly Shaw shared with people the history of the Pittsburgh struggle, detailed in Chapter 3. At the Summit, Aly discussed how Veolia did not invest anything into the Pittsburgh system. Instead, PWSA (under the management of Veolia) laid off workers and made an illegal chemical switch that likely caused spiked lead levels. The city terminated the contract with Veolia and, shortly after, the news broke of the city's lead problem. The OWC emerged soon after, and activists realized that the only way to solve the problems was to make the water authority more public and democratic. There have been subsequent attempts by water and gas companies to privatize the water, but the community has been successful at pushing back, and officials have backed off privatizing for now (Schroering, 2019b; Shaw, 2019). Veolia North America announced in February 2018 that it would stop pursuing "Peer Performance Solutions" (PPS), a form of PPPs, which industry analysts attribute to public relations difficulties in Pittsburgh and other cities (Global Water Intelligence, 2018: 12; Global Water Intelligence, 2019).

The OWC – and other participants from around the globe – were invited to the Summit to share their failed experiences with Veolia. Summit speakers noted repeatedly that PPPs never work out to the benefit of the people. As one speaker noted, "PPPs use what you have, run it down" and then leave. All of the risk turns over to the government or public side, with all of the profit given to the corporation (see also Bieler and Moore, 2023; Moore, 2018). Globalized policies of privatization threaten human rights everywhere and, as climate change progresses, resources will become even more scarce, with more of a push from corporations seeking to further consolidate control and commodify water. The Veolia/Suez merger (discussed in Chapter 2), speaks to this.

In response to resistance to privatization schemes and evidence of the failures of privatization to deliver on its promises, there is a global trend of remunicipalization. As discussed in Chapter 2, one of the principal reasons for this is because privatized water services have almost always generated an increase in price and cost-cutting that compromises water quality (Food and Water Watch, 2016). Activists use these figures to help make the case for why water privatization is undesirable and ineffective – if those who had privatized their water systems are now remunicipalizing, why is privatization being considered as a solution?

On the first day of the Summit, a participant from Los Angeles representing Black Lives Matter (BLM) Los Angeles and Corporate Accountability, said: "I am here to say that BLM stands with struggle here [in Nigeria]. [and we] see the lack of access to water as violence. [We] can't have corporations controlling this precious resource." This point resonates with what Nnimmo Bassey, Chair of the Board for Environmental Rights Action/ Friends[8] of the Earth Nigeria, asserted: "All of the polluted waters in this country have been privatized by polluters" – and he continued to explain how then oil companies use that water as a place to dump oil. This means a future of violence, illness, and poverty for children. This is why, he argued, we must defend the right to water at the regional, national, and international level. The Summit, Bassey reminded us, was a place to share strategies and prepare to defend rights. This means working to ensure the human right to water, including the need to clean up the Niger Delta and all polluted waters in this country and the world. The solution? Water systems around the world must be modernized in a way that places control in the hands of people and is both transparent and democratic. This is the only way to ensure the human right to water is recognized. Our Water, Our Right is a campaign to emphasize that no one has a right to privatize water.

This resonates with what people in Brazil told me. As one member of a human rights organization (CDDH) that partners with MAB shared with me, "violations of human rights can occur in all places … people have the right to education, health, housing, work, to not be victims of violence" (Personal interview, summer 2018). This relates to the quote illustrated earlier from one of the leaders of CAPPA who put it simply: "capitalism can kill." Or, as a social media post from OWC on 9 October 2019 put it: "No Matter How Green We Make Our Lifestyles, Capitalism is Not Sustainable."

To be clear: the violence of capitalism is not new, as Cedric Robinson so meticulously details. The current global system of racism and capitalism, as Robin D.G. Kelley writes in the foreword to *Black Marxism* "did not break from the old order but rather evolved from it to produce a modern world system of 'racial capitalism' dependent on slavery, violence, imperialism, and genocide" (2000 [1983]: xiii; see also Murphy and Schroering, 2020). Following Debadatta Chakraborty (2020), I argue we ought to add patriarchy to this list.[9] As one participant at the Summit noted, "we fight for our water [and] our life ... Need to fight for dignity for women and other disenfranchised groups."

Summit speakers noted at various points, the gendered dimensions of access to clean water and sanitation, and argued that women and children are most affected. Water justice is also racial and gender justice. Systemic injustice in its various and interrelated forms, including imperialism, colonialism, patriarchy, and racial capitalism is not new; but it is also true that the particular form of finance capital does create a different form of rapaciousness. There is a narrative that public services do not work and that the private sector can do it better, when in reality, the evidence (including the trend of remunicipalization) shows the opposite. As one of the Abuja Summit participants noted, a few decades ago, when he was a child, there was a pump at the end of each street in Lagos. Each home did not have piped water, but each street did. People had access to clean, affordable water. Now they do not. Why? Because of a complicated process of neoliberal austerity measures led by the World Bank, IMF, and other financial institutions working with governments and corporations, that has pushed to stop public investment in infrastructure, while also promoting the agenda of PPPs. This also relates to water financialization, which presents compounded challenges for all who are fighting against water privatization.

As noted in previous chapters, the financialization of water is the sixth form of water grabbing (Bieler and Moore, 2023).[10] The financialization of water is the privatization of life itself, turning this element essential for survival, one of the four elements of matter, into a commodity for financial speculation (Ideas for Development, 2020; Muehlebach, 2023: 12–18). Trading water on Wall Street began in December 2020 (Yale Environment 360, 2020). In a 132-page document published by Citigroup in 2017 entitled "Solutions for the Global Water Crisis: The End of 'Free and Cheap' Water," Citigroup's argument throughout can be summarized as "how can I make money off of water shortages?" (Citigroup, 2017). In 2011, Citigroup's top economic analyst, Willem Buiter, encouraged clients to invest in water, saying:

> I expect to see a globally integrated market for fresh water within 25 to 30 years. Once the spot markets for water are integrated, futures markets and other derivative water-based financial instruments – puts, calls, swaps – both exchange-traded and OTC will follow. There will be different grades and types of fresh water, just the way we have light sweet and heavy sour crude oil today. Water as an asset class will, in my view, become eventually the single most important physical-commodity based asset class, dwarfing oil, copper, agricultural commodities and precious metals. (Lubin, 2011: final paragraph)

As Maude Barlow noted during a webinar titled "Water Financialization 101: Water Futures, Water Markets and Reclaiming the Water Commons," coordinated by the Blue Planet Project,[11] Nestlé was recently acquired by private equity firm, One Rock Capital. This makes it even harder to fight against Nestlé's water grabs because no longer is it one company you can name and target. One Rock Capital announced the completion of its acquisition of Nestlé on 31 March 2021 (One Rock, 2021). Barlow also noted how this financialization is a form of water grabbing. Water financialization is something that we all need to be vigilant about and fight against; it demonstrates that just as people and movements are fighting to reclaim the commons of water, global finance and business interests seek to further commodify and profit off water (Muehlebach, 2023). This is especially true as these corporate interests seek to use the language of human rights and environmental responsibility and preservation to advance their cause and make a popular appeal (see Citigroup, 2017 and the language used).

The "right to water" is a message embraced by movements opposed to its privatization. A majority of these actions to date have occurred in the Global South but they are also becoming more common in the Global North, particularly in response to the intensification of neoliberal policies, aging urban infrastructure, and state austerity programs (Sultana, 2018: 486). As discussed in Chapters 2 and 3, the same austerity process is unfolding in the United States as inequities in municipal maintenance coincide with collapsing municipal budgets. I will return to this near the end of the chapter.

Water is about power (Sultana, 2019). It is instructive to think about power in the context of a space like the Summit in Abuja: on the one hand there is the power of capital, as exemplified by the Shell conference and the ongoing threat of water privatization; on the other hand, there is the power of people to bring about change, bringing together people from many different countries (mostly in Africa) and three continents (Africa, North America, and Europe). Corporations work across geographic borders, so too must the resistance. Spaces like the Summit show that movements and activists are united, and that this movement is growing. They are also tools for building unity and growing the movement. Nikhil Deb, in writing about the Bhopal disaster in India, notes that "Slow violence in Bhopal shows that suffering – growing painfully slower by the day – is not invisible by default; invisibility is the product of global neoliberalism at work in India" (2021: 14). He builds on Nixon's concept arguing that "The political economy and processes of slow violence have changed as a result because neoliberalization encourages unfettered global free trade and a healthy foreign investment climate while abandoning the state protection of the victims of economic and ecological problems" (Deb, 2021: 6). These same processes, I argue, are certainly visible in Nigeria, and around the globe.

One of the critical things that the Summit did was to make this invisibilization of injustice and the systems causing it, more visible. As one participant stated in a question-and-answer section, "we need to work together because corporations work together" (Fieldnotes, 30 January 2019). This illustrates a point made by the water justice and human rights scholar Farhana Sultana:

> Getting involved in local or regional water justice efforts can be a good start. But this requires recognition that water justice is never only local, but cross-scalar and global. It is also critical to pay attention to the ways that water is about gender, class, race, ethnicity, identity and place, and appreciate how it is linked to broader issues of social justice. Such action and advocacy can foster collectivizing, alliances, and working with others to promote equity, human rights, and justice. Changing institutions, laws and norms are long-term goals that require sustained involvement, which is important to cultivate and support. (2018: 489)

Since there are systemic forces engaged via corporations and global financial institutions, this struggle is not only local. Movements learn from each other and form coalitions through solidarity. The Summit focused on how to resist privatization of public water supplies. On our last day in Abuja, Nigeria, we learned about another dimension of water commodification and privatization: bottled water. Over a dozen of the US participants (plus members from CAPPA) rode in a van – escorted by civil police – over an hour away to where Nestlé has one of two water bottling plants in the country. When we arrived, we stood outside of Nestlé for a few minutes (surrounded by armed police) holding up signs that said, "Nestlé Take Your Hands Off Our Water" and "Water is a Human Right." We next visited a community adjacent to the Nestlé plant. While there, we met the chief. Nestlé has given him an old packing container for an office. It served, essentially, as a dehumanizing attempt to buy him off. Nestlé had built new water pumping stations, although no water flows from the taps. A plaque on the pump showed the date '30 January 2019' – two days before we had arrived.[12] When we asked one of the Nigerian activists about this, the answer was simple: "They have spies. They've been watching us and suspected we would bring you here."

Bottled water is an insidious piece of the conversation about water as a right versus commodity. Companies like Nestlé and Coca Cola have worked hard to create the idea that only commodified water (that they have often stolen from aquifers and bottled with fewer safety regulations than public tap water) is safe. Not to mention all the horrible plastic waste, which requires petroleum to produce. Nestlé (and others including Coca Cola) do this in Nigeria, in Brazil, and in the United States.[13] From Michigan, United States, to Abuja, Nigeria, to the Guarani Aquifer in Brazil, multinational companies seek to privatize the water: to bottle and to sell it.[14] These companies then use marketing to convince people bottled water is better. Sometimes bottled water is a safer option – but this is because of the lack of investment in public water infrastructure. I share this discussion of bottled water because it illustrates an important part of both how corporate players engage in similar activities transnationally, but also how activist conversations in particular spaces connect and learn from each other to fight these forces.[15] My conversations and participation with other participants from the United States highlighted how the Summit shifted their thinking about organizing and how the struggle was not just local. As one Pittsburgh activist attending the Abuja water Summit said:

> We can't drink the water here … or in Flint … or in Pittsburgh … that is [something that is] shared. So, we need to think about it globally … I'm thinking about what's going on and how I'm going to put a global spin on everything now.

This statement draws attention to the fact that around the world, people lack access to a fundamental substance for life: water. It also illustrates that this holds true in many places in the United States, the wealthiest country the world has ever known, which gained its wealth through explicit violence: theft of Indigenous peoples' land and kidnapping and enslaving Black people. This explicit violence continues today; but so too has the growth of slow violence, which is less explicit, and therefore more insidious. As discussed earlier in this chapter, slow violence is perpetrated by corporations, governments, and global financial institutions in the interest of profit, and much of this violence is concentrated in the Global South. But it is also occurring in the Global North, and that process is classed, raced, and gendered. The water *is* now drinkable in Pittsburgh, and Flint has replaced most of the lead lines – but as a recent article in *The Guardian* is titled "Flint residents grapple with water crisis a decade later: 'If we had the energy left, we'd cry'" (Beaumont, 2024). In the state of Jackson, Mississippi, a record amount of rainfall hit the city in August 2022, causing the water supply system to fail, leaving 150,00 residents without water. As of February 2023, many residents remain without safe water. But as an article written by Hadas Thier (2023) shows, this failure is not simply due to "natural" causes. It is due to human decisions, including decades of disinvestment, which has disproportionately harmed Black people. Thier writes:

> The water infrastructure in Jackson – a city that is 83 percent Black – has been underfunded and crumbling for decades. Now the intensifying impacts of a changing climate are delivering a final blow. Whether in New Orleans in 2005, Flint, Mich., in 2014, or Jackson today, Black Americans are disproportionately affected by these system failures. Abre' Conner, the NAACP's

director of environmental and climate justice, testified during a congressional hearing on water infrastructure in September: 'The effect of climate change on Black people has finally come into national focus, because Black people experience the most horrific impacts from historic disinvestment from communities. (2023: paragraph 4)

Thier ends the piece with the following:

The Rev. William Barber II, who cochairs the Poor People's Campaign and travels regularly from North Carolina to Jackson to help lead rallies at the governor's mansion, tells me that residents there are fed up. But their efforts to save the city from state neglect could inspire the growing number of communities in similar fights. "The people in Jackson have come to a place where Fannie Lou Hamer was at when she said, 'I'm just sick and tired of being sick and tired.' They're sick and tired of being forced to drink and bathe and wash in nasty water," Barber says. "But this is not an isolated battle. In some ways, Jackson may become a launching pad for more movements across the country, wherever this problem exists." (2023: paragraph 52)

These words remind me of a statement by another Pittsburgh organizer on the first day of the Abuja Summit; they noted that participating in the Summit lead to "a different way of seeing the world, which leads to a different way of organizing." Another person asserted: "Corporations want us to feel small and like we don't have power but when we come together, we do have power" (Schroering, 2019b, 2021a). When I asked about the role of international solidarity, OWOR activists said that international solidarity needs to not just be a moment, but something sustained. I also met people at the Summit who know and work with MAB, and we discussed the importance of movements in the Global North learning from and working with Global South movements. It relates to the Latin American history of Diálogo de Saberes (discussed in Chapters 4 and 5). The Summit served as a space where alternatives to the current world could be imagined. It is illustrative of how Rossett and Martinez-Torres (speaking about La Vía Campesina, discussed in previous chapters) note that "movements and organizations are constantly creating new, emergent knowledges and collective readings of reality" (2013: 4).

The right to water is a global fight to create another world(s)

The Summit served as a place to collectively create a path for solutions. One aspect of this is the public statement that participants drafted through a collective process on the last day. This statement affirmed the human right to water and opposed all privatization and corporate control of this life

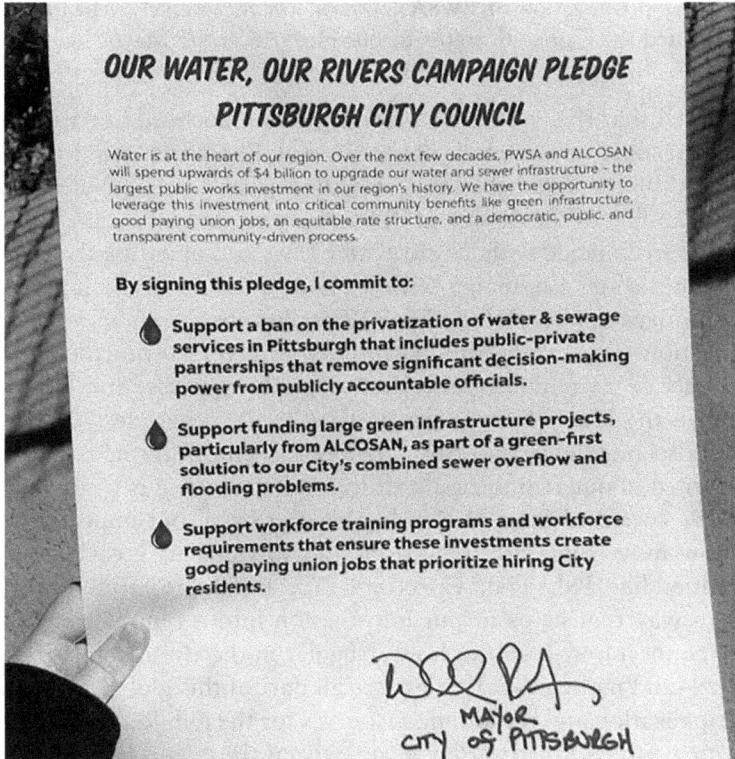

Figure 6.4 Pittsburgh Mayor pledge

sustaining substance ("Communique," 2019). Shortly after returning from Nigeria, OWC planned a lobby day training with local officials (discussed in Chapter 3) and created a pledge for officials to sign committing they were against privatization – and detailing exactly what that meant. We visited with over a dozen public officials, many of whom signed the pledge. The biggest victory, perhaps, was that the mayor – to everyone's surprise – signed the pledge (see Figure 6.4). As OWC leader, Tom Hoffman, wrote:

> The most exciting and newsworthy visit was to Mayor Bill Peduto of Pittsburgh. The group outlined our positions and then the Mayor grabbed a blue marker and signed his name to the bottom of the pledge. After much applause and hand shaking (and the obligatory selfies) we filed out of the office and headed home. Less than a week later we got an email from Neil Gupta of our partner organization Corporate Accountability with some very exciting news. He monitors the activities of the national industry trade journal Global Water Intelligence (GWI). They maintain a tracker that ranks the likelihood that a public water authority will be privatized. As a direct result of our lobbying Mayor Peduto about keeping PWSA public, GWI updated their tracker

to say that privatization of PWSA is "now looking unlikely." In the notes they credited the change in status to our pledge that the Mayor had signed. (Hoffman, 2019)[16]

I observed that this event and planning was influenced in part from the transnational connections made at the Summit: Pittsburgh activists returned energized, thinking about the issue in new ways and strengthened in a better understanding of the threats of PPPs; planning and scheduling a week of lobby visits to coincide with World Water Day; and updating the Facebook page for Our Water Campaign with a photo from the Summit with us all holding up signs reading "United For Water Justice."

Connections made at the Summit resulted in TNI featuring the Pittsburgh OWC as a case of remunicipalization of public services, and Pittsburgh's inclusion in the Water Remunicipalisation Tracker website (Shaw, 2019). This site also highlights two cases of remunicipalization in Brazil (where I first learned about remunicipalization) and the writer is a part of MAB (Itu, 2019; Tocantins State, 2019).[17] This is a small but important example of how movements are organizing and working with each other, and with entities like PSI, TNI, Corporate Accountability, and others, who work in a way that helps to put information into a central place, and to enhance connections. It shows how struggles in the United States, Nigeria, and Brazil (and many other locales) are all part of this global movement of remunicipalization and reclaiming resources for the public good rather than for private gain. As noted earlier, as a result of the connection with Veolia, Corporate Accountability is also a partner of the Our Water Campaign in Pittsburgh, bringing national and transnational aspects to an otherwise local campaign. Many (if not most) of the examples of anti-water privatization movements qualify as place bound because they focus on local (or national) struggles for control of water. Yet their issue identification is not bound only to place, as these groups articulate an interest in connecting their local effort to a broader, global struggle for water as a human right.

The focus in social movement studies is often on outcomes (Amenta et al., 2018; Piven, 2006; Staggenborg and Lecomte, 2009; Wood et al., 2017). For sure, outcomes matter, but outcomes can also be challenging to measure or see. How many movements did in fact change something, but it cannot easily be proven or measured? Does it count? If so, how do we measure it? Is it possible that the focus on specific policy outcomes perhaps misses other less easily measured but still transformational changes? Many outcomes are invisible if not examined in the context of the complex and long-term processes they involve. As Robin D.G. Kelley puts it:

> Unfortunately, too often our standards for evaluating social movements pivot around whether or not they "succeeded" in realizing their visions rather than on the merits or power of the visions themselves. By such a measure, virtually

every radical movement failed because the basic power relations they sought to change remain pretty much intact. And yet it is precisely these alternative visions and dreams that inspire new generations to continue to struggle for change. (2002: vii; see also Rabaka, 2006: 738)[18]

Indeed, the mere presence of counter-hegemonic projects arguably reflects some success in mobilizing opposition to capitalist hegemony. The translocal movements I discuss here move beyond mere existence and further contribute to the project of contesting hegemony and building alternatives (including skills and methods that enable democratic governance). One essential aspect of these right to water movements is tangible policy and system-level changes; another aspect is the path of getting there, of envisioning a new world. As MAB activists would say, it is a process of creating a "novo caminho" – a new path (MAB, 2017: 32). This work can go by various names including "alter-globalizations," "globalization from below," or "counter-hegemonic globalization."[19] I have not often heard these terms used by movement actors; instead, I hear the same sentiment expressed in different forms: the idea of "creating a new world," "another world is still possible,"[20] or a "new path" (see Figure 6.5).

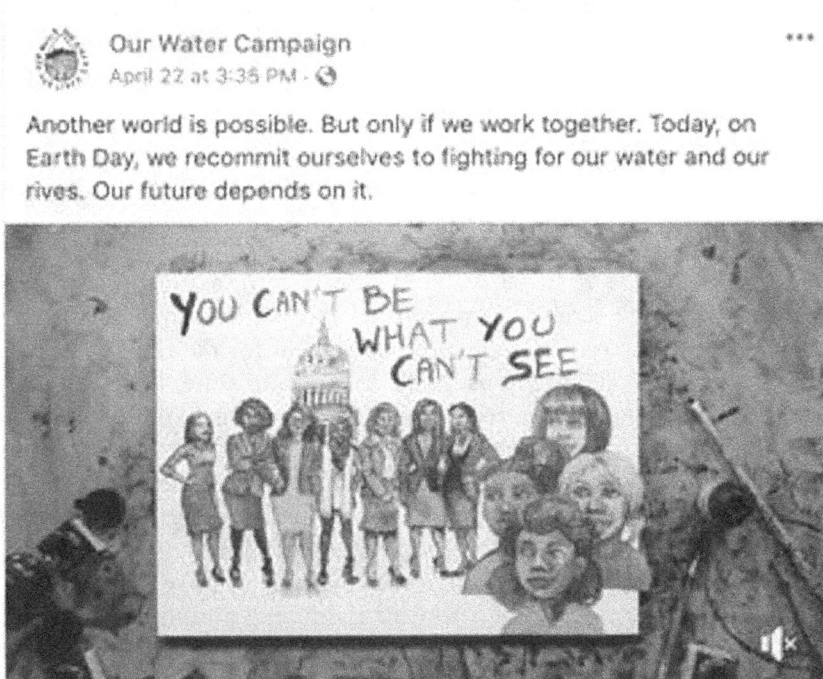

Figure 6.5 Another world is possible

Or, as Kelley wrote, articulating a new vision is the first step in build-ing a new world; a revolution is a process and that process is transforma-tional (2002: xi; see also Rabaka, 2006: 737). As Sabrina Fernandes writes, "Resistance and revolution are different things, but they must be intercon-nected in a dialectical process" (Fernandes, 2020: 168).[21] The work described here is about creating new forms of living and relationships in the present moment, a piece of which includes people developing shared understandings of oppression and exploitation and becoming leaders in their communities to stand up together against greed and for the right to survive and thrive. The potential transformative capacity of that ought not to be overlooked.

As one presenter at the Abuja Summit asserted: "[We] need to build revo-lutionary force. But today … we will use a rights-based approach." Another person stated, "We want to put alternatives on the table that aren't avail-able to the ruling class!" (Fieldnotes, 30 January 2019). One of the most powerful short-term results of this Summit was how it served as a place for international solidarity to be built. For people not to just hear of struggles elsewhere, but for people from Flint and Pittsburgh to meet people from Lagos and vice versa, and to learn about how much we share in our struggle. The discussions at the Summit relate also to Marina Sitrin's (2012) work on autonomous movements in Argentina, introduced in the previous chapter. She writes about new solidarities and "el otro soy yo"[22] (the other is me) (Sitrin, 2012: 47–8). This relates to MAB's "todos somos atingidos," which means "we are all affected."

Conclusion

The struggle for the right to water is driven by grassroots movements demanding that democracy, transparency, and the human right to water are above corporate profit. I argue the movement for the right to water is important for three main reasons. First, attention to water is critical in the face of climate change. Some regions will have too much, others too little, and conflicts will worsen. Second, conflicts around water are also about equity, power, and access. Organizing around water implicates a range of other important dynamics, including trends of market deregulation, privati-zation, and austerity measures. Third, movements fighting for the human right to water today represent a radical and transformative position in the face of recent government trends toward right-wing authoritarian govern-ments that run on rhetoric of "law and order" and seek to further shrink the public safety net and impose harsh penalties on social movements fighting for the basic right to survival.

When I think about the most basic things to survival, air and water are what come to mind. And in so many places around the globe, both of those things are polluted. Air and water do not know geographic and political boundaries, and they flow where they want. The number of people on the globe suffering the consequences of polluted air and polluted water is only increasing. Of course, the other truth is that the communities disproportionately affected – both in the United States and globally – are poor, are Black, are Indigenous, are brown, and many are geographically in the "Global South." Each community, each country, certainly has its own histories and present realities in which colonialism and racial capitalism play a significant role that do mean we should be cautious with making broad brush-stroke comparisons. Each locality has its own distinct challenges.

Yet there is a need to acknowledge how these problems are global and develop an analysis that addresses the root of the problem: capitalism. As discussed earlier in the chapter, capitalism uses racism, white supremacy, patriarchy, xenophobia, colonialism, imperialism, and other systems of oppression to operate and grow. It always has, and it always will.[23] We cannot recycle our way out of the problem or make individual choices that are going to fix it. The OWC post I noted earlier put it succinctly: "capitalism is not sustainable" (Fieldnotes, 9 October 2019). In other words, we need a paradigm shift, and we need to de-theorize and to reinvent new ways of understanding and living in our world (Goodman and Salleh, 2013: 413). As Leonard Figueroa-Helland, Cassidy Thomas, and Abigail Pérez Aguilera put it:

> Anticipating the global convergence of crises,[24] counterhegemonic social forces have solidified their challenge against the anthropocentric/patriarchal/ (neo)colonial/capitalist world-system. LVC and affiliates like Brazil's Landless Workers' Movement (MST), or others like the Zapatistas (Chiapas, Mexico), tie food sovereignty to defending Mother Earth, decolonization, depatriarchalization, and indigenous revitalization. (2018: 182)

MAB also succinctly makes similar arguments in a statement produced at the end of a Summit on water, held in the United States in 2017:

> Our analysis is that capitalism is going through a productive crisis of character and provokes terrible consequences in society, spreading itself into a crisis of civilization and proving that, besides being unsustainable, it expands armed conflicts around the world, intensifies the destruction of nature and increases societal inequality, religious persecution and persecution of people of different sexual orientations, racism, patriarchy, sexism, xenophobia and all kinds of discrimination. This system is not able to provide for the basic demands of humanity such as food for all the population, health, education, dignity, liberty and justice. Therefore, it is the working class who pay the bill of the

crisis and suffer the consequences of capitalism, especially Black and immigrant populations and traditional and indigenous peoples. ("Letter From The II International Seminar," 2017)

To be sure, the challenges are many: in the case of Lagos, there continues to be a lack of transparency as it relates to the privatization project, and where that stands. The global firm Metito (which counts the International Finance Corporation (IFC), a member of the World Bank, as one of its key shareholders) has launched a new "partnership" with the United Kingdom that targets water infrastructure and systems on the African continent (Metito, 2023), and could have repercussions related to the drive to further privatize resources such as water. Further, the Lagos Water Corporation (LWC) announced a "partnership" with USAID (which CAPPA and Corporate Accountability learned the details of only through a Freedom of Information Act), which contains pro-privatization plans. The Lagos government worked to keep this out of the public eye, until CAPPA exposed it (Oboh, 2023). It is another example of how "aid" organizations, and USAID specifically, continue to perpetrate new forms of colonialism under the guise of "development." It illustrates the slow violence of capitalism and neocolonialism, discussed earlier in this chapter and throughout the book.

Still, OWOR continues to fight and to build power. The OWOR movement has now grown to a continent-wide movement under the banner of the Our Water, Our Right Africa Coalition (OWORAC), which spans eight countries (including Nigeria). This serves as a further example of how the Lagos campaign served as a model for effective anti-privatization campaigns in other parts of the continent. In 2021, OWORAC produced a 24-page booklet entitled Africa Must Rise & Resist Water Privatisation. It is free and accessible online (CAPPA, 2021b). OWORAC also created a website in 2021 with content in English, French, and Portuguese, which contains an abundance of information and resources (CAPPA, 2022).

In 2020, it appeared that there was a growing global movement against police brutality, racism, and anti-Blackness (including in the United States, Brazil, and Nigeria), building momentum and gaining more attention (A Planet, n.d.; Yancy, 2022). As noted earlier in this chapter, BLM is a movement linked – at least tangentially – to OWOR and to the Nigeria Summit. While this movement has ceased to receive as much attention post-2020 and the wave of mass, visible protests ended, it is not over. The struggle continues, *and* points to a challenge: how can social movement momentum be sustained? This is a question I will turn to in more depth in the concluding chapter. Yet it remains the case that just because the ongoing daily resistance and struggles are not in the national and international news, does not mean they are not ongoing. The struggle for the right to water is connected to this fight. This fight for the right to water and sanitation is also a fight for the right to education, transportation, and healthcare. It is the right to be free from police violence. It is a fight against the systemic realities that produce violence in all its forms, a point discussed in Chapter 4 (see also Figure 6.6).

BLM and other activists called for the diversion of money from policing into other places like housing and education. The excuse that there is not

Figure 6.6 OWOR (CAPPA spearheads the OWOR campaign) post on social media on 13 October 2020

money to invest in these things, including public water infrastructure, simply is not true. The questions are: who has the power? Who is choosing where to spend money? Who is profiting off the current socio-economic-political system? Who is not? And how can the many seeds of resistance and imagining of a new world be nurtured? In the previous chapter, I discussed how a MAB leader noted the political moment, including BLM, in August 2020, and how he said it presented opportunities for transformation. Further, he discussed the importance of popular education in political formation, which itself has three main parts: the struggle, the organization, and the political formation and training (Fieldnotes, August 2020). The Summit provided a space for better understanding the struggle and organization, and the work continued as people dispersed back to their home countries, campaigns, and movements.

This ties back into discussion of social movement outcomes, and how we measure them, discussed earlier in this chapter and throughout the book: the moment and visibility of BLM has diminished, however, we cannot argue whether a movement has failed or succeeded just because the change is less visible, or the media's focus has shifted. Much counter-hegemonic work is not always visible to those outside the movements. This chapter represented one moment of a translocal learning network around fighting water privatization, and it explored how it is connected to other struggles that transcend geographic borders.[25] The fight against water grabbing in all its forms, and the struggle to build a new world, is connected to a larger counter-hegemonic movement, and is an ongoing and non-linear process. As Flávia Braga Vieira writes of Vía Campesina writes, the struggle is one of creating internationalism and building a "globalization of hope" (Vieira, 2011). Other worlds *are* possible, and the roots to create those worlds are planted and growing. In the words of Arundhati Roy, "Another world is not only possible, she's on her way."[26]

Notes

1 CAPPA was created in 2020 but it was formerly known as Environmental Rights Action (ERA) Nigeria, which was founded in 1993. At the time of the Summit, CAPPA was known as ERA, but I use the current name here (CAPPA, 2021a).

2 This chapter builds on a previously published paper (see Schroering, 2021a; Schroering, 2019b).

3 As discussed in Chapter 2, Corporate Accountability is connected to the OWC in Pittsburgh and with Flint Rising in Michigan, both places with water contamination crises involved Veolia.

4 Veolia is discussed in Chapters 2 and 3.

5 While the Covid-19 pandemic disrupted/delayed the building of some of these connections, virtual meetings and conversations have occurred.

6 See also my discussion in Chapter 2 about rights language.

7 I recommend looking into the life and work of Ken Saro-Wiwa to learn more about this history, including SaroWiwa's diary, *A Month and a Day: A Detention Diary* (1995) and *Ogoni's Agonies: Ken Saro Wiwa and the Crisis in Nigeria* (1998), edited by Abdul Rasheed Na'allah.

8 He held this position at the time of the Summit.

9 This relates as well to Lugones' coloniality of gender, discussed in Chapter 1, as well as Kara Ellerby's use of the term "kyriarchy," which is defined as "interlocking structures of domination" to name the sexist, racist, heterosexist, and imperialist system(s) of subordination central to understanding how gender equality has come to represent add-women/gender policies, rather than address the intersecting system that causes gender inequality (Ellerby, 2017: 6–7). Kyriarchy was originally coined in English by theologian Elisabeth Schussler Fiorenza (1992).

10 The other five are privatization of drinking water and sanitation; bottled water; water for extractive industry; land grabbing for export agriculture; and large dam constructions.

11 The video can be found here: https://fb.watch/log_OHQOlr/?mibextid= v7YzmG

12 It warrants mentioning that Nestlé had also publicly announced (and made a video) that they would provide water to around 1,000 people via the taps placed at the front of the plant. After a report by an investigative journalist (who was with us on the visit to the community) with the International Center for Investigative Reporting called them out on this (Abba, 2019), Nestlé issued a statement saying the pumps are now working (see Issa, 2019).

13 Nestlé, for example, owned 51 different brands of water in 2019 (Perkins, 2019a). Pepsi and Coca Cola are also in the lucrative bottled water industry, making billions of dollars from, in many cases, tap water that they bottle. For example, Coca Cola owns, among others, the popular brand Dasani, which is actually just tap water (Felton, 2020).

14 A 2019 ruling from a Michigan court, however, asserted that Nestlé cannot claim their activities constitute an "essential public service" (Perkins, 2019b).

15 It is also one of the forms, as noted in Chapter 2, of water grabbing, as argued by Bieler and Moore (2023).

16 See also Global Water Intelligence 2019.

17 At the time of this writing, this tracker was offline; it will hopefully be back online in the near future. In the interim, the following website provides some (abbreviated) details on the cited cases. You are able to search for those and others here: https://publicfutures.org/

18 Conway's (2017) critique of how social movements are studied, discussed in Chapter 1, also parallels Kelley's arguments.

19 See Chapter 1 and Chapter 4.

20 This comes from the 2001 World Social Forum slogan, "Another World Is possible."
21 Sabrina Fernandes is a sociologist and eco-socialist whose work was introduced to me by someone in MAB.
22 Language that comes from the Zapatistas.
23 See Cedric Robinson's (2000) work on racial capitalism and the Combahee River Collective (1986).
24 These crises include the following: global food, water, environment and climate, economic inequality and financial instability, energy and other resource exhaustion or depletion, livelihood and health, and refugees and displaced populations (Figueroa-Helland et al., 2018: 174).
25 That said, I argue that organizing to sustain long-term movements is a challenge in the United States; we see moments of mobilization today, but struggle to turn that into an ongoing and organized movement. MAB is an example of how you build a popular social movement organization that has been sustained for over three decades. The conclusion will touch on this point.
26 Roy made this statement in the epilogue of her book *Capitalism: A Ghost Story* (2014).

7

Um novo caminho

Eduardo Galeano argues that writing can be a platform – dare we say a social movement – for change.[1] In his book, *Days and Nights of Love and War,* he examines the role that writing – in a world filled with strife – can play. Does it make sense to write? This is a question that I have grappled with, and with which I continue to struggle. Galeano writes: "One writes out of a need to communicate and to commune with others, to denounce that which gives pain and to share that which gives happiness" (2000 [1983, 1978]: 169). Writing can be a powerful force for recreating our social reality.

This book examined how people organize and create solidarities between movements and across national borders, especially in this political moment where authoritarian governments are making a resurgence, and corporate greed appears limitless. There are three main takeaways from this study: 1) Global communications and social movement organizing are occurring around water in the form of translocal struggles; 2) Global North movements are engaging with and learning from the Global South, with Global South movements playing a more prominent and innovative role; and 3) The struggle for water as a human right, a public good, and a commons, rather than a commodity, is connected to a broader anti-systemic and anti-capitalist fight for livelihood that spans well beyond water.

Through translocal right to water organizing, people from the Global North have shared experiences with people in the Global South regarding corporate power that results in unsafe water. These interactions challenge nationalist identities and alignments, and center resistance to capitalist expansion and exploitation around the world. Translocality also allows for the maintenance of local specificity (Banerjee, 2011, 2018), in line with Banerjee's (2011, 2018) argument of translocal resistance, understanding what is shared while also acknowledging and centering differences based on class, gender, race, geographic location, etc. The cases discussed in this book exemplify how people are resisting existing power relations and structures based on competition and extraction.

Global solidarities against water grabbing contributes to ongoing methodological and theoretical discussions about knowledge production and decolonial/anti-colonial research methodologies. Taking a collaborative and solidarity-based approach to knowledge production – and being driven by my ongoing history as an organizer and militant committed to advancing the idea of water as a right for all – directly shaped the theories and methods of analysis that I used. In this work, I am a participant in and with the movements I discuss, and how I engage and participate is always under the invitation and guidance of the movements. In this sense, as I noted in Chapter 1, I am also a subject of my analysis.

Chapter 1 provided a literature review of political economy, resource conflicts, and social movement resistance, and overviewed my cases and chapters. It also discussed my theoretical and methodological approach, the methods used and data collected, and the importance of anti-colonial and co-research methodologies. In Chapter 2, I discussed the broader landscape of resistance to water grabbing, especially in the United States and Brazil. Chapter 3, the first of my four main empirical chapters, argued that in the case of the OWC in Pittsburgh, Pennsylvania, what impelled people to organize constituted *political* rather than just *pragmatic* concerns (González Rivas and Schroering, 2021). Organizing pressure prevented another PPP, and resident/activist pressure shaped this process of public water governance. As such, the OWC serves as a counterexample to what previous research (McDonald, 2018) has found to be true in the United States context. I also argued that the OWC is an example of translocal activism, with movement actors focused on a local issue but engaging with the state, markets, and other movements at a national and global level. In Chapter 4, drawing on fieldwork with Brazil's MAB, I contended that the standpoint offered by MAB offers crucial insights into the operation of systems of power and strategies of anti-capitalist resistance. Further, the work points to how the underlying systemic realities that cause struggles around water must be acknowledged by all – the problem is not solely one of scarcity versus abundance. Chapter 5 examined how social identities, understandings of interests, and translocal connections are a part of how MAB builds a global struggle against water privatization and contributes to a broader effort at redefining and reshaping globalization. The chapter provided a "backstage" or "power from below" (Banerjee, Maher, Krämer, 2023: 265 and 282) look of how movements produce narratives and shape their struggle. Chapter 6 examined how the Water Summit, held in Abuja, Nigeria, in 2019 served as a specific convergence space of translocal organizing for the human right to water and served as a space in which to build global solidarities and imagine alternatives to current socio-economic relations.

Water as an entry point for a larger anti-systemic struggle

We cannot separate the fight for water from broader conversations about struggles for survival and livelihood. The book shares important lessons on effectively fighting global water privatization and increasing access to safe water. Yet, it is not only about water, given that understanding water conflicts also has broader lessons for understanding austerity, market deregulation, resource privatization, and resistance. This is true in Brazil and the United States. There are differences in the locales, and one challenge – especially in the United States – is seeing problems (such as lack of safe water and lack of housing) as connected. As much as it is about resistance to water grabbing, *Global solidarities against water grabbing* is about resistance to capitalism, imagining new social relations, understanding how power works and operates, and the role of education and organization in building counter-hegemonic movements. I argue that through the struggle for water, people also become engaged in the broader structural fight for rights and justice: for housing, land, food sovereignty, education, and freedom from police brutality. In this sense, this book also becomes a portal to understanding how all these struggles are interconnected. What I have seen in my work with OWC is how the thinking of movement activists evolves from the starting place of saying water should be accessible to all to the perspective that to realize this goal, requires thinking about access to land, access to housing, and the abolition of systems of oppression. This work expands the empirical foundations that can help illuminate the complex and multifaceted ways by which information and knowledge flows through transnational movement networks, thereby contributing to learning that can disrupt prevailing power alignments and social relations.

In Chapter 1, I noted how scholars have called for social movement theory to be more attuned to economy and structure (Bieler, 2021; Englehardt and Moore, 2022; Hetland and Goodwin, 2013; McAdam and Boudet, 2012); to listen to what social movements themselves are teaching and calling for (Barbosa, 2016; Bringel and Vieira, 2016; Cox, 2014; Cox and Flesher Fominaya, 2009; Holt-Giménez, 2006; Icaza and Vásquez, 2013; Rosset et al., 2021); to address continued legacies of epistemic erasure, racism, colonialism, and imperialism; and to necessitate for white scholars and those from the Global North to think about whiteness, positionality, and decolonial frameworks (Bracey, 2016; Go, 2020; Silva, 2016, 2018).

People from the Global South, Indigenous movements, Black movements, and others from outside the centers of power have felt the exploitation of capitalism first and hardest for centuries. Many movements have also noted that the rapaciousness of our global system means that it is constantly seeking new frontiers to exploit, and that the effects of this will increasingly be felt by most people. Water grabbing in its multitude of forms is a perfect illustration of this. The Global South has been sounding the alarm on the political/ecological crisis and warning that the current socio-economic system is not sustainable. My argument that knowledge flows South to North is important for this reason. This flow is not a "new" phenomenon, but it is one that continues not to be noticed, including by scholars in the North, especially in the United States, and particularly in social movement studies. Yet, to change this system requires the participation of all of us, including those of us from the Global North. Moreover, systemic injustices are woven into the very fabric of the United States and most people on this planet – including the United States – are not actually benefitting from this capitalist system in the first place.

One of the main differences between the OWC and MAB has to do with civil and political society, by which I mean the different historical, national, political, cultural, and economic contexts,[2] and a limitation of this book is that I do not delve into them that much. Even though NGOs are prevalent in Brazil, the country has a popular social movement community (including MAB) that simply does not exist in the United States. Pittsburgh United, which houses the OWC, is not a popular social movement in the form of MAB. In the United States, we do not have any organized, leftist political parties. Further, we do not have mass social movements (organized with decades of history) akin to those in Brazil. Most of our coordinated, long-term campaigns, including around water, are tied to 501(c)(3)'s legally prohibited from taking explicit partisan political stances. Unions are also more robust in Brazil. While they vary in their political leanings, to a much greater extent than in the US, there is a stronger organized leftist labor movement in Brazil that MAB and other popular movements align with when being strategic. It is also relevant that during most of the fieldwork process for this book, and some of its writing, Brazil faced the right-wing administration of Bolsonaro, and the United States, Trump. This further necessitated the need to build coalitions across differences, to attempt to combat the concerted effort to dismantle and weaken unions and public-run systems. While the OWC is a part of Pittsburgh United (see Chapter 3 for organizational structure), whose board includes trade unions, that presence did not actively engage in the day-to-day work of the OWC. Despite the differences, however, what has repeatedly been shown to me in my work is the similarities: this is a fight for water and livelihood. Both the OWC and MAB work with a broad coalition of unions, organizations, and other movements with national and international connections.

As Gianpaolo Baiocchi (2018: 104) writes, contrasting the United States labor landscape to that of much of Latin America, "US labor, too, shows signs, often below the surface, of a radicalism that may not always be apparent at the level of national leadership." He also argues that what the United States lacks is "a structure of political representation – whether it takes the form or name of a party or not – that amplifies and connects these struggles" (Baiocchi, 2018: 106). Baiocchi contends that:

> Sometimes observers from the Global North are surprised to find the fluid merging of class, ethnic, and popular identities in social justice struggles in Latin America, but they seldom look at the political parties that make this merging possible. The intersectionalism that observers sometimes find so admirable seldom happened by itself – it appeared in the context of a broad, transformative vision of social justice. (2018: 70)

He continues to say that "Re-imagining political parties and their relationships to social movements is an ongoing and urgent task, even if we acknowledge that it is full of contradictions" (2018: 70–1). These insights resonate with what I have observed. People from MAB (and others I interviewed, including those who are a part of organized labor in Brazil) talked about how during the administrations of Lula and Dilma, they were critical of the policies and pushed them to be more responsive to the people, more to the left, more democratic. In the face of Temer and Bolsonaro, they also joined in active efforts to support democracy, including to "free Lula," to preserve public education and health systems, and to tackle ongoing systemic inequalities. In interviews and conversations, people acknowledged the importance of the PT (Worker's Party) and alliances created by different leftist/socialist/communist parties. Political parties – and working together in an organized fashion on the left – is important. This political organization also worked to ultimately defeat another term of Bolsonaro.

This is not a critique of the OWC or other campaigns like it in the United States. Instead, it is an observation of the differences in political systems and civil society, and the reality that much organizing work in the United States is tied to non-profits.[3] In many ways, this is the most significant difference that I perceive between the right to water movement in Brazil and the one in the United States. People in both places are calling for similar things. Both see water as a right and not a commodity and even use similar language in talking about the struggle. Both also organize in communities and do political education and hold trainings. But the larger civil society structure in Brazil allows for the formation of a more robust social movement (rather than a coalition or campaign) that provides space for the type of liberatory pedagogy and consciousness raising of "building the base" that I discuss in Chapters 4 and 5, that links with other popular social movements, unions, and various forms of state institutions from universities to political parties. This is an area that I hope to explore more in my future work.

Connecting with others in the global struggle against water privatization and water grabbing is something that both MAB and OWC understand, even though the formal scale of each (national versus local) is different. The OWC has had various moments of strong connection and organizing solidarity with other campaigns, such as Flint Rising and CAPPA (discussed in Chapter 6), and in smaller ways. For example, in 2020, the EJ organizer for the OWC at the time (through the relationship with Corporate Accountability), spoke on a virtual panel in 2020 to a movement in Chile fighting for water justice. Though small-scale, this is an example of the translocality highlighted throughout this book. Translocalism helps us to think through how we can organize in a way that doesn't lose the local while connecting it to the global, and to be able to engage with state and market structures – just as the transnational corporations seeking to privatize water do. Afterall, even a "local" company such as Peoples Gas in Pittsburgh is not truly local and is tied to national and international firms and structures.[4]

An organizer in Pittsburgh once commented about wanting to take on the larger energy structure and have a campaign to remunicipalize all of our resources, but they noted that we do not currently have the people power to do that. I think that's one of the things, going back to my question of what Global North movements can learn from the Global South, that we in the United States can learn: how MAB and other Global South movements build people power, and how solidarity, education, training, and consciousness-raising function in organizing. How do we build a national popular social movement to have the capacity to take on the struggle of reclaiming (or claiming) control of our energy and resource structures? Can we do so in a way that can serve the people and provide for needs, while also caring for the planet and other-than-human life?

Connecting all forms of oppression together in the struggle is also a strategy for building people power: the systems that oppress us also divide us, which is an intentional strategy. The oppressor tells us to focus on our fight – that if we let in the "other," we will lose. Might that be because the powers that be fear what would change if we united? To address the problems everyone is naming, we must come alongside each other, even when the struggle seems like it isn't the one we are most concerned about. I think that's the thing that is most powerful to me about MAB (or LVC), but I also observed it in OWC: spaces where we engage with each other can be transformational because they are spaces that give us the chance to hear and understand our differences, and that we are stronger when we work together. It is in these spaces that worlds beyond the racial capitalist, colonial, imperial, cisheteropatriarchal one we currently inhabit can be imagined and created.

MAB's fight links to patterns described in research on the importance of Global South peasant movements as sites for constructing grassroots democracy, alter-globalizations, and knowledge production (see Chapters 1 and 4). In Chapters 4 and 5, I noted the importance of the history of liberation theology in Brazil's popular movements, including MAB. Elisabeth Wood discusses the role of liberation theology in shaping resistance. Wood argues three main reasons why campesinos supported the insurgent resistance in the El Salvador Civil War. First, that social justice is seen as the will of God, thus leading to campesino participation (Wood, 2003: 232). Next, and related, liberation theology is important in understanding the second reason: defiance. People defied the authorities because of their interpretation of liberation theology and continued the struggle for justice of fallen families and comrades. Finally, Wood argues the third reason people participated is because of "the pleasure in together changing unjust social structure through intentional action" (2003: 235). These three observations from Wood are insightful and apply to MAB, too. The last also applies to all the water justice activists I have met around the world. In future work, I would like to explore more: what makes people come together to fight against oppression and injustice, and how are those connections solidified and sustained?

The history of liberation theology is undoubtedly critical to MAB's struggle. Liberation theology also exists and has played a role in struggles for social justice in the United States, including in the Civil Rights Movement and anti-war/peace movement. Indeed, James Cone[5] talked about how Martin Luther King, Jr. was a liberation theologian before the term even existed (Burrow, 1994; Cone, 2010 [1970]). However, the history of liberation theology takes a specific form in Latin America that substantially informs movement organizing there today. As I argued in my M.A. thesis, liberation theology is not "dead" (as some have suggested), and its history was and remains vital to popular social movements in Brazil (Schroering, 2015). In this book, I did not dwell on the role of religion much, aside from the importance of liberation theology in shaping MAB's focus on popular education and consciousness-raising (in Chapters 4 and 5). Still, I do see that as a fruitful area of exploration in the future. Indeed, a congregation-based community organization in Pittsburgh was influential in the early years of the CRC (which later merged with the OWC, as noted in Chapter 1), and MAB works closely with churches (both Catholic and Protestant), which continue to serve as sites for organization. The importance of religious leaders in giving legitimacy to MAB's work (such as Boff, noted in earlier chapters, but this extends to many others) is also noteworthy.

What MAB does so well is connect the movement to people's self-interests and needs and then relate those to a broader movement for justice. I think that MAB's model is one from which movements in the United States could learn.[6] While the shape and form would inevitably be different to fit the specific context, the core ideas are applicable. However, even as I make this contrast and suggest that movements in the US might learn from movements in Brazil, there are also similarities between MAB and OWC. The OWC has relied on community town halls, trainings, canvassing, and other meetings and educational events to talk to people and hear their concerns and provide education about the more significant structural problems. From an organizing perspective, building people power is everything, and mechanisms to teach and develop these skills are critical (Ganz and Lin, 2011). More so than what I observe in the United States, MAB also sees the need to include building not just national but international alliances. It is a local, national, and global fight. This analysis – which comes from an interrogation of political economy – makes seeing these connections more accessible. The individualism and the privilege for many (especially white and affluent) people in the United States to ignore exploitative systems because they are personally shielded from the impacts, arguably make it harder to organize and build mass movements here. In this sense, the different political and cultural contexts do matter. This is one place where I see that the role of academics and social movement scholars – who have learned skills of translation and analysis/synthesis – is needed. These are important for coalition work and broadening the base. This is also why I contend it is imperative to move away from the notion of objectivity and to work in collaboration and solidarity with movements. As I note early on in this book, knowledge is not an individual, but rather a collective and iterative process.

This collective process is also evident in how MAB draws on the history of other struggles, including the United States Civil Rights Movement. In MAB there is an egalitarian idea that says there is a place (and need) for everyone to be a leader. Ganz and McKenna (2019: 190) argue that leaders engage in relationship building, storytelling, strategizing, structuring, and action. In my own organizing work, I was taught that a leader is someone who has a following of people (not in some charismatic sense, but relationships of friends, family, neighbors, etc.) that they can call on and engage in the work of building people power to place demands upon public officials to make changes. I observed that through consciousness raising, base building, and popular education (discussed in Chapters 4 and 5). MAB facilitates the critical work necessary to move people to be even more effective as leaders. There is an understanding that this is a crucial part of building communal, national, and even transnational power. To relate it to United States social movement literature on leadership, it is a type of participatory and decentralized leadership that Polletta discusses is comprised of: "Making decisions jointly, rotating leadership, and taking turns articulating the group's position to the public" (2002: 160).[7]

While the content, intensity, and frequency of how it was done varied, both the OWC and MAB understand the importance of building people power. Further, both also did this through engaging with people and holding trainings: "base building." While the OWC did at times use this term, its focus on it ebbed and flowed (again, I think this speaks to the difference between a national social movement and a campaign situated within a larger non-profit movement community), but both do what MAB calls "strengthening the base" or base building.

Water privatization in the time of Covid

Some of the fieldwork, and much of the writing, of this manuscript took place during the Covid-19 pandemic. The pandemic highlighted existing injustices, and increased the precarity faced by those who lack access to clean water. How do you wash your hands without water? How do you care for the sick without water? Covid-19 also showed the brutality of capitalism, and the slow violence that its ever expanding and rapacious forms perpetrate. Water grabbing in all its various forms is one of these forms of capital accumulation. The Covid-19 pandemic represented a moment when choices could have been made to prioritize people over profit, though for the most part, this did not happen. The few protections that did emerge, such as moratoriums on water shut offs, are now being rolled back.

At the same time, the pandemic did draw more attention to the crisis of water affordability, including in the United States, as revealed in *The Guardian's* series on water affordability.[8] Further, many social movements and water justice groups (including MAB and OWC) built and participated in mutual aid/solidarity networks, and their organizing work undoubtedly saved lives. The work also built solidarity and created moments to focus on our common humanity, fragility of life, and interdependence. Ashish Kothari writes of the pandemic:

> The need for fundamental change has not escaped the attention of northern scholars. Sandbrook et al. (2020) examined the likely political and economic responses to the COVID-19 pandemic, and stressed the need for transformative economic reconstruction, noting that green recovery approaches will simply not be enough. But even they limit their horizon to approaches to degrowth emanating from the Global North, and do not mention the radical approaches emerging or resurfacing in the Global South. Some of us have recently laid out key principles for a new, post-growth approach to conservation (Fletcher et al., 2020): conviviality, diversity, decommodification, valuing the sacred in nature, decolonization, social justice, direct democracy, redistribution, subsidiarity, global interconnectedness, linking conservation and resistance,

and redefining power. These come from listening closely, being involved with grassroots movements, but it is not an attempt to speak on behalf of these movements. They must be enabled to speak for themselves in debates on the future of conservation, or indeed the future of Earth. (2021: 162)

Kothari's last sentence is particularly critical. In writing this book, I share the work the movements are doing. I do not think that MAB – or any other Global South-led movement – requires the analysis and critiques of a Northern scholar. Yet I also know that people in MAB want their work and struggle shared, and believe in the importance of connection and solidarity with others around the globe – including from the "belly of the beast" that is now called the United States – to hear about their struggle and join in solidarity. So, what I have sought to do is to tell MAB's story – albeit through my eyes – and make connections between their struggle and those of other movements fighting for water, including and especially that of the OWC (which in turn taught me about the work of OWOR). Writing much of this book amidst a pandemic made me grapple even more with the questions that guide my scholarship and my movement through the world: what place does research and writing have in my militancy? How do we create a world where life – human and other than human – might matter more than profit? I write because I have been entrusted with stories, and my positionality as an organizer, researcher, teacher, and writer means that I can tell them to an audience that otherwise might not hear them or see how the multitude of voices are connected.

Water as an entry point to a larger anti-systemic struggle?

When I began the initial research for this book in 2015/2016, I asked: does the threat to water privatization compel people to react – to resist and/ or organize – more so than does the threat of other forms of privatization? Today, my answer to this is both yes and no. Indeed, my research both confirms and challenges that of other scholars' who have argued that water privatization or the threat of water privatization elicits more resistance than other forms of privatization. On the one hand, there is evidence that resource conflicts involving water produce more resistance (Almeida, 2014; Subramaniam, 2014), and that struggles against water privatization are a part of a larger fight to transform capitalist relations into new ways of being and living (Bieler, 2021; Bieler and Moore, 2023). My work with the OWC, including how various public officials changed their stance on the matter, suggests this is true. My findings show that people in the United States who are not necessarily against privatization or hold an anticapitalist position find the idea of privatizing water problematic. Research on remunicipalization suggests that popular opinion supports public over private water, and this can be used to suggest that globally public opinion veers in support of public water (Rapid Transition Alliance, 2019). There are no large-scale public opinion polls, however, that show the percentage of people who support/oppose privatization on a national or global scale, but remunicipalization efforts – including in the United States – suggest growing support for water and other utilities to be managed by public governance.[9] Similarly, in Pittsburgh, the water has remained public only due to the mobilization of residents demanding that it remain so.

Every person who sat at the OWC table (be they individual residents or representing organizations) came to the topic out of a broader commitment to various environmental and social justice struggles. That is, water is not what brought them to the table. A few people in my interviews in Brazil noted that water specifically was their interest; but most people came to the struggle because they are atingidos/as/es directly impacted by dam projects or had a commitment to fighting for social justice, land reform, resource conflicts, and environmental issues. Even MAB's motto "water and energy aren't commodities" connects the fight to larger energy structures.

The fight for the right to water is one connected to other struggles. MAB articulates a clear and intentional fight against interlocking systems of oppression: classism, racism, heterosexism, and patriarchy. These are all seen as interlinked with capitalism, viewed as the root cause of the problem. Articulating a different model for how we structure our world is a process of education and growth, where people learn through lectures, conversations, and discussions. The literature examining drivers of remunicipalization in the United States has argued that efforts are more pragmatic rather than political. Yet the Pittsburgh case is, in fact, political. The OWC also used the argument that water is a human right and has confronted the idea that water is "not an inalienable right that should be free," as discussed in Chapter 3. Pittsburgh United, which houses the OWC, is also engaged in other campaigns, including housing and economic justice. In this sense, both MAB and the OWC view water as something that should not be a commodity, and that is connected to other struggles.

Yet, even as the fight against water privatization is linked to other struggles, there is something special about water. Indeed, water is, quite literally, a required substance for life. I do think the threat of losing access to water catches people's attention more than the threat of other forms of privatization. My observations are drawn from working within movements themselves.[10] In terms of a national conversation in the United States, water is receiving more attention, as noted earlier in this chapter. When I started this project, there was not much of a national conversation around water privatization in the United States. In 2016, a sociologist and water scholar

at the American Sociological Association Conference told me in conversation that they constantly had to argue the broader sociological significance
of studying water to their peers. Today, this is changing. Flint played a role
in drawing more attention to municipal water issues in the United States.
Of course, the residents of Flint still lack safe water, so attention does not
necessarily mean change. Still, it's not just Flint: it is a symptom of decades
of austerity measures and disinvestment that have led to a breaking point of
decaying infrastructure in the United States and worldwide.

Austerity and disinvestment are national and global problems. It is also
the case that the effects of these measures are not always felt equally by all.
For example, as I discussed in Chapter 6, state violence against Black and
brown people and the "slow" violence of water injustice are connected. In
the United States, Pittsburgh's replacement of lead lines recently received
national attention. On 16 June 2022, Vice President Kamala Harris visited
Pittsburgh and held a press conference with the Pittsburgh Water and Sewer
Authority (PWSA). There, she lauded the public utility for its leadership in
replacing lead service lines. To date, PWSA has replaced 9,100 lead lines,
and the authority has pledged to replace all lead lines in the service area
using funds provided by a $17 million grant from the American Rescue Plan
Act of 2021 (PWSA, 2022b). This success occurred because of the sustained
and organized community work to make it so, and it should be celebrated.[11]
This initiative, which is projected to be complete within the next 10 years, is
a long-awaited victory of environmental justice advocates, and will ensure
cleaner and safer water for more than 10 million homes.

But where do those used lead pipes go? In an article published in the
Spanish newspaper, *El País,* Isabella Cota notes that as part of United
States President Joe Biden's plan to stimulate the economy (and address
the environmental injustice of lead pipes), the United States has announced
plans to spend $15 billion to replace the country's remaining lead pipes.
However, as Cota notes, the afterlife of these pipes presents a much less
rosy picture. These lead pipes will be shipped to other countries via the
international secondary lead waste market, which supplies companies that
refine and smelt lead reclaimed from items such as car batteries and pipes
(Cota, 2022).

This illustrates why translocal organizing and resistance is so critical: without it, there is a risk of environmental injustice being "fixed" in one
place but exported to another. It also exemplifies how even with something
as "issue specific" as water, the organizing is not simply about water. The
United States is finally correcting an environmental injustice, but exporting
that injustice to other places in the world. It is an example of environmental imperialism and state violence, which disproportionately impacts Black
and brown communities (Togami, Schroering, Musil, and González Rivas,

2023). This elucidates another reason for the importance of global political economy and translocal organizing.

Translocal organizing is about knowledge production and the role of information sharing and popular education in anti-systemic struggles. As Choudry put it, when writing about two disparate organizing spaces (La Vía Campesina and the Highlander School), popular education is critical, and everywhere, but is often "not necessarily documented. Systematizing popular education and movement experiences remain a challenge" (2015: 89–90). What I have observed in my own organizing work and scholarship, and what I hope to have shown and documented a slice of here, is the critical role that popular education – whether explicitly called that, as in the case of MAB, or not – plays in the struggle for water.

Translocalism and global solidarities

The OWC says that water is a human right that should be available to all. MAB argues that water is a right and not a commodity, and they treat the production of knowledge as communal, constant, and interrelated with creating anti-systemic struggle. As the title of a 2021 article by MAB puts it, "Water is the right of humanity and not the property of private capital" (Calisto and Paulino, 2021). I have found the idea of translocality fruitful – even though it is *not* a word I hear movements using – because I think the term does capture multiple ideas and processes that are coming from movements.

In the case of MAB, they use the language of "global" or "international." In the OWC, both of those words are used (though less frequently), and generally in terms of talking about the role of transnational corporations in privatizing water. What I see happening with this expression and my application of it is that people understand how Veolia, Nestlé, and other corporations operate across (or without) state borders. In turn, this relates to how under the present form of capitalism (neoliberalism, speculative finance, and the financialization of water to name some), geographic and state boundaries are in some cases dissolved. I am not arguing that nation-states no longer matter – they do. But corporate power transcends these borders. And so too does people power. What the term translocal captures is that people understand that their struggle might be local, with a local target like the mayor, while at the same time understanding that the pressure creating the need for the fight is coming from corporate power that is seeking to exploit communities around the globe, albeit in varying forms. Translocal resistance thus allows for local autonomy and specificity while also creating learning networks that allow for movements to come together with others to build solidarity. Just as corporations operate together, so too does the resistance. How is this different from a transnational social movement? One key distinction is that transnational social movements privilege the nation state as the unit of analysis (see Banerjee, 2011).

I do not suggest that we eliminate the term transnational from our lexicon, largely because that is how we refer to corporations. In theory, it is states that can regulate corporations within their so-called borders; part of the challenge of corporate power is that it is able to elude and evade national boundaries to escape regulation and extract profit – which speaks to how states are also complicit in allowing this. While many of these corporations and their CEOs are concentrated in the United States, they span the world. It is present day imperialism, where the corporation is the primary instrument of imperial extraction. This suggests that we need to reimagine how we think about states today – especially as many movements fighting against corporate power and engaged in counter-hegemonic struggles are also fighting for a world that does not have the type of borders and boundaries that exist today. At the same time, many of these movements are fighting to place demands upon nation-states to provide for social welfare. These concepts and processes are complicated and, at times, contradictory. Part of the explanatory power of the term translocal is that it captures these contradictions in a way that transnational does not. I also observe that the term is specific to describing resistance and social movements – it cannot be used to describe a corporation, for example. This speaks to the point made by Ramachandra Guha, as discussed in the introduction, that the forms of domination shape the forms of resistance (Guha, 1989: 98). But resistance also shapes the domination, as is demonstrated by the corporate use of the term "PPP," noted in Chapter 3. While transnational capital and neoliberal restructuring (including transnational corporations) drive water privatization and shape the resistance to it, the resistance also shapes economic processes (Bieler, 2021; Bieler and Moore, 2023).

As Emerson, Fretz, and Shaw write, "writers do more than inscribe the world. Just as the ethnographer-as-observer participates with members in constructing a social reality, so, too, the ethnographer-as-writer creates the world through language" (2011: 126). In this book, I describe the world(s) that I have observed and participated in and hope that my words might be a part of creating the world I would like to see, even if in a small way. At this moment in time, language – words – are my weapon of resistance. This book attempts to bridge these worlds of organizer and scholar. To understand resource conflicts, we need to realize that the core of these conflicts goes much deeper than the surface of the water. The lack of safe drinking water, commodification of water, and dam projects for mining that cause displacement and destruction – all of these things result from systemic realities. As MAB asserts, "justice only with struggle and organization."

MAB's struggle spans beyond its own fight and beyond the fight against water privatization. It is part of a global resistance effort to reclaim (or claim) the commons of water and fight against the commodification and privatization of life. MAB's insistence that all forms of oppression are interconnected and that the struggles of those who have died in their fight for a better world serve as seeds of resistance is also a statement of hope and a catalyst for envisioning a different world – and imagining new possibilities is a prerequisite for creating them. It relates to a statement that Ignacio,[12] a MAB militante, made to the two other people from the United States participating in the Course on Energy[13] and me: "I've noticed that people from the United States seem to have less hope" (Fieldnotes, July 2019). He said this in the context of a conversation about what we all thought the world might look like in ten years' time. And he noted that he thought Brazilians had more hope, suggesting that hope, even when all the evidence points against it, is essential. The statement reminded me of these words by Galeano: "If, as we believe, hope is preferable to nostalgia, perhaps that nascent literature may come to deserve the beauty of the social forces which, sooner or later, by hook or by crook, will radically alter the course of our history" (2000: 178).

The tone of this book has been intentionally optimistic; amidst all that is broken, there are always glimmers of hope, flowers growing in a crack in the pavement. Hope is necessary. Even if small, temporary, or not translated into policies, claiming wins in terms of organizing, evolution and expansion of relationships, and connections that form in the struggle, are essential. I believe (and this is the organizer in me, as the researcher in me is often more despondent than hopeful) in the power of organized people. I may not be able to prove that it can work, and for sure, more often than not, there are defeats and also debates questioning the impact that social movements can have. Yet, I continue to believe in people power; I believe it is the engine that changes history, and I keep hope that we can create a different world. It is a dangerous trap to decide that just because things have always been terrible, or just because we can only imagine things to be a certain way, that they will stay that way. One of the things we can learn from movements like MAB is how our knowledge production and thinking might serve to disrupt the hegemonic narratives and not further reproduce it; it's about breaking the hold of cultural hegemony (see Chapters 1, 4, and 6 for more about cultural hegemony). A key component of this is popular education, which is more explicitly seen in MAB's work, but my chronicle of the OWC also centers the role of community/public education in the organizing process. Counter-hegemonic work is about knowledge and imagination: we must believe a different world is possible and imagine what it looks like; and then fight to create it. "Internationalize the struggle, internationalize hope!"

Notes

1 A New Path.
2 I would argue, for example, that the United States is the most individualistic society that has ever existed, and so building the idea of the collective is particularly challenging.
3 This also speaks to the "non-profit industrial complex" that shapes – and often limits – how campaigns organize and seek change in the United States (Choudry, 2015: 94). There is a growing awareness and discussion of this reality, that is incredibly important, but beyond the main focus of this book.
4 And as discussed in Chapter 3, was since acquired by Aqua America, which is now known as Essential Utilities (ITPI, 2021).
5 Paulo Freire (1985: 145–148) also wrote about the importance of James Cone's work to the struggle for liberation in the United States.
6 The most similar process for building people power to MAB's organizing that I have seen here in the US was during my time working as a community organizer with a congregation-based community organization in Jacksonville, Florida. I mean this not just in the sense of theologies of liberation, but in organizing structures that do not have anything to do with religion per se, but focus on listening to people's needs and concerns, education, reflection, research on the problems, and then coming together to demand change, focused on building grassroots democracy and leadership.
7 Polletta was writing of women in leadership in the Student Non-Violent Coordinating Committee (SNCC).
8 Discussed in Chapter 3.
9 I noted this previously, but the Water Remunicipalisation Tracker offers a visual way to see some of these examples. Although, at the time of publication of this book, the website was not working. However, there are plans to revive it. www.remunicipalisation.org/front/page/home
10 Further work is required to determine whether these are broader trends. I encourage other researchers to consider how water serves as an inciting issue – pragmatic or political – for individuals outside the social movement community
11 The role of the community mobilization around the topic, however, was not mentioned at the press conference.
12 A pseudonym.
13 Discussed in Chapter 5.

Appendix A

Fieldwork background and reflections

During the summer of 2018, I received funding through the Center for Latin American Studies/Tinker Grant and Nationality Rooms Scholarship from the University of Pittsburgh. From 12 June - 18 July 2018, I conducted field-work in Brazil. My on-the-ground fieldwork took place in various locales, including the city of Belém in the state of Pará and the states of Rio de Janeiro and São Paulo and, in subsequent visits, Brasília and Minas Gerais. Relying on the connections of Rob Robinson, a founding member of the US Solidarity Network for MAB, I established contacts with two key leaders of MAB. These leaders facilitated making more contacts, and I had the opportunity to research MAB and other partner organizations and unions. Movement leaders also shared an abundant amount of published material, including books, pamphlets, posters, and other literature.

I conducted open-ended, semi-structured interviews in Portuguese, guiding the conversations toward the specific areas listed in Appendix D (see Appendix E for English version). I relied on my principal contacts (described in more detail under case selection and feasibility) and then used snowball sampling to identify key informants. I conducted 24 formal semi-structured interviews that lasted between 25 minutes and 2 hours (with the average being an hour). Before each interview, I read a script (see Appendix B and C for English and Portuguese versions) to respondents explaining the purpose of the research. During this first fieldwork trip, I also conducted 140-plus hours of participant observation, as well as over a dozen informal interviews.

I returned to Brazil for seven weeks during the summer of 2019 to conduct more fieldwork. I completed seven additional formal semi-structured interviews (using the same protocol as discussed above), three of which were with individuals I had previously interviewed, and four with new partici-pants (including a leader with an environmental NGO that works on water, the former head of the water regulatory commission, and the president of a water and sanitation workers' union). However, early in this second trip, I decided to focus on ethnographic participant observation rather than interviews. The initial interviews allowed me to meet people and to gain trust and gain valuable insight and understanding of the various and complex dynamics around the struggle for the right to water. As I was invited into more organizing spaces and spent less time in interviews, I started to question the top-down format of interviews and its efficacy in my particular research project (interviews are an essential and valid tool, I am speaking to my specific research, which also comes out of my own positionality as someone who came to this work initially as an organizer and activist, rather than researcher).

As I had many informal conversations (including with people I had interviewed the year before), I also started to think how much I had "missed" by jumping right in and doing interviews before people knew me well or trusted me. There was also a practical reason for not doing more formal interviews: after 14–18-hour days, I did not feel comfortable asking people if I could interview them, nor did I frankly have the capacity to be a good interviewer after those long days of constant activity and "observant participation."

In 2019, I had the opportunity to observe four trainings held by MAB that spanned each from two to 12 days. In addition, I attended various other events and activities led by MAB leaders and others in the broader movement community. MAB also extended an invitation for me to participate in a two-year, four-part course that is a partnership between MAB and the Universidade Federal do Rio de Janeiro (Federal University of Rio de Janeiro or UFRJ). It brings together more than 70 people from 21 organizations, social movements, and unions from five countries across the Americas. The goal is to make the university more accessible to workers and the public, and in the process, strengthen the struggle for the human right to water and fight against the privatization of resources and education. While there are activists from the United States who participate in this course, I am the first academic from the United States to be invited. From 15 to 26 July 2019 I attended the first 10-day part of this course, with sections on the following themes: Capitalism, nature, and scarcity; The State and classes in modern society; Energy and industrialization in the modern world; Methodology of scientific work; and Basic principles of economics.

I returned to Brazil for another four weeks in January–February 2020. During this time, I continued my participation in intensive ethnographic and participant observation. I participated with MAB and partners from around the world in multiple activities (including days-long planning and strategizing meetings between international partners and marches, seminars, and other actions to commemorate the one-year anniversary of the Brumadinho dam collapse, discussed in Chapters 2 and 5). From 4 to 15 February, I attended the second part of the Course on Energy. The themes for it included: History of energy in Brazil; Imperialism and other theories about global capitalism; The state and revolutions; and The history of the environmental question and its institutional apparatus. I had planned to return to Brazil for at least another 4–6 months, which would have included in-person participation in the third portion of the Course on Energy, but the Covid-19 pandemic disrupted this plan. The course moved to a less concentrated (meeting every other Saturday for four hours each time over the course of five months in 2021),online format, in which I continued to participate. This portion focused on the following themes: Social democracy and the welfare state; Social struggles and environmental justice; The State and Revolutions II; and The geopolitics of energy in the contemporary world. I participated and graduated from the course in July 2022, where we had gathered in person for two weeks outside of the city of Rio for the fourth and final time. The topics covered the following: Energy in contemporary Brazil; The State and classes in contemporary society; Human rights and the environment; and globalization and contemporary capitalism.

Since its inception in January 2017, I have been involved in the Our Water Campaign, participating in meetings, community outreach and actions, canvassing, town halls, and other meetings and events. When I first moved to Pittsburgh in 2015, I learned about the work of the OWC predecessor campaign, the Clean Rivers Campaign (CRC). At this time, I did not think my dissertation project would be around water, but issues of environmental justice and water were important to me. In addition to fulfilling the requirements of my course work, my primary motivation was that I hoped to find ways to become engaged in local social movement work in my new home of Pittsburgh. The CRC agreed to let me work with them as a "participant observer," for a qualitative methods class I was taking at the time.

In early discussions in 2016 with the leadership of the water coalition in Pittsburgh, there was a back-and-forth negotiation surrounding whether to allow me to attend meetings and be involved; there was suspicion of an academic – even a student – sitting in the corner "scribbling notes." There were also questions about what I might contribute to the work – and how my writing could be a part of that. One of the Pittsburgh leaders said to me that it would be great to have someone who understands organizing to write a report of the campaign, which would chronicle the history, the organizing strategies and, also perhaps, be used as a toolkit for other communities who want to follow suit. When I began this project, even though I had been an organizer for years before, on multiple issues, I thought that to be a "good" scholar, to publish, to get a PhD, I had to separate – at least a little – my researcher self from my political work. I spent the first two plus years participating in water justice work in Pittsburgh and would always sit quietly, taking notes, only speaking if someone called on me. I felt pressure from the academy that I had to separate my scholarship from my activism and militancy.

I would show up early and stay late to events, helping with setting up and cleaning up. I would use my citizen role to speak at public meetings, and people saw me showing up consistently to protests and take action (not just related to water) around the city. But in the back of my mind was a voice saying, "you aren't doing this right according to academic norms. You have to separate these two worlds, be more 'objective,' less engaged."

I had been quiet. I didn't want to overstep because I was the outsider. And I do think that was appropriate because I was an outsider to this particular organizing space and community. But after a couple of years, while constantly juggling the "insider/outsider" status, I was not an outsider – I had been engaged in the campaign since its inception. And people – especially those newer to the table who had not known me for a few years – probably wondered why I didn't speak more. Professional norms often encourage the idea of a neutral outsider when in fact, through the eyes of many outside the academia, as researchers, we are a part of an extractive university industrial complex (or edu-factory), who extract knowledge and benefit from it, at the expense of the "community."

After some time, I noted that organizers and activists in Pittsburgh who had known me now for a few years would make statements to me such as, "I think you have some valuable insight – you should speak more." The same held during my time in Brazil. One thing that does not receive sufficient discussion is how in qualitative research (including social movement studies), one's positionality always informs what you hear and learn. By not taking a public stance on the topic, you are also skewing your research: whether it gets stated or not, people are likely not trusting the researcher and probably guarding what conversations they are privy to (Bell, 2019; Snow, Benford, and Anderson, 1986; This is especially the case if the scholar seems only to be taking from and not contributing to the struggle. My work with MAB also helped to teach me that there is a history (and present) of scholars coming out of social movements, and whose scholarship is rooted to their commitment to advance movements. I grew into my role, understanding that just as I would receive pushback from some outside the movements, as long as I was transparent with them all about my positionality, I did not – in fact, could not – separate these two parts of myself.

In 2016, I participated in around a dozen meetings and events with the CRC, and I interviewed six critical leaders in the campaign. In early 2017, the OWC officially coalesced (and I was present for many of the early founding conversations that took place in the CRC), and I became actively engaged with that campaign, seeing the fight against water privatization and the right to water as critically important. I continued to participate in both campaigns but became more committed to the OWC. As noted in Chapter 1, the OWC and CRC ultimately merged into one campaign in early 2019. Between January 2017 and June 2020, I attended over 85 bi-weekly meetings, strategizing retreats, board meetings with water authorities, meetings with public officials, public actions, and community events and canvassing.

My engagement with OWC led to my participation as an invited delegate from Pittsburgh with three other Pittsburgh organizers connected to the OWC to a Water Summit in Nigeria. I was invited to attend pre- and post-strategy meetings of OWOR, and I spent two weeks in Nigeria, visiting Lagos, Ibadan, Calabar, and other towns, meeting with Nigerian environmental activists, and seeing firsthand some of the challenges around gaining socio-environmental justice. Chapter 6 focuses on that period.

Data analysis

I kept detailed notes and daily memos throughout my time in the field to help build my theories, both from inductive analysis of data and thinking about theoretical ideas, and have employed an inductive approach to analysis. When I first went to Brazil in 2018 to conduct preliminary dissertation fieldwork, I used my pre-existing knowledge of the water movements and other activist spaces to establish codes. My general categories included: Participant demographics and biographical history/involvement in other movements; Perception of Scale and Struggle; Movement characteristics; Forms of leadership; and, Types of outcomes. I relied on an open/inductive approach to data collection, remaining open to the unexpected, and incorporating a grounded and inductive approach to my findings (Maxwell, 2013). As such, my research and practice shifted throughout time, as I discuss in the chapters of this book. While I initially planned on using a software analysis program, I decided to create my system, manually going through my fieldnote interviews and written documents to see what themes emerged. The idea of water as a right and not a commodity; the importance of linking struggles, international solidarity, and translocality; the importance of seeing the right to water as one inseparable from other efforts (including around gender, economic, and racial justice); and the idea that the fight against water privatization is part of a larger anti-capitalist struggle, are what emerged. In addition, Chapters 4, 5, and 7 also discuss themes that emerged and foci of MAB that inform the core of their work and that I think are examples of how academics (and activists) from the US might learn from movements from the so-called Global South.

The words and stories shared with me by every interviewee informed this book, and the perspective from each individual informed and enlightened my understanding of the broader movement community in Brazil. Everyone gave similar responses in terms of seeing the fight for the right to water as a local, national, and international struggle; spoke of their involvement in the struggle due to the belief that humans have a right to water and to livelihood (the specific reasons for their involvement did vary, just as it does in the US, and I do think that this would be an interesting future paper); most people did not get explicitly involved because of the topic of water[1] but were more broadly engaged in social, environmental, and revolutionary struggles; and people saw the objective of the fight to be so that people can have control of their resources, and that those resources – including and especially water – are for all, not just a wealthy few.

While I do include interview data where I think it helps to paint a clearer picture of the landscape for the reader, the more profound stories came from conversations and interactions with people after building relationships and trust or turning off the tape recorder. In terms of methodology, in future projects (time permitting), I would choose to conduct interviews at the end, rather than the beginning, of my research process, after my knowledge and understanding of the topic had grown, and people had gained trust in me. Because this project was mainly an ethnographic one, I do not include a list of interviews in the bibliography. In the few cases where I do cite from interview data, I introduce the speaker in the body of the text. In most cases when referencing an interview, I provide the exact date; in a few cases, I keep it to the general time period; this is intentional, and to protect anonymity. I utilize in-text citations noting fieldwork as well; when there is not an exact date it is either because a) it is referencing a recurring point that I encountered during that time period (for example, "summer 2018") or b) for the reason noted above regarding interview dates.

Note

1 I discuss how this both is and is not consistent with existing literature on right to water movements in the conclusion.

Appendix B

Interview script (English)

The purpose of this study is to examine "right to water" or anti-water privatization movements in the United States and Brazil. Specifically, I am interested in the following questions: 1) Do members of these mobilizations see their efforts as an isolated local struggle, or as connected to a larger national and/or global network of activists? 2) What are the reasons that individuals are engaged with this work? 3) Did the issue of water impel people to become engaged in organizing work, or had they been involved in mobilizations around other issues previously? 4) What do they understand to be the goals of their work? 5) What types of campaigns and movements have activists been involved in?

Participants will receive no compensation for participation. Participants will be asked to partake in a semi-structured interview. Interview questions will allow participants to elaborate on the five themes stated above. Interviews will typically last 30 minutes to 2 hours, and most individuals will only be interviewed once. There is no anticipated risk from participation in this study. Participants will have the option of choosing if they prefer their identity to remain anonymous. Names will not be used in research paper or dissertation unless consent is given by the research participant. The researcher will be the only person to have access to the audio recorded interviews. The interview transcripts will only be read by the researcher, who will store hard copies of the interviews in a secure cabinet. Participation in this study is completely voluntary. You do not have to respond to any questions that you do not wish to answer. You have the right to withdraw from this study at any time without consequence.

If you have any questions, you may contact Caitlin Schroering, a graduate student in sociology at the University of Pittsburgh. Email: chs203@pitt.edu

Appendix C

Interview script (Portuguese)

O objetivo deste estudo é examinar os movimentos de "direito à água" ou movimentos contra a privatização da água nos Estados Unidos e no Brasil. Especificamente, estou interessada nas seguintes questões: 1) Os participantes dessas mobilizações vêem seus esforços como uma luta local isolada ou conectada com a uma grande rede de ativistas nacional e/ou global? 2) Quais são as razões que indivíduos estão envolvidos com este trabalho? 3) As pessoas se envolveram em ativismo por causa da questão da água ou já tinham se envolvido em outros tipos de mobilizações? 4) O que eles entendem como objetivos de seu trabalho? 5) Perguntas sobre ativismo de água e em que tipos de campanhas e movimentos os activistas estiveram envolvidos?

Os participantes não serão remunerados pela sua participação. Participantes serão convidados a participar de uma entrevista semi-estruturada. As perguntas da entrevista vão permitir que os participantes elaborarem sobre os temas referidos acima. Uma entrevista pode durar de 30 minutos a 2 horas, e a maioria dos indivíduos serão intrevistados somente uma vez. Não há antecipação de risco na participação deste estudo. Os participantes terão a opção de escolher sua preferencia em manter sua identidade anônima. Os nomes não serão utilizados a menos que a permissão seja explicitamente oferecida pelo participante da pesquisa. A pesquisadora será a única pessoa a ter acesso as entrevistas gravadas. As transcrições das entrevistas serão lidas exclusivamente pela pesquisadora que armazenará cópias dentro de um arquivo trancado. Você tem o direito de retirar-se do estudo a qualquer momento, sem prejuízo.

Contato em caso de dúvidas sobre o estudo: Caitlin Schroering, estudante de pós-graduação, Universidade de Pittsburgh, chs203@pitt.edu

Appendix D

Perguntas para entrevistas semi-estruturadas com ativistas da agua

1 Qual é o seu trabalho com o movimento?
2 Como você se envolveu? Quanto tempo?
3 Quais são as razões que você está envolvida/o com este trabalho/ movimento?
4 Você já trabalhou em outros movimentos antes? Que tipo? Você ainda está envolvido com isso?
5 Você está envolvida/o em ativismo por causa da questão da água ou já tinham se envolvid/ao em outros tipos de mobilizações?
6 Na sua opinião, quais são os objetivos do movimento?
7 O que você acha que são os principais alvos da sua campanha?
8 Pensando sobre os atores diferentes / indivíduos / grupos quanto a unidade que você acha que existe no entendimento da questão e / ou destino das pessoas?
9 Você vê o movimento como uma luta local isolada ou conectada com a uma grande rede de ativistas nacional e/ou global?

Appendix E

Questions for semi-structured interviews with water activists

1 What is your work with the movement?
2 How did you get involved and for how much time?
3 What are the reasons that you are involved in this work/with this movement?
4 Had you worked in other movements previously? What type? Are you still involved in that work?
5 Did the problem of water cause you to get involved in movement work or were you involved in other types of mobilizations?
6 In your opinion, what are the objectives of the movement?
7 What do you think are the main targets of your campaign?
8 Thinking about the different actors/individuals/groups, how much unity do you think there is in people's understanding of the issue and/or target?
9 Do you see the movement as a local and isolated fight or as connected to a larger national, or even global, network?

References

A Planeta n.d. "This Police Planet Has to End!" *A Planeta*. Retrieved 1 July 2023 (https://web.archive.org/web/20230701142148/http://aplaneta.org/this-police-planet-has-to-end/).

Abba, Amos. 2019. "How Nestle Nigeria Contaminates Water Supply of Its Host Community in Abuja." *International Centre for Investigative Reporting*. Retrieved 3 July 2024 (https://web.archive.org/web/20190710185316/ https:// www.icirnigeria.org/how-nestle-nigeria-contaminates-water-supply-of-its-host-community-in-abuja/).

Addison, Rebecca. 2017. "While PWSA and Veolia Squabble over Who's to Blame, Some Call for Quicker Action to Address Pittsburgh's Lead Crisis." *Pittsburgh City Paper*, August 16. Retrieved 23 June 2023 (https://web.archive.org/web/2023070 1162046/https://www.pghcitypaper.com/news/while-pwsa-and-veolia-squabble-over-whos-to-blame-some-call-for-quicker-action-to-address-pittsburghs-lead-crisis-3813202).

Alatas, Syed Farid. 2003. "Academic Dependency and the Global Division of Labour in the Social Sciences." *Current Sociology* 51(6):599–613.

Alatas, Syed Hussein. 2000. "Intellectual Imperialism: Definition, Traits and Problems." *Southeast Asian Journal of Social Science* 28(1):23–45.

Almeida, Paul. 2014. *Mobilizing Democracy: Globalization and Citizen Protest*. Baltimore, MD: Johns Hopkins University Press.

Almeida, Paul. 2019. *Social Movements: The Structure of Collective Mobilization*. Oakland, CA: University of California Press.

Altieri, Miguel A. and Victor Manuel Toledo. 2011. "The Agroecological Revolution in Latin America: Rescuing Nature, Ensuring Food Sovereignty and Empowering Peasants." *The Journal of Peasant Studies* 38(3):587–612.

Amenta, Edwin, Kenneth T. Andrews, and Neal Caren. 2018. "The Political Institutions, Processes, and Outcomes Movements Seek to Influence." Pp. 449–65 in *The Wiley Blackwell Companion to Social Movements*, edited by David A. Snow, Sarah A. Soule, Hanspeter Kriesi, and Holly J. McCammon, 2nd ed. John Wiley & Sons.

Amin, Samir. 2022. *The Agrarian Question Beyond Neoliberalism: Essays on the Peasantry, Sovereignty and Socialism*. Harare. New Delhi, India, and São Paulo:, Brazil Agrarian South Network in collaboration with Sam Moyo African Institute for Agrarian Studies, Centre for Agrarian Research and Education for South, and Coletivo Novo Bandung. Retrieved 25 June 2023 (https://web.archive.org/web/ 20220704025546/http://www.agrariansouth.org/wp-content/uploads/2022/06/ SAMIR-AMIN__The-Agrarian-Question-Beyond-Neoliberalism__ASN-e-Book-2022.pdf).

ANA (Agência Nacional de Águas e Saneamento Básico). 2020. "Relatório de Segurança de Barragens 2019." Brasília: ANA. Retrieved 23 June 2023 (https://web.archive.org/web/20220713092532/https://www.snisb.gov.br/relatorio-anual-de-seguranca-de-barragem/2019/rsb19-v0.pdf).

Anderson-Sherman, Arnold and Doug McAdam. 1982. "American Black Insurgency and the World-Economy: A Political Process Model." Pp. 165–88 in *Ascent and Decline in the World System*, edited by Edward Friedman. Beverly Hills, CA: SAGE Publications.

Andreoni, Manuela and Leticia Casado. 2021. "Vale Mining Company to Pay $7 Billion in Compensation for Brazil Dam Collapse." *The New York Times*, 4 February. Retrieved 23 June 2023 (https://web.archive.org/web/20210219002454/https://www.nytimes.com/2021/02/04/world/americas/vale-brazil-dam-collapse-7-billion-compensation.html).

Appadurai, Arjun. 2000. "Grassroots Globalization and the Research Imagination." *Public Culture* 12(1):1–19.

Appe, Susan. 2022. "South-South Networks among NGOs." Pp. 49–61 *Beyond the Boomerang: From Transnational Advocacy Networks to Transcalar Advocacy in International Politics,* edited by Christopher L. Pallas and Elizabeth A. Bloodgood. Tuscaloosa, AZ: University of Alabama Press. Retrieved 25 June 2023 (https://ebookcentral.proquest.com/lib/uncc-ebooks/detail.action?docID=28870496).

Aun, Heloisa. 2020. "Brumadinho: Quais as Reivindicações dos Atingidos um Ano Após Desastre." *Catraca Livre*, 25 January. Retrieved 23 June 2023 (https://web.archive.org/web/20220223004805/https://catracalivre.com.br/cidadania/brumadinho-quais-as-reivindicacoes-dos-atingidos-um-ano-apos-desastre/).

Baiocchi, Gianpaolo 2018. *We, the Sovereign*. Medford, MA: Polity Press.

Bakker, Karen. 2007. "The 'Commons' versus the 'Commodity': Alter-Globalization, Anti-Privatization and the Human Right to Water in the Global South." *Antipode* 39(3):430–55.

Bakker, Karen and Richard Hendriks. 2019. "Contested Knowledges in Hydroelectric Project Assessment: The Case of Canada's Site C Project." *Water* 11(3):406.

Bandy, Joe. 2004. "Paradoxes of Transnational Civil Societies under Neoliberalism." *Social Problems* 51(3):410–31.

Banerjee, Subhabrata Bobby. 2011. "Voices of the Governed: Towards a Theory of the Translocal." *Organization* 18(3):323–44.

Banerjee, Subhabrata Bobby. 2018. "Transnational Power and Translocal Governance: The Politics of Corporate Responsibility." *Human Relations* 71(6):796–821.

Banerjee, Subhabrata Bobby, Rajiv Maher, and Romy Krämer. 2023. "Resistance is Fertile: Toward a Political Ecology of Translocal Resistance." *Organization* 30(2):264–87.

Barbosa, Lia Pinheiro. 2016. "Educación, conocimiento y resistencia en América Latina: por una teoría desde los movimientos sociales." *Revista De Raíz Diversa* 3(6):45–79.

Barlow, Maude and Tony Clarke. 2002. *Blue Gold: The Fight to Stop The Corporate Theft of The World's Water*. New York: New Press.

Barna, Mark. 2019. "Momentum Builds Across US to Replace Lead Water Pipes: Water Contamination an Issue For Millions." *The Nation's Health* 49(5):1–8.

Bartling, Sönke and Sascha Friesike. 2014. "Towards Another Scientific Revolution." Pp. 3–15 in *Opening Science* edited by S. Bartling and S. Friesike. Springer Open.

Baviskar, Amita. 2004 [1995]. *In the Belly of the River: Tribal Conflicts over Development in the Narmada Valley*. New Delhi, India: Oxford University Press.

Bayram, Seyma. 2023. "Billions of People Lack Clean Drinking Water, UN Report Finds." *NPR*, 22 March. Retrieved 23 June 2023 (https://web.archive.org/web/20230405013059/https://www.npr.org/2023/03/22/1165464857/billions-of-people-lack-access-to-clean-drinking-water-u-n-report-finds).

BBC News. 2020. "Marielle Franco Murder: Suspect Shot Dead by Police." *BBC News*, 9 February. Retrieved 23 June 2023 (https://web.archive.org/web/20230327203407/http://www.bbc.com/news/world-latin-america-51439016).

BBC News. 2021. "Uttarakhand Dam Disaster: Race to Rescue 150 People in India," *BBC News*, 8 February. Retrieved 23 June 2023 (https://web.archive.org/web/20230503152141/https://www.bbc.com/news/world-asia-india-55975743).

Beaumont, Hilary. 2024. "Flint Residents Grapple with Water Crisis a Decade Later: 'If We Had the Energy Left, We'd Cry.'" *The Guardian*. Retrieved 3 July 2024 (https://web.archive.org/web/20240512000438).

Bejarano, Carolina Alonso, Lucia López Juárez, Mirian A. Mijangos García, and Daniel M. Goldstein. 2019. *Decolonizing Ethnography: Undocumented Immigrants and New Directions in Social Science*. Durham, NC: Duke University Press.

Bel, Germà. 2020. "Public Versus Private Water Delivery, Remunicipalization and Water Tariffs." *Utilities Policy* 62.

Bel, Germà, Paula Bel-Piñana, and Jordi Rosell. 2017. "Myopic PPPs: Risk Allocation and Hidden Liabilities for Taxpayers and Users." *Utilities Policy* 48:147–56.

Bell, Kirsten. 2019. "The 'Problem' of Undesigned Relationality: Ethnographic Fieldwork, Dual Roles and Research Ethics." *Ethnography*, 20(1):8–26.

Berkes, Fikret and Carl Folke. 1998. "Linking Social and Ecological Systems for Resilience and Sustainability." Pp. 1–27 in *Linking Social and Ecological Systems,* edited by F. Craig, C. Folke, and J. Colding. Cambridge: Cambridge University Press.

Bevington, Douglas and Chris Dixon. 2005. "Movement-Relevant Theory: Rethinking Social Movement Scholarship and Activism." *Social Movement Studies: Journal of Social, Cultural and Political Protest* 4(3):185–208.

Bezerra, Camila. 2023. "Dados Mostram Que Privatizacões Não Salvam a Economia do Brasil." *Movimento dos Atingidos por Barragens*, 9 May. Retrieved 29 June 2023 (https://mab.org.br/2023/05/09/dados-mostram-que-privatizacoes-nao-salvam-a-economia-do-brasil/).

Bhalla, Nita. 2015. "World Has Not Woken up to Water Crisis Caused by Climate Change." *Scientific American*, 3 February. Retrieved 23 June 2023 (https://web.archive.org/web/20230509080750/https://www.scientificamerican.com/article/world-has-not-woken-up-to-water-crisis-caused-by-climate-change/).

Bieler, Andreas. 2021. *Fighting for Water: Resisting Privatization in Europe*. New York: Zed Books.

Bieler, Andreas and Madelaine Moore. 2023. "Water Grabbing, Capitalist Accumulation and Resistance: Conceptualising the Multiple Dimensions of Class Struggle." *Global Labour Journal* 14(1):2–20.

BlackRock. 2023. "Delivering on Our Commitment to Sustainability and Stewardship." Retrieved 23 June 2023 (https://web.archive.org/web/20230517175021/https://www.blackrock.com/corporate/about-us/mission-and-principles).

Blue Ribbon Panel. 2017. "Report of the Mayor's Blue Ribbon Panel Restructuring the Pittsburgh Water and Sewer Authority." Retrieved 23 June 2023 (https://web.archive.org/web/20220320232441/https://www.puc.pa.gov/pcdocs/1552668.pdf).

BNDES. n.d. "Histórico." Retrieved 29 June 2023 (https://web.archive.org/web/20230208111102/https://www.bndes.gov.br/wps/portal/site/home/transparencia/desestatizacao/processos-encerrados/Historico).

Boelens, Rutgerd, Esha Shah, and Bert Bruins. 2019. "Contested Knowledges: Large Dams and Mega-Hydraulic Development." *Water* 11(3):416.

Boff, Leonardo. 1997. *Cry of the Earth, Cry of the Poor*. Maryknoll, NY: Orbis Books.

Boff, Leonardo. 2014. "Leonardo Boff: A Luta pela Reforma Agrária É Uma Luta por Vida." *Movimento dos Trabalhadores Rurais*, 21 January. Retrieved 29 June 2023 (https://web.archive.org/web/20230329003810/https://mst.org.br/2014/01/21/leonardo-boff-a-luta-pela-reforma-agraria-e-uma-luta-por-vida/).

Bonnie Watson Coleman. 2023. "Rep. Watson Coleman, Sen. Sanders Introduce Water Act to Improve Water Safety, Affordability, Access." Retrieved 23 June 2023 (https://web.archive.org/web/20230529061217/https://watsoncoleman.house.gov/newsroom/press-releases/rep-watson-coleman-sen-sanders-introduce-water-act-to-improve-water-safety-affordability-access).

Bracey, Glenn E. 2016. "Black Movements Need Black Theorizing: Exposing Implicit Whiteness in Political Process Theory." *Sociological Focus*, 49(1):11–27.

Brand, Ulrich and Patrick Makal. 2022. "A Brief History of the Alter-Globalization Movement." Rosa Luxemburg Stiftung. Retrieved 23 June 2023 (https://web.archive.org/web/20230129133943/https://www.rosalux.de/en/news/id/46700).

Brandão, Carlos Rodrigues. 2008. *Minha Casa o Mundo*. Aparecida, SP: Ideias & Letras.

Bringel, Breno, and Flávia Braga Vieira. 2015. "Movimientos internacionalistas y prácticas de cooperación Sur-Sur: brigadas y experiencias formativas del Movimiento de los Sin Tierra de Brasil y La Vía Campesina." *Revista Española de Desarrollo y Cooperación* 36:65–79.

Bringel, Breno and Flávia Braga Vieira. 2016. " 'We Must Never Forget, So It Never Happens Again:' Brazil's Peasant Internationalism." *Open Democracy*, 17 April. Retrieved 23 June 2023 (https://web.archive.org/web/20230610233907/https://www.opendemocracy.net/en/we-must-never-forget-so-it-never-happens-again-brazil-s-peasant-in/).

Brito, Camilla Larangeira. 2022. "Mulheres Atingidas Pelo Crime da Samarco (Vale/BHP): O Caso da Região do Médio Rio Doce em Minas Gerais." Trabalho de Conclusão de Curso (Curso em Especialização e Extensão em Energia e Sociedade no Capitalismo Contemporâneo), Universidade Federal do Rio de Janeiro.

Britto, Ana Lucia and Patricia Finamore. 2023. "Access to Water Supply in Rio de Janeiro: The Urban Poor Affordability Issue in a Privatization Context." Presented at the annual congress of the Latin American Studies Association. Vancouver, 27 May.

Broad, Robin. 2006. "Research, Knowledge, and the Art of 'Paradigm Maintenance': the World Bank's Development Economics Vice-Presidency (DEC)." *Review of International Political Economy* 13(3):387–419.

Broad, Robin, and John Cavanagh. 2021. *The Water Defenders: How Ordinary People Saved a Country from Corporate Greed*. Boston, MA: Beacon Press.

Brown, Colin, Priscila Neves-Silva, and Léo Heller. 2016. "The Human Right to Water and Sanitation: A New Perspective for Public Policies." *Ciencia & Saúde Colectiva* 21(3):661–670.

Brown, Maia. 2019. "Stopping Veolia: A Report from Seattle." *E-flux Architecture*. Retrieved 25 June 2023 (https://web.archive.org/web/20211214141158/https://power.buellcenter.columbia.edu/essays/stopping-veolia-report-seattle).

Brulle, Robert J, and David N. Pellow. 2006. "Environmental Justice: Human Health and Environmental Inequalities." *Annual Review of Public Health* 27:103–24.

Bullard, Robert. 1993. "Anatomy of Environmental Racism and the Environmental Justice Movement." Pp. 15–39 in *Confronting Environmental Racism: Voices from the Grassroots,* edited by R. Bullard. Boston, MA: South End Press.

Burrow, Rufus, Jr. 1994. *James H. Cone and Black Liberation Theology.* Jefferson, NC: McFarland & Company.

Byrd, Ayana. 2018. "New Legislation Aims to Prevent the Next Fling Water Crisis." *Colorlines,* 25 April. Retrieved 25 June 2023 (https://web.archive.org/web/202 30209133326/https://colorlines.com/article/new-legislation-aims-prevent-next-flint-water-crisis/).

Calisto, Dalila and Iury Paulino. 2021. "Água É Direito da Humanidade e Não Propriedade Privada do Capital." *Conselho Nacional de Igrejas Cristãs do Brasil,* 27 March. Retrieved 25 June 2023 (https://web.archive.org/web/20230701164 652/https://conic.org.br/portal/conic/noticias/agua-e-direito-da-humanidade-e-nao-propriedade-privada-do-capital).

CAPPA. 2021a. "Our Water Our Right Campaign." Retrieved 25 June 2023 (https:// web.archive.org/web/20230424224013/http://cappaafrica.org/social-justice-and-public-services/our-water-our-right-campaign/).

CAPPA. 2021b. "Africa Must Rise & Resist Water Privatisation." Retrieved 30 June 2023 (https://web.archive.org/web/20230424224048/http://africawateract ion.org/wp-content/uploads/2021/10/Africa-Must-Rise-Resist-Water-Privatisat ion-final11.pdf).

CAPPA. 2022. "About." *Africa Week of Action against Water Privatization.* Retrieved 30 June 2023 (https://web.archive.org/web/20230324023833/https:// africawateraction.org/about/).

Cárdenas Grajales, G.I. 2010. "El conocimiento tradicional y el concepto de territorio." NERA (Brazil), pp. 1–12. Retrieved 25 June 2023 (https://web.archive.org/web/ 20220127214134/http://www2.fct.unesp.br/nera/artigodomes/2artigodomes_ 2010.pdf).

Carr, Dillon. 2021. "How Much Are Penn Hills' Sewers Worth? Officials to Discuss Privatizing the Municipality's System." *Trib Live,* 17 February. Retrieved 25 June 2023 (https://triblive.com/local/penn-hills/how-much-are-penn-hills-sewers-worth-officials-to-discuss-privatizing-the-municipalitys-system/).

Carruthers, David V. 2008. "Introduction: Popular Environmentalism and Social Justice in Latin America." Pp. 1–22 in *Environmental Justice in Latin America: Problems, Promise and Practice,* edited by D.V. Carruthers. Cambridge, MA: MIT Press. Retrieved 25 June 2023 (https://ebookcentral.proquest.com/lib/ unccebooks/reader.action?docID=3338776&ppg=12).

Carter, Miguel. 2011. "The Landless Rural Workers Movement and Democracy in Brazil," Special Issue: Living in Actually Existing Democracies, *Latin American Research Review*, 45:187–217.

Carvalho, Arnaldo V. 2021. "Não São de Paulo Freire." Retrieved 23 June 2023 (https://web.archive.org/web/20230701170225/https://arnaldovcarvalho.wordpr ess.com/tag/a-educacao-nao-muda-o-mundo/).

Case, Benjamin S. 2022. *Street Rebellion: Resistance Beyond Violence and Nonviolence.* AK Press.

Central Única dos Trabalhadores de São Paulo. 2017. *Água No Estado de São Paulo,* edited by Fundação Friedrich-Ebert-Stiftung. São Paulo, SP: Friedrich-Ebert-Stiftung Brasil.

Chakraborty, Debadatta. 2020. "Racial-Patriarchal Capitalism: Implications for The Global Capitalist Crises." Presented at the Annual Meeting of the American Sociological Association, Virtual, 8 August.

Chipman, Kim. 2020. "California Water Futures Begin Trading amidst Fear of Scarcity." *Bloomberg*, 6 December. Retrieved 25 June 2023 (www.bloomberg.com/news/articles/2020–12–06/water-futures-to-start-trading-amid-growing-fears-of-scarcity?leadSource=uverify%20wall).

Choudry, Aziz. 2015. *Learning Activism: The Intellectual Life of Contemporary Social Movements*. Toronto, Canada: University of Toronto Press.

Citigroup. 2017. "Solutions for the Global Water Crisis: The End of 'Free and Cheap' Water." Retrieved 25 June 2023 (https://willembuiter.com/CitiGPSWater.pdf).

City of Pittsburgh. 2020. "PWSA Continues Industry-Leading Lead Line Replacement Program." *City of Pittsburgh*. Retrieved 30 June 2023 (https://web.archive.org/web/20230331224422/https://pittsburghpa.gov/press-releases/press-releases/4177).

Clark, Anna. 2018. *The Poisoned City: Flint's Water and the American Urban Tragedy*. New York. US: Metropolitan Books.

Cohen, Donald. 2016. "Is the Tragedy in Flint an Opening for Privatization?" *In the Public Interest*, 29 January. Retrieved 25 June 2023 (https://web.archive.org/web/20230322230428/https://inthepublicinterest.org/is-the-tragedy-in-flint-an-opening-for-privatization/).

Cole, Luke and Sheila Foster. 2001. *From the Ground Up: Environmental Racism and the Rise of the Environmental Justice Movement*. New York: New York University Press.

Collado, Ángel Calle, Marta Soler Montiel, and Marta G. Rivera Ferré. 2011. "La democracia alimentaria: soberanía alimentaria y agroecología emergente." Pp. 213–38 in *Democracia radical: Entre vínculos y utopías*, edited by A. C. Collado. Vilassar de Dalt, Catalonia, Spain: Icaria.

Collins, Patricia Hill. 2002. *Black Feminist Thought: Knowledge, Consciousness, and The Politics of Empowerment*. New York: Routledge.

Collins, Patricia Hill. 2012. *On Intellectual Activism*. Philadelphia, PA: Temple University Press.

Collins, Patricia Hill. 2015. "Science, Critical Race Theory and Colour-Blindness." *British Journal of Sociology*, 66(1):46–52.

Combahee River Collective. 1986. *The Combahee River Collective statement: Black Feminist Organizing in the Seventies and Eighties*. Kitchen Table: Women of Color Press.

Communique from Abuja Water Summit. 2019. National Summit on the Human Right to Water. Retrieved 25 June 2023. (https://web.archive.org/web/20230701172830/https://rwr.fm/wp-content/uploads/Communique-from-Abuja-Water-Summit2019.pdf).

Cone, James H. 2010 [1970]. *A Black Theology of Liberation*. Mary Knoll, NY: Orbis Books.

Conway, Janet. 2006. *Praxis and Politics: Knowledge Production in Social Movements*. New York: Routledge.

Conway, Janet. 2017. "Modernity and the Study of Social Movements: Do We Need a Paradigm Shift?" Pp. 17–34 in *Social Movements and World-System Transformation*, edited by J. Smith, M. Goodhart, P. Manning, and J. Markoff. New York: Routledge.

Connell, Raewyn. 2006. "Northern Theory: The Political Geography of General Social Theory." *Theory and Society* 35(2):237–64.

Connell, Raewyn. 2007a. "The Northern Theory of Globalization." *Sociological Theory* 25(4):368.

Connell, Raewyn. 2007b. *Southern Theory*. Cambridge: Polity.

Corporate Accountability. 2021a. "Statement: Public Officials Indicted for Alleged Crimes Related to the Flint Water Crisis." Retrieved 25 June 2023 (https://corp orateaccountability.org/media/statement-public-officials-indicted-for-alleged-crimes-related-to-the-flint-water-crisis/).

Corporate Accountability. 2021b. "Organizational Support for the WATER Act of 2021." Retrieved 23 June 2023 (https://web.archive.org/web/20230325132 917/https://corporateaccountability.org/wp-content/uploads/2021/02/2.25.21-WATER-Act-Organizational-Support.pdf).

Costa, Larissa. 2021. "Atingidos por barragem da Vale em Brumadinho homenage-iam vítimas dois anos depois." *Brasil de Fato*, 26 January. Retrieved 25 June 2023 (https://web.archive.org/web/20230325053218/https://www.brasildefato. com.br/2021/01/26/atingidos-por-barragem-da-vale-em-brumadinho-homenage iam-vitimas-dois-anos-depois).

Cota, Isabella. 2022. "Cómo el plan de agua limpia de Biden puede terminar envenenando el aire en México." *Ediciones El Pais*, 30 April. Retrieved 26 June 2023 (https://web.archive.org/web/20230323134638/https://elpais.com/mexico/ 2022–04–30/como-el-plan-de-agua-limpia-de-biden-puede-terminar-envenena ndo-el-aire-en-mexico.html).

CounterPower. 2020. *Organizing for Autonomy: History, Theory, and Strategy for Collective Liberation*. Brooklyn, NY: Common Notions.

Cox, Laurence. 2014. "Movements Making Knowledge: A New Wave of Inspiration for Sociology?" *Sociology* 48(5):954–71.

Cox, Laurence and Cristina Flesher Fominaya. 2009. "Movement Knowledge." *Interface* 1(1):1–20.

Crenshaw, Kimberlé. 1989. "Demarginalizing The Intersection of Race and Sex: A Black Feminist Critique of Antidiscrimination Doctrine, Feminist Theory and Antiracist Politics." *University of Chicago Legal Forum* 140:139–67.

Crenshaw, Kimberlé. 1991. "Mapping the Margins: Intersectionality, Identity Politics, and Violence against Women of Color." *Stanford Law Review* 43(6):1241–99.

Dangl, Ben. 2014. "Introduction: Tupak Katari's Promise Lives On." Pp. 305–28 in *Until the Rulers Obey: Voices From Latin American Social Movements*, edited by C. Ross and M. Rein. Oakland, CA: PM Press.

Deb, Nikhil. 2021. "Slow Violence and the Gas Peedit in Neoliberal India." *Social Problems*. doi:10.1093/socpro/spab058.

Deemer, Bridget R., John A. Harrison, Siyue Li, Jake J. Beaulieu, Tonya DelSontro, Nathan Barros, José F. Bezerra-Neto, Stephen M. Powers, Marco A. dos Santos, and J. Arie Vonk. 2016. "Greenhouse Gas Emissions from Reservoir Water Surfaces: A New Global Synthesis." *BioScience* 66(1):949–64.

Del Bene, Daniela, Arnim Scheidel, and Leah Temper. 2018. "More Dams, More Violence? A Global Analysis on Resistances and Repression Around Conflictive Dams Through coproduced Knowledge." *Sustainable Science* 13(3):617–33.

Del Cielo, Lauren. 2021. "From Coast to Coast: A Closer Look at Lead Contamination across the Country." *WaterWorld*. Retrieved 3 July 2024 (https://web.archive.org/web/20240513154942/https://www.waterworld.com/ residential-commercial/article/14306164/from-coast-to-coast).

della Porta, Donatella and Dieter Rucht. 2002. "The Dynamics of Environmental Campaigns." *Mobilization* 7(1):1–14.

Demos. 2022. "Water as a Public Good: Pittsburgh's Our Water Campaign." Demos. Retrieved 29 June 2023 (https://web.archive.org/web/20230427224559/https://www.demos.org/research/water-public-good-pittsburghs-our-water-campaign).

Desai, Manisha. 2009. *Gender and the Politics of Possibilities: Rethinking Globalization.* Lanham, MD: Rowman & Littlefield Publishers.

Desai, Manisha. 2016. *Subaltern Movements in India: Gendered Geographies of Struggle Against Neoliberal Development.* New York: Routledge.

DiChiro, Giovanna. 1998. "Nature as Community: The Convergence of Environment and Social Justice." Pp. 120–43 in *Privatizing Nature: Political Struggles for the Global Commons,* edited by Michael Goldman. New Brunswick, NJ: Rutgers University Press.

DiFelice, Mia. 2022. "Fighting Water Privatization in Pennsylvania and Beyond." *Food & Water Watch.* Retrieved 3 July 2024 (https://web.archive.org/web/20221206213350/https://www.foodandwaterwatch.org/2022/09/14/fighting-water-privatization-in-pennsylvania-and-beyond/).

Dine, Janet. 2006. "Using Companies to Oppress the Poor." Pp. 48–79 in *Human Rights and Capitalism,* edited by J. Dine and A. Fagan. Northampton, MA: Edward Elgar Publishing.

Dine, Janet. 2009. "Rigging the Risks: Why Commercial Law Kills." *Irish Pages: A Journal of Contemporary Writing* 6(1):46–63.

Dotson, Kristie. 2011. "Tracking Epistemic Violence, Tracking Practices of Silencing." *Hypatia* 26(2):236–57.

Du Bois, W. E. B. 1952. *In Battle for Peace: The Story of My 83rd Birthday.* New York: Masses & Mainstream.

Eckel, Rianna. 2018. "Baltimore Becomes First Big U.S. City to Ban Water Privatization." *Food and Water Watch*, 8 November. Retrieved 30 June 2023 (https://web.archive.org/web/20201113063053/https://www.foodandwaterwatch.org/news/baltimore-becomes-first-big-us-city-ban-water-privatization).

EIA U.S. Energy Information Administration. 2020. "Hydropower Explained Where Hydropower is Generated." Retrieved 25 June 2023 (https://web.archive.org/web/20230619180922/https://www.eia.gov/energyexplained/hydropower/where-hydropower-is-generated.php).

Ellerby, Kara. 2017. *No Shortcut to Change: An Unlikely Path to a More Gender Equitable World.* New York: New York University Press.

Emerson, Robert M., Rachel I. Fretz, and Linda L. Shaw. 2011. *Writing Ethnographic Fieldnotes.* Chicago, IL: University of Chicago Press.

Engelhardt, Anne and Madelaine Moore. 2017. "Moving beyond the Toolbox: Providing Social Movement Studies with a Materialist Dialectical Lens." *Momentum Quarterly* 6(4):271–89.

Engelhardt, Anne and Madeleine Moore. 2022. "From Mechanisms to Dynamics: How to Embed Social Movement Studies within Historical Materialism." Pp. 75–104 in *Marxism, Social Movements and Collective Action,* edited by Adrián Piva and Agustín Santella. Cham: Palgrave Macmillan.

Environmental Rights Action/Friends of the Earth, Nigeria. 2016. *Lagos Water Crisis: Alternative Roadmap for Water Sector.* Retrieved 25 June 2023 (https://web.archive.org/web/20220308115347/https://www.tni.org/files/publication-downloads/lagos_water_book_web_publishing_version_0.pdf).

EPA. 2021. "Lead and Copper Rule." Retrieved 3 July 2024 (https://web.archive.org/web/20210325203325/https://www.epa.gov/dwreginfo/lead-and-copper-rule).

Escobar, Arturo. 1988. "Power and Visibility: Development and the Invention and Management of the Third World." *Cultural Anthropology* 3(4):428–43.

Escobar, Arturo. 2008. *Territories of Difference: Place, Movements, Life, Redes.* Durham, NC: Duke University Press.

Escobar, Arturo and Susan Paulson. 2005. "The Emergence of Collective Ethnic Identities and Alternative Political Ecologies in the Colombian Pacific Rainforest." Pp. 257–78 in *Political Ecology across Spaces, Scales, and Social Groups*, edited by Susan Paulson and Lisa L. Gezon. New Brunswick, NJ: Rutgers University Press.

Evans, Peter and Cesar Rodríguez-Garavito. 2018. "Introduction: Building and Sustaining the Ecosystem of Transnational Advocacy." Pp. 8–25 in *Transnational Advocacy Networks: Twenty Years of Evolving Theory and Practice,* edited by Peter Evans and Cesar Rodríguez-Garavito. Bogotá, Colombia: Dejusticia.

Fabricant, Nicole. 2012. *Mobilizing Bolivia's Displaced: Indigenous Politics & The Struggle Over Land.* Chapel Hill, NC: The University of North Carolina Press.

Falcón, Sylvanna M. 2016. "Transnational Feminism as a Paradigm for Decolonizing the Practice of Research: Identifying Feminist Principles and Methodology Criteria for Us- Based Scholars." *Frontiers* 37(1):174–94.

Falk, Richard. 1993. "The Making of Global Citizenship." Pp. 39–50 in *Global Visions Beyond the New World Order*, edited by J. Brecher, J. Brown Childs, and J. Cutler. Boston, MA: South End Press.

Fanon, Frantz. 2007 [1961]. *The Wretched of the Earth.* New York: Grove/Atlantic.

Fearnside, Philip. 2017. "How a Dam Building Boom Is Transforming the Brazilian Amazon." *Yale Environment 360*, 26 September. Retrieved 25 June 2023 (https://web.archive.org/web/20230525075925/https://e360.yale.edu/features/how-a-dam-building-boom-is-transforming-the-brazilian-amazon).

Fearnside, Philip. 2020. "Many Rivers, Too Many Dams." Opinion, *The New York Times*, 2 October. Retrieved 25 June 2023 (https://web.archive.org/web/20230429055712/https://www.nytimes.com/2020/10/02/opinion/amazon-illegal-dams-brazil.html).

Fearnside, Philip. 2021. "Brazil's Belo Monte Dam: Greenwashing Contested (Commentary)." *Mongabay*, 11 February. Retrieved 25 June 2023 (https://web.archive.org/web/20230601084949/https://news.mongabay.com/2021/02/brazils-belo-monte-dam-greenwashing-contested-commentary/).

Fellet, Melissae. 2016. "All or Nothing Is a Better Strategy for Keeping Drinking Water Lead Levels Low." *Chemical and Engineering News*, 13 July. Retrieved 25 June 2023 (https://cen.acs.org/articles/94/web/2016/07/nothing-better-strategy-keeping-drinking.html).

Felton, Ryan. 2020. "How Pepsi and Coke Make Millions Bottling Tap Water, as Residents Face Shutoffs." *The Guardian*, 23 April. Retrieved 25 June 2023 (https://web.archive.org/web/20230409201018/https://www.theguardian.com/us-news/2020/apr/23/pepsi-coke-bottled-water-consumer-reports).

FEMA. 2019. "Dam Safety." Retrieved 25 June 2023 (https://web.archive.org/web/20230626204149/https://www.fema.gov/emergency-managers/risk-management/dam-safety).

Fernandes, Florestan. 1986. "Para o Sociólogo, Não Existe Neutralidade Possível: O Intelectual Deve Optar Entre o Compromisso com os Exploradores ou com os Explorados." *Leia* 7(96):25.

Fernandes, Sabrina. 2020. *Se Quiser Mudr O mundo: Um Guia Político para Quem Se Importa.* São Paulo: Editora Planeta do Brasil LTDA.

Figueroa-Helland, Leonardo, Cassidy Thomas, and Abigail Pérez Aguilera. 2018. "Decolonizing Food Systems: Food Sovereignty, Indigenous Revitalization, And Agroecology As Counter-Hegemonic Movements." *Perspectives on Global Development and Technology* 17(1–2):173–201.

Fiorenza, Elisabeth Schussler. 1992. *But She Said: Feminist Practices of Biblical Interpretation*. Boston, MA: Beacon Press.

Fisher, Mark. 2009. *Capitalist Realism: Is There No Alternative?* London: O Books.

Fleming, Margaret. 2021. "PWSA Says It's Replaced Half of Pittsburgh's Lead Service Lines, on Track for 2026 Goal." *WESA*, 5 July. Retrieved 25 June 2023 (www.wesa.fm/development-transportation/2021–07–05/pwsa-says-its-replaced-half-of-pittsburghs-lead-service-lines-on-track-for-2026-goal).

Flint Rising. n.d. Retrieved 25 June 2023 (https://web.archive.org/web/2023060 1002322/https://flintrising.com/).

Fonger, Ron. 2019. "AG Claims Bad Advice from Private Companies Caused Flint Water Crisis." *MLive.com*, 22 April. Retrieved 25 June 2023 (https://web.arch ive.org/web/20230406080447/https://www.mlive.com/news/flint/2019/04/ag-claims-bad-advice-from-private-companies-caused-flint-water-crisis.html).

Food and Water Watch. 2009. "Water Privatization Threatens Workers, Consumers and Local Economies." *In the Public Interest*. Retrieved 25 June 2023 (https:// web.archive.org/web/20230322222459/https://inthepublicinterest.org/water-privatization-threatens-worker-consumers-and-local-economies/).

Food and Water Watch. 2016. "The State of Public Water in The United States." *In the Public Interest*. Retrieved 25 June 2023 (https://web.archive.org/web/ 20230702234757/https://foodandwaterwatch.org/wp-content/uploads/2021/03/ report_state_of_public_water.pdf).

Food & Water Watch. 2022. "The WATER Act: Restoring Federal Support for Clean Water Systems." *Food & Water Watch*. Retrieved 25 June 2023 (https://web.arch ive.org/web/20230529213753/https://www.foodandwaterwatch.org/2022/03/ 18/the-water-act-restoring-federal-support-for-clean-water-systems/).

Fórum Alternative Mundial da Água (FAMA). 2018. "Declaração Final." Retrieved 28 June 2023 (https://web.archive.org/web/20230331124849/http://fama2018. org/declaracao-final/).

Foster, John Bellamy. 1997. "The Crisis of the Earth Marx's Theory of Ecological Sustainability as a Nature-Imposed Necessity for Human Production." Pp. 120–36 in *Environment, Energy, and Society: Exemplary Works,* edited by C. R. Humphrey, T. L. Lewis, and F. H. Buttel. Toronto, Canada: Thomson Wadsworth.

Fox, Coleen A. and Christopher S. Sneddon. 2019. "Political Borders, Epistemological Boundaries, and Contested Knowledges: Constructing Dams and Narratives in the Mekong River Basin." *Water* 11(3):413.

Freire, Paulo. 2018 [1968]. *Pedagogy of the Oppressed*. New York: Bloomsbury Publishing USA.

Galeano, Eduardo. 2000 [1983, 1978]. *Days and Nights of Love and War*. Monthly Review Press.

Ganz, Marshall and Elizabeth McKenna. 2019. "Bringing Leadership Back In." Pp. 185–202 in *The Wiley Blackwell Companion to Social Movements,* edited by D. A. Snow, S. A. Soule, H. Kriesi, and H. J. McCammon. Hoboken, NJ: Wiley Blackwell.

Ganz, Marshall and Emily S. Lin. 2011. "Learning to Lead: Pedagogy of Practice" Pp. 353–66 in *The Handbook for Teaching Leadership: Knowing, Doing, and Being,* edited by S. Snook, N. Nohria, and R. Khurana. SAGE Publications.

Gasteyer, Stephen, Jad Isaac, Jane Hillal, and Sean Walsh. 2012. "Water Grabbing in Colonial Perspective: Land and Water in Israel/Palestine." *Water Alternatives* 5(2):450–68.

Ghiso, A. 2000. "Potenciando la Diversidad. Dialogo de saberes, una practica her-meneutica colectiva." *Revista Aportes* (53):57–70.

Glenza, Jessica. 2017. "Nestlé Pays $200 a Year to Bottle Water Near Flint – Where Water is Undrinkable." *The Guardian*, 29 September. Retrieved 25 June 2023 (https://web.archive.org/web/20230530085042/https://www.theguardian.com/us-news/2017/sep/29/nestle-pays-200-a-year-to-bottle-water-near-flint-where-water-is-undrinkable).

Global Water Intelligence. 2018. "Veolia North America Finds New Strategies for Growth After PPS Fails to Make Headway." *Global Water Intelligence* 19(2). Retrieved 25 June 2023 (www.globalwaterintel.com/global-water-intelligence-magazine/19/2/general/veolia-north-america-finds-new-strategies-for-growth-after-pps-fails-to-make-headway).

Global Water Intelligence. 2019. "Pittsburgh Restructuring, PA." Retrieved 25 June 2023 (www.globalwaterintel.com/global-water-intelligence-magazine/project-trackers/pittsburgh-restructuring-pa).

Global Water Intelligence. 2022. "The World's Top 50 Private Water Operators." *Global Water Intelligence* (23)12. Retrieved 25 June 2023 (www.globalwaterintel.com/global-water-intelligence-magazine/23/12/the-list/the-world-s-top-50-private-water-operators-12–2022).

Global Witness. 2023. "French Giant Veolia Accused of Buying 'toxic' Colombian Landfill, Failed to Address the Risks Faced by Environmental Defenders." *Global Witness*, 30 May. Retrieved 25 June 2023 (https://web.archive.org/web/20230621221757/https://www.globalwitness.org/en/press-releases/french-giant-veolia-accused-of-buying-toxic-colombian-landfill-failed-to-address-the-risks-faced-by-environmental-defenders/).

Go, Julian. 2020. "Race, Empire, and Epistemic Exclusion: Or the Structures of Sociological Thought." *Sociological Theory* 38(2):79–100.

Goldberg, David Theo. 2002. *The Racial State*. Malden, MA: Blackwell Publishers.

Gonzalez, Carmen G. 2021. "Racial Capitalism, Climate Justice, and Climate Displacement." *Oñati Socio-Legal Series, symposium on Climate Justice in the Anthropocene* 11(1):108–47.

González Rivas, Marcela. 2020. "A Tale of Two Water Operators: Legacies of Public Versus Private amidst Covid19 in Pittsburgh." Pp. 291–310 in *Public Water and Covid-19: Dark Clouds and Silver Linings*, edited by D. A. McDonald, S. J. Spronk, and D. Chavez. Kingston. Canada; Amsterdam; Buenos Aires: Municipal Services Project; Transnational Institute; Latin American Council of Social Sciences.

González Rivas, Marcela and Caitlin Schroering. 2021. "Pittsburgh's Translocal Social Movement: A Case of the New Public Water." *Utilities Policy* 71:1–8.

Goodman, James and Ariel Salleh. 2013. "The 'Green Economy:' Class Hegemony and Counter-Hegemony." *Globalizations* 10(3):411–24.

Goodwin, Jeff, James Jasper, and Francesca Polletta. 2000. "The Return of the Repressed: The Fall and Rise of Emotions in Social Movement Theory." *Mobilization: An International Journal* 5(1):65–83.

Gottesdiener, Laura. 2015. "Detroit Is Ground Zero in the New Fight for Water Rights." *The Nation*, 15 July. Retrieved 25 June 2023 (https://web.archive.org/web/20221007002754/https://www.thenation.com/article/archive/detroit-is-ground-zero-in-the-new-fight-for-water-rights/).

Gould, Deborah. 2009. *Moving Politics: Emotion and ACT UP's Fight Against AIDS*. Chicago, IL: University of Chicago Press.

Gramsci, Antonio. 2000. *The Gramsci Reader: Selected Writings, 1916–1935.* New York: New York University Press.

Griggs, Troy, Gregor, Aisch, and Sarah Almukhtar. 2017. "America's Aging Dams Are in Need of Repair." *The New York Times*, 23 February. Retrieved 26 June 2023 (https://web.archive.org/web/20230701180955/https://www.nytimes.com/interactive/2017/02/23/us/americas-aging-dams-are-in-need-of-repair.html?mtrref=undefined&assetType=PAYWALL&mtrref=www.nytimes.com&gwh=98078 4F09779E39247BD374FB929B889&gwt=pay&assetType=PAYWALL).

Gudynas, Eduardo. 2015. "Buen Vivir." Pp. 201–04 in *Degrowth: A Vocabulary for a New Era*, edited by G. D'Alisa, F. Demario, and G. Kallis. New York: Routledge.

Guha, Ramachandra. 1989. *The Unquiet Woods: Ecological Change and Peasant Resistance in the Himalaya*. Berkeley, CA: University of California Press.

Guha, Ramachandra and Juan Martinez-Alier. 1997. *Varieties of Environmentalism: Essays North and South*. London: Earthscan.

Guhin, Jeffrey, and Jonathan Wyrtzen. 2013. "The Violences of Knowledge: Edward Said, Sociology, and Post-Orientalist Reflexivity." Pp. 231–62 in *Postcolonial Sociology*, edited by Julian Go. Bingley: Emerald Group Publishing.

Guimarães, Juca. 2019. "Das 24 Mil Barragens do Brasil, Apenas 780 Passaram por Fiscalização." *Brasil de Fato*, 28 January. Retrieved 25 June 2023 (https://web.archive.org/web/20230511071912/https://www.brasildefato.com.br/2019/01/28/das-24-mil-barragens-do-brasil-apenas-780-passaram-por-fiscalizacao-em-2017/).

Hammel, Paul. 2023. "Family of Man Who Was Washed Away in Collapse of Spencer Dam Loses Court Appeal." *Nebraska Examiner*, 14 April. Retrieved 26 June 2023 (https://web.archive.org/web/20230421132326/https://nebraskae xaminer.com/briefs/family-of-man-who-was-washed-away-in-collapse-of-spen cer-dam-loses-court-appeal/).

Hart, Megan. 2020. "Green Bay Has Officially Replaced All City's Lead Pipes." Wisconsin Public Radio, 7 October. Retrieved 27 June 2023 (https://web.archive.org/web/20230127185009/https://www.wpr.org/green-bay-has-officially-repla ced-all-citys-lead-pipes).

Harvey, David. 2004. "The 'New' Imperialism: Accumulation by Dispossession." *Socialist Register* 40:63–87.

Harvey, David. 2012. *Rebel Cities: From the Right to the City to the Urban Revolution*. Brooklyn, NY: Verso.

Hess, David. 2018. "The Anti-Dam Movement in Brazil: Expertise and Design Conflicts in an Industrial Transition Movement." *Tapuya: Latin American Science, Technology and Society* 1(1):256–79.

Hetland, Gabriel and Jeff Goodwin. 2013. "The Strange Disappearance of Capitalism from Social Movement Studies." Pp. 83–102 in *Marxism and Social Movements*, edited by C. Barker, L. Cox, J. Krinsky, and A. G. Nilsen. Leiden, Netherlands: Brill.

Hoffman, Tom. 2019. "Sierra Lobbying in Pittsburgh, Echoes Nationally." *Sierra Club Pennsylvania, Allegheny Group, Pennsylvania Chapter*. Retrieved 26 June 2023 (https://web.archive.org/web/20230701181303/https://www.sierraclub.org/pennsylvania/allegheny/blog/2019/06/sierra-lobbying-pittsburgh-echoes-nationally).

Ho, Michelle, Upmanu Lall, Maura Allaire, Naresh Devineni, Hyun Han Kwon, Indrani Pal, David Raff, and David Wegner. 2017. "The Future Role of Dams in the United States of America." *Water Resources Research* 53(2):982–998.

Holden, Emily, Ron Fonger, and Jessica Glenza. 2019. "Revealed: Water Company and City Officials Knew about Flint Poison Risk." *The Guardian*, 10 December. Retrieved 26 June 2023 (https://web.archive.org/web/20230414204823/https://www.theguardian.com/us-news/2019/dec/10/water-company-city-officials-knew-flint-lead-risk-emails-michigan-tap-water).

Holmsy, George and Mildred Warner, 2020. "Does Public Ownership of Utilities Matter for Local Government Water Policies?" *Utilities Policy* 64. Retrieved 26 June 2023. doi:10.1016/j.jup.2020.101057

Holston, James. 2009. "Insurgent Citizenship in an Era of Global Urban Peripheries." *City & Society* 21(2):245–67.

Holt-Giménez, Eric. 2006. *Campesino a Campesino: Voices from Latin America's Farmer to Farmer Movement for Sustainable Agriculture*. Oakland, CA: Food First Books.

Hosea, Leana and Sharon Lerner. 2018. "From Pittsburgh to Flint, the Dire Consequences of Giving Private Companies Responsibility for Ailing Public Water Systems." *The Intercept*, 20 May. Retrieved 26 June 2023 (https://web.archive.org/web/20230203061347/https://theintercept.com/2018/05/20/pittsburgh-flint-veolia-privatization-public-water-systems-lead/).

Howell, Junia, Sara Goodkind, Leah Jacobs, Dominique Branson, and Elizabeth Miller. 2019. "Pittsburgh's Inequality across Gender and Race." Pittsburgh, PA: City of Pittsburgh's Gender Equity Commission. (www.socialwork.pitt.edu/sites/default/files/pittsburghs_inequality_across_gender_and_race_07_19_20_compressed.pdf).

Hudson, Kate. 2017. "Hydropower Is Not Clean Energy: Dams and Reservoirs are Major Drivers of Climate Change." *Waterkeeper Alliance*, 21 November. Retrieved 26 June 2023 (https://web.archive.org/web/20230330122433/https://waterkeeper.org/news/hydropower-is-not-clean-energy/).

Hughes, Melanie, Pamela Paxton, Sharon Quinsaat, and Nicholas Reith. 2018. "Does the Global North Still Dominate Women's International Organizing? A Network Analysis from 1978 to 2008." *Mobilization: An International Quarterly* 23(1):1–21.

Hylton, Forrest and Sinclair Thomson. 2007. *Revolutionary Horizons: Past and Present in Bolivian Politics*. New York: Verso.

Icaza, Rosalba, and Rolando Vázquez. 2013. "Social Struggles as Epistemic Struggles." *Development and Change* 44(3):683–704.

Ideas for Development. 2020. "The Financialization of Water: Pursuit of Profit Draining Human Rights." Retrieved 26 June 2023 (https://web.archive.org/web/20230330044137/https://ideas4development.org/en/financialization-of-water-pursuit-of-profit-draining-human-rights/).

Issa, Rabie. 2019. "Listening and Working Together in Nigeria." *3BL Media*. Retrieved 4 July 2024 (https://web.archive.org/web/20191006045422/https://www.3blmedia.com/news/listening-and-working-together-nigeria).

ITPI. 2019. "A Guide to Understanding and Evaluating Public-Private Partnerships in the Water Sector." *In the Public Interest*. Retrieved 26 June 2023 (https://web.archive.org/web/20230128103127/https://inthepublicinterest.org/wp-content/uploads/ITPI_P3WaterGuide_Nov2019.pdf).

ITPI. 2021. "Restoring and Reimagining Investment in Public Water." Report from *In the Public Interest*. Retrieved 30 June 2023.

Itu. 2019. Water Remunicipalisation Tracker, Transnational Institute and Corporate Europe Observatory. Retrieved 12 November 2020 (www.remunicipalisation.org/#case_Itu).

Jackson, Derrick Z. 2018. "The Goldman Prize Missed the Black Heroes of Flint – Just Like the Media Did." *Grist*, 23 April. Retrieved 26 June 2023 (https://web. archive.org/web/20230401200826/https://grist.org/article/the-goldman-prize-missed-the-black-heroes-of-flint-just-like-the-media-did/).

Johnston, Barbara Rose. 2018. "Large-Scale Dam Development and Counter Movements: Water Justice Struggles around Guatemala's Chixoy Dam." Pp. 169–86 in *Water Justice*, edited by R. Boelens, T. Perreault, and J. Vos. Cambridge: Cambridge University Press.

Jung, Moon-Kie, João H. Costa Vargas, and Eduardo Bonilla-Silva. 2011. *State of White Supremacy: Racism, Governance, and the United States*. Stanford, CA: Stanford University Press. Retrieved 26 June 2023 (https://ebookcentral. proquest.com/lib/uncc-ebooks/detail.action?docID=683285).

Karriem, Abdurazack. 2009. "The Rise and Transformation of The Brazilian Landless Movement Into a Counter-Hegemonic Political Actor: A Gramscian Analysis." *Geoforum* 40:316–25.

Keck, Margaret. E. and Kathryn Sikkink. 1998. *Activists Beyond Borders: Advocacy Networks in International Politics*. Ithaca, NY: Cornell University Press.

Kelley, Robin. D. G. 2002. *Freedom Dreams: The Black Radical Imagination*. Boston, MA: Beacon.

Kishimoto, Satoko, Lavinia Steinfort, and Olivier Petitjean. 2020. "Introduction." Pp. 17–31 in *The Future is Public: Towards Democratic Ownership of Public Services*, edited by Satoko, Kishimoto, Lavinia Steinfort, and Olivier Pettijean. Amsterdam, Netherlands, and Paris, France: Transnational Institute.

Kishimoto, Satoko, Olivier Petitjean, and Lavinia Steinfort. 2017. *Reclaiming Public Services: How Cities and Citizens are Turning Back Privatization*. Amsterdam: Transnational Institute.

Klein, Peter T. 2015. "Engaging the Brazilian State: The Belo Monte Dam and the Struggle for Political Voice." *The Journal of Peasant Studies* 42(6):1137–56.

Kothari, Ashish. 2021. "Half-Earth or Whole-Earth? Green or Transformative Recovery? Where Are the Voices from the Global South?" *Oryx* 55(2):161–62.

Krauss, Margaret J. 2019. "PWSA Pledges to Keep Authority Public." 90.5 WESA, 1 July. Retrieved 27 June 2023 (https://web.archive.org/web/20230701182034/ https://www.wesa.fm/development-transportation/2019–07–01/pwsa-pledges-to-keep-authority-public).

Krauss, Margaret J. 2020. "Aqua America Will Buy Peoples Gas for $4.3 Billion." 90.5 WESA, 16 January. Retrieved 27 June 2023 (https://web.archive.org/web/ 20220123054458/https://www.wesa.fm/development-transportation/2020–01–16/aqua-america-will-buy-peoples-gas-for-4-3-billion).

Krishna, Sankaran. 2001. "Race, Amnesia, and the Education of International Relations." *Alternatives: Global, Local, Political* 26(4):401–24.

La Via Campesina. 2007. "What's Missing from the Climate Talks? Justice!" La Via CampesinaInternational Peasant's Movement. Retrieved 30 June 2023 (https:// web.archive.org/web/20230530211439/https://viacampesina.org/en/whats-missing-from-the-climate-talks-justice/).

La Vía Campesina. 2008. "Food Sovereignty Now! Unity and Struggle of the People!" Declaration of Maputo: V International Conference of La Vía Campesina. Maputo, Mozambique, 19–22 October. Retrieved 30 June 2023 (https://web.arch ive.org/web/20230530203024/https://viacampesina.org/en/declaration-of-map uto-v-international-conference-of-la-via-campesina/).

Lakhani, Nina. 2020. "Revealed: Millions of Americans Can't Afford Water as Bills Rise 80% in a Decade." *The Guardian*, 23 June. Retrieved 27 June 2023 (https://web.archive.org/web/20230628232254/https://www.theguardian.com/us-news/2020/jun/23/millions-of-americans-cant-afford-water-bills-rise).

Lakhani, Nina. 2021. "Biden Urged to Back Water Bill amid Worst US Crisis in Decades." *The Guardian*, 25 February. Retrieved 27 June 2023 (https://web.archive.org/web/20230322234301/https://www.theguardian.com/us-news/2021/feb/25/joe-biden-water-act-bernie-sanders).

Laurie, Nina. 2011. "Gender Water Networks: Femininity and Masculinity in Water Politics in Bolivia." *International Journal of Urban and Regional Research*, 35(1):172–88.

Lazare, Sarah. 2015. "Ruptured Dams Engulf Brazilian Village in Toxic Mine Waste." *Common Dreams*, 6 November. Retrieved 27 June 2023 (https://web.archive.org/web/20221203021322/https://www.commondreams.org/news/2015/11/06/ruptured-dams-engulf-brazilian-village-toxic-mine-waste).

Lefebvre, Henry. 1996 [1968]. "The Right to the City." Pp. 63–181 in *Writings on Cities*, edited by E. Kofman and E. Lebas. Oxford: Blackwell.

Leo, Brooklyn. 2020. "The Colonial/Modern [Cis] Gender System and Trans World Traveling." *Hypatia* 35(3):454–74.

Leslie, Jacques. 2019. "The Dam Truth: The 91,000 Dams in the US Earned a 'D' for Safety." *Mother Jones*, 23 July. Retrieved 27 June 2023 (https://web.archive.org/web/20230625225234/https://www.motherjones.com/environment/2019/07/the-dam-truth-the-91000-dams-in-the-us-earned-a-d-for-safety/).

"Letter from the II International Seminar: Food, Water and Energy are not Commodities." 2017. International Seminar: Food, Water and Energy are not Commodities, Newark, NJ, 12–14 March. Retrieved 27 June 2023 (https://web.archive.org/web/20210412161147/https://sasn.rutgers.edu/sites/default/files/sites/default/files/inline-files/II%20International%20Seminar%20Food%20Water%20and%20Energy%20are%20not%20commodities%20-%20sintesis%20letter.pdf).

Leturcq, Guillaume. 2019. *Dams in Brazil: Social and Demographical Impacts*. Retrieved 27 June 2023. doi:10.1007/978-3-319-94628-3

Lewis, Tammy. 2016. *Ecuador's Environmental Revolutions: Ecoimperialists, Ecodependents, and Ecoresisters*. Cambridge, MA: The MIT Press.

Lidskog, Rolf., Arthur PJ Mol, and Peter Oosterveer. 2015. "Towards a Global Environmental Sociology? Legacies, Trends and Future Directions." *Current Sociology* 63(3):339–68.

Lieb, David A., Michael Casey, and Michelle Minkoff. 2019. "At Least 1,680 Dams across the US Pose Potential Risk." *Associated Press*, 11 November. Retrieved 28 June 2023 (https://web.archive.org/web/20230928084725/https://apnews.com/article/ne-state-wire-us-news-ap-top-news-sc-state-wire-dams-f5f09a300d394900a1a88362238dbf77).

Lindstrom, Natasha. 2017. "Peduto Taps 'Blue-Ribbon' Panel to Restructure Troubled PWSA." *Trib Live*, 10 March. Retrieved 27 June 2023 (https://archive.triblive.com/local/pittsburgh-allegheny/peduto-taps-blue-ribbon-panel-to-restructure-troubled-pwsa/).

Lobina, Emanuele and David Hall. 2008. "The Comparative Advantage of the Public Sector in the Development of Urban Water Supply." *Progress In Development Studies* 8(1):85–101.

Loftus, Alex. 2009. "Rethinking Political Ecologies of Water." *Third World Quarterly* 30(5):953–68.

Lopez, Oscar. 2020. "Reported Murders, Suicides of Trans People Soar in Brazil." *Reuters*. Retrieved 28 June 2023 (https://web.archive.org/web/20230202005021/ https://www.reuters.com/article/us-brazil-lgbt-murders-trfn/reported-murders-suicides-of-trans-people-soar-in-brazil-idUSKBN25Z31O).

Lubin, Gus. 2011. "Citi's Top Economist Says the Water Market Will Soon Eclipse Oil." *Business Insider*. Retrieved 28 June 2023 (https://web.archive.org/web/202 21210013017/https://www.businessinsider.com/willem-buiter-water-2011–7).

Lugones, María. 2007. "Heterosexualism and the Colonial/Modern Gender System." *Hypatia* 22(1):186–219.

Lurie, Julie. 2016. "How One Company Contaminated Pittsburgh's Drinking Water." *Wired*, 28 October. Retrieved 27 June 2023 (https://web.archive.org/ web/20230510143750/https://www.wired.com/2016/10/pittsburghs-drinking-water-got-contaminated-lead/).

MAB (Movimento dos Atingidos por Barragens). n.d. "Lutas." Retrieved 27 June 2023 (https://web.archive.org/web/20230506021415/https://www.mab.org.br/ lutas/).

MAB (Movimento dos Atingidos por Barragens). 2011. "A Onda De Privatizações e a Organização Internacional dos Atingidos." Retrieved 1 July 2023 (https:// web.archive.org/web/20171008162728/http://www.mabnacional.org.br/content/ 4-onda-privatiza-es-e-organiza-internacional-dos-atingidos).

MAB (Movimento dos Atingidos por Barragens). 2017. *Arpilleras Bordando a Resistência*.

MAB (Movimento dos Atingidos por Barragens). 2018. *Em Defesa da Petrobras e do Brasil*.

MAB (Movimento dos Atingidos por Barragens). 2019a. "A Nossa Luta É Pela Vida! Chega de Impunidade!" Movimento dos Atingidos por Barragens, Secretaria Nacional, São Paulo, Brasil. Retrieved 30 June 2023 (https://web.archive.org/ web/20221220133930/https://mab.org.br/publicacao/a-nossa-lutae-pela-vida-chega-de-impunidade/).

MAB (Movimento dos Atingidos por Barragens). 2019b. "O Lucro Não Vale a Vida: Análise do MAB Sobre O Crime da Vale em Brumadinho/MG." São Paulo: Movimento dos Atingidos por Barragens, Secretaria Nacional.

MAB (Movimento dos Atingidos por Barragens). 2020. "Retrospectiva: Relembre Aprovações do Congresso em 2020 Sobre Barragens e Saneamento." Retrieved 28 June 2023 (https://web.archive.org/web/20230331132901/https://www.mab. org.br/2020/12/30/retrospectiva-relembre-aprovacoes-do-congresso-em-2020-sobre-barragens-e-saneamento/).

MAB (Movimento dos Atingidos por Barragens). 2021a. "Nota | Barragem Rompe Em Florianópolis, No Dia Em Que O Crime Da Vale Em Brumadinho Completa Dois Anos." Retrieved 28 June 2023 (https://web.archive.org/web/20230331222 904/https://mab.org.br/2021/01/27/nota-barragem-rompe-em-florianopolis-no-dia-em-que-o-crime-da-vale-em-brumadinho-completa-dois-anos/).

MAB (Movimento dos Atingidos por Barragens). 2021b. "Campaign Collects Donations for People Affected in Godofredo Viana (MA); Contribute." Retrieved 28 June 2023 (https://web.archive.org/web/20230328185044/https://mab.org. br/2021/03/31/campaign-collects-donations-for-people-affected-in-godofredo-viana-ma-contribute/).

MAB (Movimento dos Atingidos por Barragens). 2021c. "Gold Mining Dam Breaks in Godofredo Viana, Maranhão." Retrieved 28 June 2023 (https://web.archive. org/web/20230127183911/https://mab.org.br/2021/03/30/gold-mining-dam-bre aks-in-godofredo-viana-maranhao/).

MAB (Movimento dos Atingidos por Barragens). 2021d. "Pescadores e Agricultores Ainda Lutam por Reparação Dois Anos Após Rompimento em Brumadinho." Retrieved 28 June 2023 (https://web.archive.org/web/20230331225954/https:// mab.org.br/2021/01/13/pescadores-e-agricultores-ainda-lutam-por-reparacao-dois-anos-apos-rompimento-em-brumadinho/).

MAB (Movimento dos Atingidos por Barragens). 2021e. "Note: After the Agreement On Brumadinho Between Vale and the State Government of Minas Gerais, Mab Will Appeal to the Federal Supreme Court." Retrieved 28 June 2023 (https:// web.archive.org/web/20230326051744/https://mab.org.br/2021/02/05/note-after-the-agreement-on-brumadinho-between-vale-and-the-state-government-of-minas-gerais-mab-will-appeal-to-the-federal-supreme-court/).

MAB (Movimento dos Atingidos por Barragens). 2023. "Em Dia Mundial da Água, Mab Realiza Seminário na Câmara dos Deputados, Lança Livro E Promove Atos em Todo o País." Retrieved 25 June 2023 (https://web.archive.org/web/2023032 4155532/https://mab.org.br/2023/03/23/em-dia-mundial-da-agua-mab-realiza-seminario-na-camara-dos-deputados-lanca-livro-e-promove-atos-em-todo-o-pais/).

Machado, Fernanda Amin Sampaio. 2016. "Direito À Cidade, Um Direito Humano? Reflexões À Luz Da Teoria Crítica." In *Teoria Crítica, Descolonialidade e Direitos Humanos*. Organizadoras: Vanessa Oliveira Batista Berner, Roberta Laena Costa Jucá, and Heloisa Melino de Moraes. Freitas Bastos Editora.

Macleod, Alan. 2020. "Flint-Linked Veolia Merger Brings Water Privatization Closer to "Global Reality." *MintPress News*, 7 October. Retrieved 28 June 2023 (https:// web.archive.org/web/20220126114322/https://www.mintpressnews.com/flint-lin ked-veolia-merger-brings-water-privatization-global-reality/271822/).

Manski, Ben and Jackie Smith. 2019. "Introduction: The Dynamics and Terrains of Local Democracy and Corporate Power in the 21st Century." *Journal of World-Systems Research* 25(1):6–14.

Mark, Monica. 2018. "A Company at the Center of Flint's Water Crisis Is on the Shortlist to Serve Millions in Africa." *BuzzFeed*, 9 August. Retrieved 28 June 2023 (https://web.archive.org/web/20230701185254/https://www.buzzfeednews. com/article/monicamark/lagos-flint-veolia?bftwnews).

Markoff, John. 1997. "Peasants Helped Destroy an Old Regime and Defy a New One: Some Lessons from (and for) the Study of Social Movements." *American Journal of Sociology* 102(4):1113–42.

Markoff, John. 2007. "Peasant Movements." In *Encyclopedia of Globalization*, edited by R. Robertson and J. A. Scholte. New York: Routledge.

Martinez-Alier, Joan, Leah Temper, Daniela Del Bene, and Arnim Scheidel. 2016. "Is There a Global Environmental Justice Movement?" *Journal of Peasant Studies* 43(3):731–55.

Martínez-Torres, María Elena, and Peter M. Rosset. 2010. "La vía campesina: The Birth and Evolution of a Transnational Social Movement." *The Journal of Peasant Studies* 37(1):149–75.

Marx, Karl. 1845. "Theses on Feuerbach." Marx/Engels Internet Archive. Retrieved 30 June 2023 (https://web.archive.org/web/20221210115627/https://www.marxists. org/archive/marx/works/1845/theses/theses.pdf).

Material Didático para as Oficinas Do Projeto De Extensão. 2018. *Memórias das Lutas pela Terra No Estado Do Rio De Janeiro*. Rio de Janeiro.

Maxwell, Joseph A. 2013. *Qualitative Research Design, Third Edition*. Los Angeles, CA: Sage Publications.

McAdam, Doug. 1986. "Recruitment to High-Risk Activism: The Case of Freedom Summer." *American Journal of Sociology* 92(1):64–90.

McAdam, Doug and Hilary Boudet. 2012. *Putting Social Movements in Their Place: Explaining Opposition to Energy Projects in the United States, 2000–2005*. New York: Cambridge University Press.

McCormick, Erin and Kevin G. Andrade. 2022. "Revealed: US Cities Refusing to Replace Toxic Lead Water Pipes Unless Residents Pay." *The Guardian*, 20 July. Retrieved 28 June 2023 (https://web.archive.org/web/20230608131622/https://www.theguardian.com/us-news/2022/jul/20/us-cities-force-residents-pay-thousands-replace-lead-pipes-risk-drinking-toxic-water).

McDonald, David. 2016. "To Corporatize or Not to Corporatize (and If So, How?)." *Utilities Policy* 40:107–14.

McDonald, David. 2018. "Remunicipalization: The Future of Water Services?" *Geoforum* 91:47–56.

McDonald, David and Eric Swyngedouw. 2019. "The New Water Wars: Struggles for Remunicipalisation." *Water Alternatives*, 22(2):322–333.

McDonald, David, Susan Sprunk, and Daniel Chavez, eds. 2021. *Public Water and Covid 19: Dark Clouds and Silver Linings*. Kingston; Amsterdam; Buenos Aires: Municipal Service Project, Transnational Institute, and Latin American Council of Social Sciences. Retrieved 28 June 2023 (doi:10.1080/2325548X.2021.1960032).

McMichael, Philip. 2008. "Peasants Make Their Own History, But Not Just as They Please …" Pp. 37–60 in *Transnational Agrarian Movements: Confronting Globalization*, edited by S. Borras, Jr, M. Edleman, and C. Kay. Chichester: Wiley-Blackwell.

Melucci, Alberto. 1996. *Challenging Codes: Collective Action in the Information Age*. New York: Cambridge University Press.

Members of the Mayor's Blue Ribbon Panel. 2018. "Privatization is Not the Answer for the Pittsburgh Water and Sewer Authority." Opinion, *Pittsburgh Post-Gazette*, 11 March. Retrieved 28 June 2023 (https://web.archive.org/web/20230331092454/https://www.post-gazette.com/opinion/Op-Ed/2018/03/11/Privatization-is-not-the-answer-for-the-Pittsburgh-Water-and-Sewer-Authority/stories/201803110009).

Menendian, Stephen. n.d. "Structural Racism in Flint, Michigan." Blog, *Othering & Belonging Institute*. Retrieved 29 June 2023 (https://web.archive.org/web/20230322084247/https://belonging.berkeley.edu/structural-racism-flint-michigan).

Metito. 2023. "Africa Receives Investment Boost to Develop Water Infrastructure." *Metito*, 15 March. Retrieved 30 June 2023 (https://web.archive.org/web/20230513122341/https://www.metito.com/news-detail/africa-receives-investment-boost-to-develop-water-infrastructure/).

Mignolo, Walter D. 2007. *The Idea of Latin America*. Oxford: Blackwell Publishing.

Mignolo, Walter D. 2009. "Epistemic Disobedience, Independent Thought and Decolonial Freedom." *Theory, Culture & Society* 26(7–8):159–81.

Miraftab, Faranak. 2004. "Public-Private Partnerships: The Trojan Horse of Neoliberal Development?" *Journal of Planning Education and Research* 24(1):89–101.

Mirzoeff, Nicholas. 2018. "It's Not the Anthropocene, It's the White Supremacy Scene; or, The Geological Color Line." Pp. 123–50 in *After Extinction*, edited by R. Grusin. Minneapolis, MN: University of Minnesota Press.

Moghadam, Valentine M. 2005. *Globalizing Women: Transnational Feminist Networks*. Baltimore, MD: The Johns Hopkins University Press.

Mohandesi, Salar and Asad Haider. 2018. "Workers' Inquiry: A Genealogy." *Notes from Below*, 29 January. Retrieved 29 June 2023 (https://web.archive.org/web/20230601090228/https://notesfrombelow.org/article/workers-inquiry).

Mohanty, Chandra Talpade. 2003a. "'Under Western Eyes' Revisited: Feminist Solidarity Through Anticapitalist Struggles." *Signs* 28(2):499–535.

Mohanty, Chandra Talpade. 2003b. *Feminism Without Borders: Decolonizing Theory, Practicing Solidarity*. Durham, NC: Duke University Press.

Mohler, Jeremy. 2019. "In the Public Interest – People Are Fighting Water Privatization Right Now from Chile to the Rust Belt." *In the Public Interest*. Retrieved 27 June 2023 (https://web.archive.org/web/20230322223507/https://inthepublicinterest.org/people-are-fighting-water-privatization-right-now-from-chile-to-the-rust-belt/).

Moore, Deborah, Michael Simon, and Darryl Knudsen. 2021. "Damming Rivers is Terrible for Human Rights, Ecosystems and Food Security." *Truthout*, 21 February. Retrieved 29 June 2023 (https://web.archive.org/web/20230327201926/https://truthout.org/articles/damming-rivers-is-terrible-for-human-rights-ecosystems-and-food-security/).

Moore, Donald. 1996. "Marxism, Culture, and Political Ecology." Pp. 125–147 in *Liberation Ecologies: Environment, Development, Social Movements* edited by R. Peet and M. Watts. New York: Routledge.

Moore, Madelaine. 2018. *Wellsprings of Resistance: Struggles Over Water in Europe*. Brussels: Rosa-Luxemburg-Stiftung Brussels. Retrieved 30 June 2023 (www.rosalux.eu/en/article/1366.wellsprings-of-resistance.html).

Moore, Madelaine. 2023. *Water Struggles as Resistance to Neoliberal Capitalism: A Time of Reproductive Unrest*. Manchester: Manchester University Press.

Montag, Corey. 2019. *Water/Color: A Study of Race and the Water Affordability Crisis in America's Cities*. NAACP Legal Defense & Educational Fund. Retrieved 29 June 2023 (www.naacpldf.org/wp-content/uploads/Water_Report_Executive-Summary_5_21_19_FINAL-V2.pdf).

Moraga, Cherríe and Gloria Anzaldúa, eds. 1981. *This Bridge Called My Back: Writings by Radical Women of Color*. New York: Persephone Press.

Morland, Sarah and Dagmarah Mackos. 2022. "Veolia Sees 2022 Profit Rising to $1.2 Bln after Suez Takeover." *Nasdaq.com*, 17 March. Retrieved 29 June 2023 (https://web.archive.org/web/20220610010115/https://www.nasdaq.com/articles/veolia-sees-2022-profit-rising-to-%241.2-bln-after-suez-takeover).

Moten, Fred and Stefano Harney. 2004. "The University and the Undercommons: Seven Theses." *Social Text* 22(2):101–15.

MST. 2023. "Quem Somos." Retrieved 29 June 2023 (https://web.archive.org/web/20230604233759/https://mst.org.br/quem-somos//).

Muehlebach, Andrea. 2023. *A Vital Frontier: Water Insurgencies in Europe*. Durham, NC: Duke University Press.

Murphy, Michael Warren. 2020. "Notes Toward an Anticolonial Environmental Ecology of Race." *Environmental Sociology*, 1–12.

Murphy, Michael Warren and Caitlin Schroering. 2020. "Refiguring the Plantationocene: Racial Capitalism, World-Systems Analysis, and Global Socioecological Transformation." *Journal of World Systems Research* 26(2):400–15.

Na'allah, Abdul Rasheed, ed. 1998. *Ogoni's Agonies: Ken Saro-Wiwa and the Crisis in Nigeria*. Africa World Press.

National Fisherman and National Oceanic and Atmospheric Administration. 2023. "Federal Approvals Clear Way for Klamath River Dam Removals." *National Fisherman*, 17 January. Retrieved 29 June 2023 (https://web.archive.org/web/20230208185400/https://www.nationalfisherman.com/west-coast-pacific/federal-approvals-clear-way-for-klamath-river-dam-removals).

Nixon, Rob. 2011. *Slow Violence and the Environmentalism of the Poor*. Cambridge, MA: Harvard University Press.

Nowak, Manfred. 2016. *Human Rights or Global Capitalism: The Limits of Privatization*. Philadelphia, PA: University of Pennsylvania Press.

Oboh, Agbonkhese. 2023. "MoU between Lagos, USAID Targets Water Privatisation, Coalition Raises Alarm." *Vanguard*, 26 April. Retrieved 29 June 2023. (https://web.archive.org/web/20230428174850/https://www.vanguardngr.com/2023/04/mou-between-lagos-usaid-targets-water-privatisation-coalition-raises-alarm/).

Office of City Controller. 2017. *Performance Audit Pittsburgh Water and Sewer Authority*. Retrieved 29 June 2023 (https://apps.pittsburghpa.gov/co/Pittsburgh_Water_and_Sewer_Authority_June_2017.pdf).

Olivera, Oscar and Tom Lewis. 2004. *Cochabamba: Water War in Bolivia*. Cambridge, MA: South End Press.

One Rock Capital Partners. 2021. "One Rock Capital Partners and Metropoulos & Co. Complete Acquisition of Nestlé Waters North America." Retrieved 29 June 2023 (https://web.archive.org/web/20220124222340/https://www.onerockcapital.com/news/one-rock-capital-partners-and-metropoulos-co-complete-acquisition-of-nestle-waters-north-america).

Orbach, Rebecca, Owen Minott, Lily Reckford, James Torres, and Erin Barry. 2022. "Status of Federal Low Income Household Water Assistance Program." Blog, *Bipartisan Policy Center*, 12 December. Retrieved 29 June 2023 (https://web.archive.org/web/20230208162733/https://bipartisanpolicy.org/blog/low-income-water-assistance-program/).

Our Water Campaign. 2019. "Our Water Campaign Statement on Attorney General's PWSA Charges." *Pittsburgh United*. Retrieved 21 March 2021 (https://web.archive.org/web/20190314190951/https://pittsburghunited.org/ourwater/).

Pagliarini, Andre. 2023. "A Crucial Test for Lula." *Dissent*, 5 May. Retrieved 29 June 2023 (https://web.archive.org/web/20230627151151/https://www.dissentmagazine.org/online_articles/a-crucial-test-for-lula).

Patel, Raj and Jason W. Moore. 2017. *A History of the World in Seven Cheap Things: A Guide to Capitalism, Nature, and the Future of the Planet*. Oakland, CA: University of California Press.

Pearson, Bethia, Franziska Paul, Andrew Cumbers, and Laura Stegemann. 2021. "Public Futures Database Report." University of Glasgow and European Research Council. Retrieved 29 June 2023 (www.gla.ac.uk/media/Media_782991_smxx.pdf).

Pennsylvania American Water. 2019. "Mckeesport Water." Retrieved 30 June 2023 (https://web.archive.org/web/20230306164557/https://www.amwater.com/corp/resources/McKeesport_Wastewater_CaseStudy.pdf).

Pennsylvania Department of Environmental Protection. 2021. "Lead in Drinking water." Retrieved 1 July 2023 (www.dep.pa.gov/Citizens/My-Water/Public DrinkingWater/pages/lead-in-drinking-water.aspx#:~:text=Pennsylvania's%20Lead%20and%20Copper%20Rule%20establishes%20an%20action%20level%20of,(once%20every%203%20years).

Perkins, Tom. 2019a. "The Fight to Stop Taking America's Water to Sell in Plastic Bottles." *The Guardian*, 29 October. Retrieved 29 June 2023 (https://web.arch ive.org/web/20230619174321/https://www.theguardian.com/environment/2019/ oct/29/the-fight-over-water-how-nestle-dries-up-us-creeks-to-sell-water-in-plas tic-bottles).

Perkins, Tom. 2019b. "Nestlé Cannot Claim Bottled Water Is 'Essential Public Service', Court Rules." *The Guardian*, 5 December. Retrieved 29 June 2023 (https://web.archive.org/web/20230604102305/https://www.theguardian.com/ business/2019/dec/05/nestle-bottled-water-michigan-osceola-private-public).

Pertierra, Raul. 1988. "The Rationality Problematique: An Anthropological Review of Habermas' 'The Theory of Communicative Action' Volume I." *Social Analysis: The International Journal of Social and Cultural Practice* 23:72–88.

Phillips, Dom. 2020. " 'It Tastes like Smelly Clay': Residents of Rio Alarmed by Murky, Smelly Tap Water." *The Guardian*, 16 January. Retrieved 29 June 2023 (https://web.archive.org/web/20221208073020/https://www.theguardian.com/ world/2020/jan/16/brazil-rio-de-janeiro-tap-water-pollution).

Pinheiro, Larissa Souza. 2016. "Águas, Mulheres e Energia Não São Mercadorias: A Participação Política das Mulheres no Movimento dos (as) Atingidos (as) por Barragens (MAB)." Undergraduate Thesis, Centro de Estudos Sociais Aplicadas da Universidade Estadual do Ceará. Retrieved 29 June 2023 (www.academia.edu/43733622/%C3%81GUAS_MULHERES_E_ ENERGIA_N%C3%83O_S%C3%83O_MERCADORIAS_A_PARTIC IPA%C3%87%C3%83O_POL%C3%8DTICA_DAS_MULHERES_NO_ MOVIMENTO_DOS_AS_ATINGIDOS_AS_POR_BARRAGENS_MAB_).

Piper, Nicola and Anders Uhlin. 2004. "New Perspectives on Transnational Activism." Pp. 1–25 in *Transnational Activism in Asia* edited by N. Piper and A. Uhlin. New York: Routledge.

Pittsburgh United. n.d.a. "Our Water." Pittsburgh United. Retrieved 30 June 2023 (https://web.archive.org/web/20180510234858/https://pittsburghunited.org/ ourwater/).

Pittsburgh United. n.d.b. "About." Pittsburgh United. Retrieved 30 June 2023 (https://web.archive.org/web/20190413131629/https://pittsburghunited.org/ about/).

Piven, Frances Fox. 2006. *Challenging Authority: How Ordinary People Change America*. Lanham, MD: Rowman & Littlefield.

Piven, Francis Fox and Richard Cloward. 1977. *Poor People's Movements: Why They Succeed, How They Fail*. New York: Vintage Books.

Planas, Míriam and Juan Martínez. 2020. "A New Water Culture: Catalonia's Public CoGovernance Model in The Making." Pp. 153–64 in *The Future is Public: Towards Democratic Ownership of Public Services*, edited by S. Kishimoto, L. Steinfort, and O. Petitjean. Amsterdam: Transnational Institute.

Plataforma Operáia e Camponesa da Energia. 2014. *Propostas para um Projeto Energético Popular com Soberania, Distribuição da Riqueza e Controle Popular*. Retrieved 29 June 2020 (https://web.archive.org/web/20211203095655/https:// mab.org.br/publicacao/propostas-para-um-projeto-energetico-popular-com- soberania-distribuicao-da-riqueza-e-controle-popular/).

Polletta, Francesca. 2002. *Freedom Is an Endless Meeting: Democracy in American Social Movements*. Chicago, IL: University of Chicago Press.

Polletta, Francesca. 2009. *It was Like a Fever: Storytelling in Protest and Politics*. Chicago, IL: University of Chicago Press.

Presidency of the Republic of Brazil. 2019. "Mining Sector Had US$ 23.4 Billion Trade Surplus in 2018." Retrieved 30 June 2023 (https://web.archive.org/web/20230701160919/https://gestaoconteudo.presidencia.gov.br/gestao_brazilgovnews/about-brazil/news/2019/03/mining-sector-had-us-23-4-billion-trade-surplus-in-2018).

Pulido, Laura. 2016. "Flint, Environmental Racism, and Racial Capitalism." *Capitalism, Nature, Socialism* 27(3):1–16.

PWSA. 2017. "PWSA to Temporarily Suspend Partial Lead Line Replacements." *Pittsburgh Water & Sewer Authority*. Retrieved 29 June 2023 (https://web.archive.org/web/20230401020932/https://lead.pgh2o.com/pwsa-to-temporarily-suspend-partial-lead-line-replacements/).

PWSA. 2022a. "PWSA Maintains Low Lead Levels in Drinking Water." *PGH2O*, 21 January. Retrieved 29 June 2023 (https://web.archive.org/web/20230101113855/https://www.pgh2o.com/news-events/news/press-release/2022-01-20-pwsa-maintains-low-lead-levels-drinking-water).

PWSA. 2022b. "Vice President, Cabinet Members Visit Pittsburgh to Discuss Lead Remediation, Infrastructure Investment." *PGH2O*, 16 June. Retrieved 29 June 2023 (https://web.archive.org/web/20220815134458/https://www.pgh2o.com/news-events/news/press-release/2022-06-16-vice-president-cabinet-members-visit-pittsburgh-discuss).

Quijano, Aníbal. 2000. "Coloniality of Power, Eurocentrism, and Latin America." *Nepentla: Views from the South* 1(3):533–80.

Quijano, Aníbal. 2007. "Coloniality and Modernity/Rationality." *Cultural Studies* 21(2–3):168–78.

Rabaka, Reiland. 2006. "The Souls of Black Radical Folk: W. E. B. Du Bois, Critical Social Theory, and the State of Africana Studies." *Journal of Black Studies* 36(5):732–63.

Rajagapol, Balakrishnan. 2006. "Counter-Hegemonic International Law: Rethinking Human Rights and Development as a Third World Strategy." *Third World Quarterly*, 27(5):767–83.

Rapid Transition Alliance. 2019. "Turning the Tide of Water Privatization: The Rise of the New Municipal Movement." Retrieved 29 June 2023 (https://web.archive.org/web/20230530184610/https://rapidtransition.org/stories/turning-the-tide-of-water-privatization-the-rise-of-the-new-municipal-movement/).

Ren, Xiang and Lucy Montgomery. 2015. "Open Access and Soft Power: Chinese Voices in International Scholarship." *Media, Culture & Society* 37(3):394–408.

REVE. 2020. "The Global Hydropower Installed Capacity is 1,150 GW." Retrieved 29 June 2023 (https://web.archive.org/web/20230202205921/https://www.evwind.es/2020/07/07/the-global-hydropower-installed-capacity-is-1150-gw/75616).

Ribeiro, Ana Maria Motta, Fabricio Teló, Leonilde Medeiros, Paulo Alentejano, and Ricardo Braga Brito. 2020. *Contando Histórias da Terra e das Águas*. Erechim, RS: Associação Nacional dos Atingidos por Barragens. Retrieved 29 June 2023 (www.academia.edu/44865039/Contando_hist%C3%B3rias_da_terra_e_das_%C3%A1guas).

Richter, Jennifer, Flóra Faragó, Beth Blue Swadener, Denisse Roca-Servat, and Kimberly A. Eversman. 2020. "Tempered Radicalism and Intersectionality: Scholar-Activism in the Neoliberal University." *Journal of Social Issues*, 76 (4):1014–1035.

Rivera-Cusicanqui, Silvia and Virginia Aillón-Soria. 2015. *Antología del Pensamiento Crítico Boliviano Contemporáneo*. Buenos Aires, Argentina: CLACSO.

Robbins, Paul. 2012. *Political Ecology: A Critical Introduction*. Malden, MA: J. Wiley & Sons.

Roberts, J. Timmons and Nikki Demetria Thanos. 2003. *Trouble in Paradise: Globalization and Environmental Crises in Latin America*. New York: Routledge.

Robinson, Cedric. J. [1983] 2000. *Black Marxism: The Making of The Black Radical Tradition*, 2nd ed. Chapel Hill, NC: University of North Carolina Press.

Robinson, Joanna L. 2013b. *Contested Water: The Struggle Against Water Privatization in the United States and Canada*. Cambridge, MA: MIT Press.

Robinson, William. 2013a. "Global Capitalism and Its Anti-'Human Face': Organic Intellectuals and Interpretations of the Crisis." *Globalizations* 10(5):659–71.

Robnett, Belinda. 1996. "African-American Women in the Civil Rights Movement, 1954–1965: Gender, leadership, and Micromobilization." *American Journal of Sociology* 101(6):1661–93.

Roggero, Giggi. 2014. "Notes on Framing and Re-inventing Co-research." *Ephemera: Theory & Politics in Organization*, 14(3):515–23.

Rosset, Peter, and Maria Elena Martinez-Torres. 2013. "Rural Social Movements Diálogo de Saberes: Territories, Food Sovereignty, and Agroecology" Conference Paper for Discussion at Food Sovereignty: A Critical Dialogue: International Conference, Yale University, New Haven, CT, 14–15 September. Retrieved 30 June 2023 (https://web.archive.org/web/20221103132910/https://www.iss.nl/sites/corporate/files/4_Rosset_Torres_2013.pdf).

Rosset, Peter M., and Miguel A. Altieri. 2017. *Agroecology: Science and Politics*. Canada: Fernwood Publishing and Practical Action Publishing.

Rosset, Peter M., Lia Pinheiro Barbosa, Valentín Val, and Nils McCune. 2021. "Pensamiento Latinoamericano Agroecológico: The Emergence of a Critical Latin American Agroecology?" *Agroecology and Sustainable Food Systems* 45(1):42–64.

Sacchetto, Devi, Emiliana Armano, and Steve Wright. 2013. "Coresearch and Counter-Research: Romano Alquati's Itinerary Within and Beyond Italian Radical Political Thought." *Viewpoint*, 27 September. Retrieved 29 June, 2023 (https://viewpointmag.com/2013/09/27/coresearch-and-counter-research-romano-alquatis-itinerary-within-and-beyond-italian-radical-political-thought/).

Sager, Tore. 2011. "Neo-Liberal Urban Planning Policies: A Literature Survey 1990–2010." *Progress in Planning* 76(4):147–99.

Said, Edward W. 1993. *Culture and Imperialism*. London: Chatto & Windus.

Salvador, Gilberto Nepomuceno, Cecilia Gontijo Leal, Gabriel Lourenço Brejão, Tiago Casarim Pessali, Carlos Bernardo Mascarenhas Alves, Gustavo Ribeiro Rosa, Raphael Ligeiro, and Luciano Fogaca de Assis Montag. 2020. "Mining Activity in Brazil and Negligence in Action." *Perspectives in Ecology and Conservation*, 18(2):139–44.

Sanders, Bernie and Brenda Lawrence. 2020. "Clean Water Is a Human Right. In America It's More a Profit Machine." *The Guardian*, 23 June. Retrieved 29 June 2023 (https://web.archive.org/web/20230530152849/https://www.theguardian.com/us-news/commentisfree/2020/jun/23/clean-water-should-be-an-american-human-right-not-a-government-profit-machine).

Saro-Wiwa, Ken. 1995. *A Month and a Day: A Detention Diary*. London: Penguin Books.

Sassen, Saskia. 2006. *Territory Authority Rights: From Medieval to Global Assemblages*. Princeton: Princeton University Press.

Sassen, Saskia. 2013. "Expelled: Humans in Capitalisms Deepening Crisis." *Journal of World Systems Research* 19(2):198–201.

Sassen, Saskia. 2014. *Expulsions: Brutality and Complexity in the Global Economy.* Cambridge, MA: Harvard University Press.

Sawyer, Suzana. 2004. *Crude Chronicles: Indigenous Politics, Multinational Oil, And Neoliberalism In Ecuador.* Durham, NC: Duke University Press.

Scalabrin, Leandro Gasper and Tchenna Fernandes Maso. 2015. *The People Affected by Dams and the Violations of Human Rights.* Movement of People Affected by Dams, National Secretariat: São Paulo, Brazil.

Schnaiberg, Allen, David Pellow, and Adam Weinberg. 2002. "The Treadmill of Production and the Environmental State." Pp. 15–32 in *The Environmental State Under Pressure,* edited by A. P. J. Mol and F. H. Buttel. Leeds: Emerald Group.

Schroering, Caitlin. 2015. "Green Theology and Social Justice Movements in Brazil." Master thesis, Department of Latin American Studies, University of Florida. Retrieved 29 June 2023 (https://ufdcimages.uflib.ufl.edu/UF/E0/04/91/65/00001/SCHROERING_C.pdf).

Schroering, Caitlin. 2019a. "Resistance and Knowledge Production: Social Movements as Producers of Theory and Praxis." *Revista CS* 29:73–102.

Schroering, Caitlin. 2019b. "Water Is a Human Right! Grassroots Resistance to Corporate Power." *Journal of World-Systems Research* 25(1):28–34.

Schroering, Caitlin. 2019c. "Brazil Dam Collapse Is a Human Rights Disaster and Crime." *Truthout,* 3 March. Retrieved 29 June 2023 (https://web.archive.org/web/20220901092746/https://truthout.org/articles/brazil-dam-collapse-is-a-human-rights-disaster-and-crime/).

Schroering, Caitlin. 2020a. "A Year After Brazil Dam Collapse, Communities Still Calling for Accountability." *Truthout,* 9 February. Retrieved 29 June 2023 (https://web.archive.org/web/20230528132152/https://truthout.org/articles/a-year-after-brazil-dam-collapse-communities-still-calling-for-accountability/).

Schroering, Caitlin. 2020b. "À Beira Do Colapso: A Situação Das Barragens Nos Estados Unidos." *MAB,* 8 June. Retrieved 29 June 2023 (https://web.archive.org/web/20230602090206/https://mab.org.br/2020/06/08/a-beira-do-colapso-a-situacao-das-barragens-nos-estados-unidos/).

Schroering, Caitlin. 2021a. "Constructing Another World: Solidarity and the Right to Water." *Studies in Social Justice* 15(1):102–28.

Schroering, Caitlin. 2021b. "Inside the Struggle for Water Sovereignty in Brazil." *Roar Magazine,* 12 June. Retrieved 29 June 2023 (https://web.archive.org/web/20230305174430/https://roarmag.org/essays/brazil-mab-water-sovereignty/).

Schroering, Caitlin and Suzanne Staggenborg. 2021. "Volunteer and Staff Participants in Social Movements: A Comparison of Two Local Coalitions." *Social Movement Studies* 21(6):782–797.

Schroering, Caitlin, Dalila Alves Calisto, Tamires Almeida Cruz de Paula, and Gabriel A. Gonçalves. 2023. "Das considerações": o fazer-se da escala e da consciência da luta socioambiental. Três experiências das expressões dos conflitos envolvendo o direito à água, Movimento dos Atingidos por Barragens (MAB)." Pp 183–200 in *Educação Cidadã: Experiência de Formação Profissional e Articulação Intersetorial na Cidade de São Paulo,* edited by Cláudia Graziano Paes de Barros and Valter de Almeida Costa. Campinas, SP: Pontes Editores.

Scurr, Ivy and Vanessa Bowden. 2021. "'The Revolution's Never Done': The Role of 'Radical Imagination' within Anti-Capitalist Environmental Justice Activism." *Environmental Sociology* 7(4):316–26.

Septoff, Alan. 2020. "Minas Gerais, Brazil: A State of Ticking Time Bombs." Earthworks. Retrieved 27 June 2023 (https://web.archive.org/web/20230621083 343/https://earthworks.org/blog/minas-gerais-brazil/).

Shah, Esha, Jeroen Vos, Gert Jan Veldwisch, Rutgerd Boelens, and Bibiana Duarte-Abadía. 2019. "Environmental Justice Movements in Globalising Networks: A Critical Discussion on Social Resistance Against Large Dams." *The Journal of Peasant Studies* 48(5):1008–32.

Shaw, Alyson. 2019. "Pittsburgh." Water Remunicipalisation Tracker, Transnational Institute and Corporate Europe Observatory. Retrieved 21 March 2021 (www.remunicipalisation.org/#case_Pittsburgh).

Shields, Doug. 2019. "The Stealthy Corporate Scheme to Privatize Pittsburgh's Water System." *In These Times*, 14 January. Retrieved 29 June 2023 (https://web.archive.org/web/20230331100804/https://inthesetimes.com/article/pittsbu rgh-water-system-corporate-privatization-peoples-gas-aqua-america).

Shiva, Vandana. [2002] 2016. *Water Wars: Privatization, Pollution, and Profit.* Berkeley, CA: North Atlantic Books.

Shiva, Vandana. 2005. *Earth Democracy: Justice, Sustainability, and Peace.* Cambridge, MA: South End Press.

Shoemaker, J. Dale. 2018a. "Peoples CEO Is Working to Gain Trust as the Company Vies to Run Pittsburgh's Water Utility." *Public Source*, 3 July. Retrieved 29 June 2023 (https://web.archive.org/web/20230329135409/https://www.publicsource. org/peoples-ceo-is-working-to-gain-trust-as-the-company-vies-to-run-pittsbur ghs-water-utility/).

Shoemaker, J. Dale. 2018b. "Activists, Public Officials Protest Peoples' Proposal to Overhaul Pittsburgh Water Authority." *Public Source*, 13 June. Retrieved 30 June 2023 (https://web.archive.org/web/20210303122954/https://www.publi csource.org/activists-public-officials-protest-peoples-proposal-to-overhaul-pit tsburgh-water-authority/).

Silva, Denise Ferreira da. 2016. "Fractal Thinking." *ACCeSsions, The Center for Curatorial Studies, Bard College* 27. Retrieved 1 July 2023 (https://web.archive. org/web/20230519022605/https://accessions.org/article2/fractal-thinking/).

Silva, Denise Ferreira da. 2018. "On Heat." *Canadian Art*, 29 October. Retrieved 29 June 2023. (https://web.archive.org/web/20230614145251/https://canadian art.ca/features/on-heat/).

Sitrin, Marina. 2012. *Everyday Revolutions: Horizontalism and Autonomy in Argentina.* New York: Zed Books.

Sklair, Leslie. 1997. "Social Movements for Global Capitalism: The Transnational Capitalist Class in Action." *Review of Int'l Political Economy* 4:514–38.

Skocpol, Theda. 1979. *States and Social Revolutions: A Comparative Analysis of France, Russia And China.* Cambridge: Cambridge University Press.

Smith, Jackie. 2008. *Social Movements for Global Democracy.* Baltimore, MD: The Johns Hopkins University Press.

Smith, Jackie. 2017a. "Part I Dialogue: Disrupting Hegemonic Discourses and Modes of Thought." Pp. 54–57 in *Social Movements and World-System Transformation,* edited by J. Smith, M. Goodhart, P. Manning, and J. Markoff. New York: Routledge.

Smith, Jackie. 2017b. "Local Responses to Right-Wing Populism: Building Human Rights Cities." *Studies in Social Justice* 11(2):347–68.

Smith, Jackie. 2021. "A Post-Election Strategy for National Unity: Focus on Future Generations." Opinion, *Common Dreams,* 7 January. Retrieved 30 June 2023 (https://web.archive.org/web/20230517152625/https://www.commondreams.org/views/2021/01/07/post-election-strategy-national-unity-focus-future-gene rations).

Smith, Jackie. 2022. "Power Shifts, Paradigm Shifts, and Transnational Advocacy Ecosystems." Pp. 81–94 in *Beyond the Boomerang: From Transnational Advocacy Networks to Transcalar Advocacy in International Politics,* edited by E. Bloodgood and C. Pallas. Tuscaloosa, AL: University of Alabama Press.

Smith, Jackie and Dawn Wiest. 2005. "The Uneven Geography of Global Civil Society: National and Global Influences on Transnational Association." *Social Forces* 84(2):621–52.

Smith, Jackie and Dawn Wiest. 2012. *Social Movements in the World-System: The Politics of Crisis and Transformation.* New York: Russel Sage Foundation.

Smith, Jackie, Samantha Plummer, and Melanie Hughes. 2017. "Transnational Social Movements and Changing Organizational Fields in the Late-20th and Early-21st Centuries." *Global Networks* 17(1):3–22.

Snitow, Alan, Deborah Kaufman, and Michael Fox. 2007. *Thirst: Fighting the Corporate Theft of Our Water.* Chichester: John Wiley & Sons.

Snow, David A., Burke E. Rochford, Steven K. Worden, and Robert D. Benford. 1986. "Frame Alignment Processes, Micromobilization, and Movement Participation." *American Sociological Review* 51(4):464–81.

Snow, David A., Robert D. Benford, And Leon Anderson. 1986. "Fieldwork Roles and Informational Yield: A Comparison of Alternative Settings and Roles." *Urban Life* 14 (4):377–408.

Sondarjee, Maïka and Nathan Andrews. 2023. "Decolonizing International Relations and Development Studies: What's in a Buzzword?" *International Journal* 77(4):551–71.

Spivak, Gayatri. 1998. "Can the Subaltern Speak?" Pp. 271–316 in *Marxism and the Interpretation of Culture,* edited by C. Nelson and L. Grossberg. Urbana: University of Illinois Press.

Stacey, Judith. 2007. "If I Were the Goddess of Sociological Things." Pp. 91–100 in *Public Sociology,* edited by D. Clawson, R. Zussman, J. Misra, N. Gerstel, R. Stokes, D. L. Anderton, and M. Burawoy. Berkeley, CA: University of California Press.

Staggenborg, Suzanne and Josée Lecomte. 2009. "Social Movement Campaigns: Mobilization and Outcomes in The Montreal Women's Movement Community." *Mobilization* 14(2):163–80.

Stewart, James. B. 1984. "The Legacy of W. E. B. Du Bois for Contemporary Black Studies." *Journal of Negro Education* 53(3):296–311.

Stropasolas, Pedro. 2020. "One Year Since the Brumadinho Disaster: Locals Struggle, Vale Profits." *Brasil de Fato,* 27 January. Retrieved 30 June 2023 (https://web.archive.org/web/20230325055156/https://www.brasildefato.com.br/especiais/one-year-since-the-brumadinho-disaster-locals-struggle-vale-profits).

Subramaniam, Mangala. 2004. "The Indian Women's Movement." *Contemporary Sociology* 33(6):635–39.

Subramaniam, Mangala. 2014. "Neoliberalism and Water Rights: The Case of India." *Current Sociology* 62(3):393–411.

Subramaniam, Mangala. 2018. *Contesting Water Rights: Local, State, and Global Struggles.* Basingstoke: Palgrave Macmillan.

Sultana, Farhana. 2018. "Water Justice: Why It Matters and How To Achieve It." *Water International* 43(4):483–93.

Sultana, Farhana. 2019. *Human Right to Water and Water Justice*. Public lecture, Carnegie Mellon University, 25 September.

Sultana, Farhana and Alex Loftus. 2012. *The Right to Water: Politics, Governance and Social Struggles*. New York: Earthscan.

Tarlau, Rebecca. 2014. "'We Do Not Need Outsiders to Study Us.' Reflections on Activism and Social Movement Research." *Postcolonial Directions in Education* 3(1):63–87.

Tarlau, Rebecca. 2019. *Occupying Schools, Occupying Land: How the Landless Workers Movement Transformed Brazilian Education*. New York: Oxford University Press.

Tarrow, Sidney. 2001. "Transnational Politics: Contention and Institutions in International Politics." *Annual Review of Political Science*, 4(1):1–20.

Taylor, Dorceta. 1993. "Environmentalism and the Politics of Inclusion." Pp. 53–62 in *Confronting Environmental Racism: Voices from the Grassroots*, edited by R. Bullard. Boston, MA: South End Press.

Taylor, Dorceta. 2016. *Power, Privilege, and Environmental Protection: Social Inequality and the Rise of the American Conservation Movement*. Durham, NC: Duke University Press.

Thier, Hadas. 2023. "Jackson's Water System Is Broken by Design." *The Nation*, 22 February. Retrieved 28 June 2023 (https://web.archive.org/web/20230326205706/https://www.thenation.com/article/society/jackson-mississippi-water-infrastructure/).

Tilly, Charles, and Lesley J. Wood. 2015. *Social Movements, 1768–2012*. New York: Routledge.

Tocantins State. 2019. Water Remunicipalisation Tracker, Transnational Institute and Corporate Europe Observatory. Retrieved 31 March 2021 (www.remunicipalisation.org/#case_Tocantins%20State).

Togami, Chie, Caitlin Schroering, Marcela González Rivas, and Talor Musil. 2023. "Environmental Justice Victory? Waste Colonialism and the Afterlife of Lead Water Pipes." Working paper.

Törnberg, Anton. 2021. "Prefigurative Politics and Social Change: a Typology Drawing on Transition Studies." *Distinktion: Journal of Social Theory* 22(1):83–107.

Tricontinental: Institute for Social Research. 2019. "It Was Not an Accident, It Was a Crime! The Collapse of a Dam in Brumadinho, Brazil." *Brasil de Fato*, 8 February. Retrieved 30 June 2023 (https://web.archive.org/web/20230325033726/https://www.brasildefato.com.br/2019/02/08/it-was-not-an-accident-it-was-a-crime-the-collapse-of-a-dam-in-brumadinho-brazil/).

Trocate, Charles. 2019. "Quem São os Donos da Vale S.A.?" *Brasil de Fato*, 2 April. Retrieved 20 April 2021 (https://web.archive.org/web/20230325180649/https://www.brasildefato.com.br/2019/04/02/artigo-or-quem-sao-os-donos-da-vale-sa/).

Tsutsui, Kiyoteru. 2017. "Human Rights and Minority Activism in Japan: Transformation of Movement Actorhood and Local-Global Feedback Loop." *Annual Review of Social Movements* 34:393–412.

The Undercommoning Collective. (2016). "Undercommoning within, against, and beyond the University-as-Such." *ROAR Magazine*, 5 June. Retrieved 30 June 2023 (https://web.archive.org/web/20230205082143/https://roarmag.org/essays/undercommoning-collective-university-education/).

United States Department of Environmental Protection. 2021. "Drinking Water Requirements for States and Public Water Systems." Retrieved 1 July 2023 (https://web.archive.org/web/20230619191741/https://www.epa.gov/dwreginfo/lead-and-copper-rule).

Vale. n.d. "Investidores: Composição Acionária." *Vale.* Retrieved 30 June 2023 (https://web.archive.org/web/20170731020154/http://www.vale.com/brasil/PT/investors/company/shareholding-structure/Paginas/default.aspx).

Vale. 2019. Annual Report. Retrieved 1 July 2023 (https://web.archive.org/web/202 20119014939/http://www.vale.com/PT/investors/information-market/annual-reports/reference-form/Documents/docs-en/FR_2019_i.pdf).

Vanderwarker, Amy. 2012. "Water and Environmental Justice." Pp. 52–89 in *A Twenty-First Century U.S. Water Policy*, edited by J. Christian-Smith and P. H. Fleick. New York US: Oxford University Press.

Vanguard. n.d. "Building a Sustainable Future." Vanguard. Retrieved 30 June 2023 (https://web.archive.org/web/20230529093844/https://corporate.vanguard.com/content/corporatesite/us/en/corp/who-we-are/we-care-about/sustainability.html).

Veolia. 2020. "Veolia Acquires 29.9% of Suez's Capital from Engie and Confirms Its Intention to Acquire Control." Press release, 5 October. Retrieved 30 June 2023 (https://web.archive.org/web/20230324053834/https://www.veolia.com/en/newsroom/press-releases/veolia-acquires-299-suezs-capital-engie-and-confi rms-its-intention-acquire).

Vieira, Flávia Braga. 2011. *Dos Proletários Unidos À Globalização Da Esperança: Um estudo sobre internacionalismos e a Via Campesina*. São Paulo, SP: Alameda.

Vieira, Pedro Antonio. 2015. "O Nacionalismo Metodológico Na Economia e a Economia Política Dos Sistemas-Mundo Como Possibilidade De Sua Superação." *Estudos do CEPE* 42:78–94.

Wait, Isaac and William Adam Petrie. 2017. "Comparison of Water Pricing for Publicly and Privately Owned Water Utilities in the United States." *Water International* 42(8):967–80.

Wallerstein, Immanuel. 2004. *World-Systems Analysis: An Introduction*. Durham, NC: Duke University Press.

Wallerstein, Immanuel. 2014. "Antisystemic Movements, Yesterday and Today." Keynote address delivered at the 38th Annual Political Economy of the World-System conference, Pittsburgh, PA, 10 April.

Warner, Mildred and Austin Aldag. 2019. "Re-municipalization in the US: A Pragmatic Response to Contracting." *Journal of Economic Policy Reform* 24(3):1–14.

Watkins, Rachel. 2018. "Anatomical Collections as the Anthropological Other: Some Considerations." Pp. 27–47 in *Bioarchaeological Analyses and Bodies,* edited by P. Stone. Cham, Swizerland: Springer.

Watkins, Rachel. 2019. "The Power of Erasure and Memory: Re-imagining the Subjugation of Black Bodies, Spaces, and Places." Plenary Panel at 2019 Dimensions of Political Ecology Conference, Lexington, KY, 22 February.

Weinman, Alissa. 2019a. "Victory! Public Ownership of Water System Enshrined in Pittsburgh." *Corporate Accountability*, 10 June. Retrieved 30 June 2023 (https://web.archive.org/web/20230329060411/https://corporateaccountability.org/blog/pittsburg-water-victory/).

Weinman, Alissa. 2019b. "Water Justice for All: Report-back from the National Water Summit in Abuja, Nigeria." *Corporate Accountability*, 21 February. Retrieved 24 April 2021 (https://web.archive.org/web/20230329060411/https://corporateaccountability.org/blog/pittsburg-water-victory/).

Weinman, Alissa and Madeline Weiss. 2019. "Statement: AG Shapiro's Lawsuit Fail to Address Rotten Core of Pittsburgh's Lead Crisis." *Corporate Accountability*,

1 February. Retrieved 30 June 2023 (https://web.archive.org/web/20230128165 411/https://www.corporateaccountability.org/media/shapiro-fails-to-address-rot ten-core-of-pgh-lead/).

Weiss, Madeline and Erika Strassburger. 2021. "Other Voices: Residents Deserve Public Water, not Corporate Lies." Opinion, *Pittsburgh Post-Gazette*, 7 February. Retrieved 30 June 2023 (https://web.archive.org/web/20221127200131/https:// www.post-gazette.com/opinion/Op-Ed/2021/02/07/Other-Voices-Residents-dese rve-public-water-not-corporate-lies/stories/202102070035).

White, Sarah and Sudip Kar-Gupta. 2021. "Veolia, Suez Agree $15 Billion Utilities Merger after Bitter Spat." *Reuters*, 12 April. Retrieved 30 June 2023 (https://web.archive.org/web/20230530025419/https://www.reuters.com/busin ess/veolia-suez-agree-15-billion-utilities-merger-after-bitter-spat-2021-04-12/).

Whyte, Kyle Powys. 2017. "The Dakota Access Pipeline, Environmental Injustice, and U.S. Colonialism." *Red Ink: An International Journal of Indigenous Literature, Arts, & Humanities* 19(1). Retrieved 30 June 2023 (https://papers. ssrn.com/sol3/papers.cfm?abstract_id=2925513).

Women for a Healthy Environment. 2021. *Something's in the Water*. Retrieved 1 July 2023 (https://web.archive.org/web/20211102185006/https://womenforahea lthyenvironment.org/wp-content/uploads/2021/06/2020159_WHE_WaterRe port_FA3_SINGLE.pdf).

Wood, Elizabeth Jean. 2003. *Insurgent Collective Action and Civil War in El Salvador*. New York: Cambridge University Press.

Wood, Lesley. 2005. "Bridging the Chasms: The Case of Peoples' Global Action." Pp. 95–117 in *Coalitions Across Borders*, edited by J. Bandy and J. Smith. Lanham, MD: Rowman and Littleman.

Wood, Leslie J., Suzanne Staggenborg, Glenn Stalker, and Rachel Kutz-Flamenbaum. 2017. "Eventful Events: Local Outcomes of G20 Summit Protests in Pittsburgh and Toronto." *Social Movement Studies* 16(5):595–609.

Wright, Angus and Wendy Wolford. 2003. *To Inherit the Earth: The Landless Movement and the Struggle for a New Brazil*. Oakland, CA: Food First Books.

Wright, Steve. 2002. *Storming Heaven: Class Composition and Struggle in Italian Autonomist Marxism*. London: Pluto Press.

Yale Environment 360. 2020. "Wall Street Begins Trading Water Futures as a Commodity." *E360*, 8 December. Retrieved 24 March 2021 (https://web.archive. org/web/20230401141648/https://e360.yale.edu/digest/wall-street-begins-trad ing-water-futures-as-a-commodity).

Yancy, George. 2022. "Anti-Black Racism Is Global. So Must Be the Movement to End It." *Truthout*. Retrieved 3 July 2024 (https://web.archive. org/web/20240408180034/https://truthout.org/articles/anti-black- racism-is-global-so-must-be-the-movement-to-end-it/).

Zibechi, Raúl. 2014. *The New Brazil: Regional Imperialism and the New Democracy*. Oakland, CA: AK Press.

Zibechi, Raúl. 2017. *Movimientos Sociales en América Latina: El "Mundo Otro" En Movimiento*. Málaga, Spain: Zambra.

Zimmerer, Karl S. 2015. "Environmental Governance through 'Speaking Like an Indigenous State' and Respatializing Resources: Ethical Livelihood Concepts in Bolivia as Versatility or Verisimilitude?" *Geoforum* 64:314–24.

Index

242   *Index*

EU authorised representative for GPSR:
Easy Access System Europe, Mustamäe tee 50,
10621 Tallinn, Estonia
gpsr.requests@easproject.com

www.ingramcontent.com/pod-product-compliance
Lightning Source LLC
Chambersburg PA
CBHW051957270326
41929CB00015B/2689